T0178969

Revisionaries

Revisionaries

What We Can Learn from
the Lost, Unfinished,
& Just Plain Bad Works
S.O.
of great writers

By Kristopher Jansma

QUIRK BOOKS
PHILADELPHIA

Library of Congress Cataloging-in-Publication Data
Names: Jansma, Kristopher, author.
Title: Revisionaries : what we can learn from the lost, unfinished, and just plain bad work of great writers / by Kristopher Jansma.
Description: Philadelphia : Quirk Books, 2024. | Includes bibliographical references and index. | Summary: "An exploration of the rejected drafts and abandoned projects of famous authors that dispels the myth of the creative genius and offers lessons for aspiring writers based on these setbacks and missteps"—Provided by publisher.
Identifiers: LCCN 2023053804 (print) | LCCN 2023053805 (ebook) | ISBN 9781683693734 (hardcover) | ISBN 9781683693741 (ebook)
Subjects: LCSH: Fiction—Authorship. | Editing.
Classification: LCC PN3383.E35 J36 2024 (print) | LCC PN3383.E35 (ebook) | DDC 808.02/7—dc23/eng/20231213
LC record available at https://lccn.loc.gov/2023053804
LC ebook record available at https://lccn.loc.gov/2023053805

ISBN: 978-1-68369-373-4

Printed in China
Typeset in Braisetto, Drip Splatters, Kingthings Trypewriter 2, Mr Eaves Mod OT, Recoleta, and Sabon LT Pro

Designed by Paige Graff
Cover photography from Texturelabs
Some material adapted from work previously published in *Electric Literature*

Quirk Books
215 Church Street
Philadelphia, PA 19106
quirkbooks.com

10 9 8 7 6 5 4 3 2 1

For Leah

Contents

Introduction

Revising Genius

When I was a young college student studying creative writing, I begged my way into a graduate-level English literature course called "Faulkner, Fitzgerald, and Hemingway." The class met in the clock tower of an old brick and marble building. Each week I climbed five flights of stairs to sit in a beautiful sky-blue room with huge windows that opened out over the century-old campus. Twelve of us gathered there on Wednesdays for three hours around a long table to discuss some of the best novels ever written.

Very quickly I realized I was in way over my head. Not only was I considerably younger than my classmates, not only had I read nearly nothing in my life compared to them, but I was not trained in formal literary theory at all. Unlike them, I was not a scholar but a writer, and I had enrolled in the course hoping to figure out one thing and one thing only.

Faulkner, Fitzgerald, and Hemingway. Would I ever become as good as them? Or had these three masters been gifted at birth with talents that I simply would never possess?

All I knew was that I had fallen blindly in love with writing. Growing up, I'd always enjoyed reading and entertained myself by scribbling little stories. I'd filled notebooks and floppy disks with weird attempts at novels and my own imaginary TV episodes. But in college, it all became much more. My creative writing classes were serious work. We were not playing around anymore. In that room, fiction was an art form. A *craft*. Short stories were miraculous constructions. Great novels changed people. The history of the world was marked not just by wars and governments, but by literary turning points and the movements that followed, or even led, the greatest thinkers of every civilization. Authors became towering figures in my mind. I saw that my professors had spent their whole lives in deep study of these writers, and suddenly I wanted to study them as well.

But I nursed another wish: to be one of them myself.

I wanted to do something that mattered. I wanted to write something lasting, that asked big questions. At least I could tell stories about the people I loved and admired, whose lives had changed mine for the better. What if, writing about them, I could share that with others? What if I could immortalize them in some way?

Increasingly, writing was all I thought about. My freshman year, I'd nearly ended up on academic probation because I was barely showing up to my other classes. Meanwhile, I was exceeding the length requirements for every assignment in Introduction to Fiction and Poetry. I eagerly churned out stories, plays, poems, essays. On whiteboards in my dorm room, I plotted screenplays and then novels. Ideas came faster than I could keep up. There was so much to learn and read and try, and I was excited to begin.

But I also knew none of that meant I had what it took to be great—or even just *good*.

Like many people, at that moment I was suffering from quite a few delusions about the way art is made. My view of the creative landscape back then was that there were certain immortal artists who possessed superhuman abilities, and then a whole lot of mere mortals without the requisite mystical talents. From the way my professors lectured about Vladimir Nabokov and Flannery O'Connor and Zora Neale Hurston, I gathered that these geniuses naturally spouted flawless prose and effortlessly manifested vivid and human characters on the page, while people like me could only hope to follow in their stylistic footsteps.

In my creative writing classes, we'd read short fiction and novels each week, pulling the prose apart to see why it worked. But we never discussed *how* it had been done.

How many drafts did it take for James Baldwin to finish "Sonny's Blues"? Did Truman Capote use an outline to organize *Breakfast at Tiffany's*? Was it a good idea to write longhand and then type it up later? Or just dive straight into Microsoft Word? Should you carry around a notebook all the time to scribble down ideas, or was that pretentious?

After breathlessly discussing the perfection of many master works, we'd eventually turn to our own shambolic attempts at writing fiction. Silently, we'd sit there and be workshopped. For anyone who's never had the pleasure, back then this meant that our instructor and peers talked at us, pointing out every character inconsistency, plot hole, awkward phrase, and lamentable word choice. After a lot of laughing and eye-rolling and insincere complaints, my pages would be returned to me, bathed in red ink, inevitably revealed to be a hopeless mess.

We hoped to emerge with thicker skins, the creative light inside us not wholly snuffed out, but this was a constant struggle.

There was praise in our workshops too, but I noticed that a writer's successes were nearly always described as having been achieved effortlessly, because of something *innate* in them.

"You've got a great eye for detail!" a professor might say. "A real feel for the language!" Strong scenes were "lifelike" and great sentences "had a natural flow."

When it was good, in other words, it was just *good*, and little was said about how it had gotten that way.

Once more it seemed that there was something innate in rare, genius writers that we either had or didn't have, something that no amount of revision or practice could replace.

Hoping to trick everyone into believing I was one of these talented few, I began finishing my workshop pieces a few days early and asking my girlfriend to give me feedback, so that I could patch up all the worst mistakes before our class met.

This worked. Steadily, I began to earn praise in class for my "sense of humor" and my "ear for dialogue." Just one problem: I felt like I was cheating. No one knew I'd had to work so *hard* to get the humor and the dialogue right. If anyone ever saw my first drafts, I feared, they'd realize I was still a talentless hack. My determination rose, even as, after three years of workshops, I still had no idea if I was any good or not.

We celebrate the *genius* in both the arts and the sciences, the singular, brilliant mind that can do what everyone else has failed to accomplish: invent a light bulb, compose Symphony no. 40, see inside a black hole, write *Hamlet*, discover the electron. We lionize prodigies who perform with the philharmonic and then finish college before age ten. We speak of the "once-in-a-generation mind." We uphold the myth of genius even as it reinforces the narrative that the rest of us will most likely fail unless we happen to share in their gifts. Yes, we might read that a now-famous actress stumbled in auditions early on, or that a tech wizard flunked out of college before creating the app that made him a billionaire. We recognize that hard work and persistence are important to accomplishment. But these are billed as mere prologue to the massive success we already know has occurred. In retrospect we think they were always remarkable, just unappreciated at first.

Similarly, we are aware that we, and lots of people around us, work quite hard and still never reach great success in the end. Is it all luck? Or is there some X factor? Some genetic advantage, some divine gift, that separates the true stars from the rest?

This was why I'd talked my way into the Faulkner, Fitzgerald, and Hemingway class. I hoped that if I took the hardest possible class about the very best of the best, then the secret to genius would at last be revealed.

It would be—just not in the way I expected.

At first, reading William Faulkner, I got badly lost in the dense worldbuilding and wild language and was more certain than ever that he was simply a higher life-form. How was I supposed to write *Absalom, Absalom!* when I could barely read it?

This fear doubled as we dug into F. Scott Fitzgerald, and I became intimidated by the lush beauty of his novels. Now I could follow the sentences, but their perfection made me hopeless.

Then we came to *The Love of the Last Tycoon.*

Our professor explained that Fitzgerald's last novel had been left unfinished at the time of his death, and that the edition we were reading came with a long section reproducing the author's notes on what the remainder would have involved. Fitzgerald's biographer, Matthew J. Bruccoli, introduced the book as one that—had it been completed—would have surely become yet another masterpiece by the great genius.

But when I began reading, I discovered it was anything but.

It was a trainwreck. A total disaster. A hot, hot mess.

The novel, set in the Hollywood of the 1930s, is narrated by a woman named Cecelia, though sporadically Fitzgerald spells her name "Cecilia" instead. She tells the story in the first person, but in several chapters, the story is randomly in the third person. The central figure in the novel, a love interest for Cecelia/Cecilia, is a handsome and charismatic movie producer whose name is Monroe Stahr—because he's a *star*, get it? The writing is great in some places but in the majority it either drags or feels far too light.

Overall, the story is rough and unready. There are large plot holes and minor characters whose names aren't consistent. In the introduction, Bruccoli clarifies that spelling and grammatical errors had to be addressed before the book was published, and that Fitzgerald "expected and required" editorial help and "spelled and punctuated by ear . . . Fitzgerald never mastered the rules for punctuating dialogue, and these flaws have been corrected here."

He didn't know how to punctuate *dialogue*?

In short, if F. Scott Fitzgerald had been taking Advanced Fiction Workshop with me, my classmates would have shredded *The Love of the Last Tycoon* to pieces.

At first, reading Fitzgerald's final novel depressed me even more than the works of genius that had preceded it. The deeply messy manuscript seemed to prove that even if someone did manage to be born with a massive talent, it could still be lost to drink, despair, and financial distress.

This is probably true enough in its own way. But in the years since then, I've traveled around the world to read dozens more unfinished novels like *The Love of the Last Tycoon*, and I've discovered that they prove something else of far greater value. Examining these works, each frozen in progress in some way, has revealed to me that our best writers all had their limits and flaws. Most didn't have some inborn "perfect pitch" when it came to their craft—no innate sense of plot, or ear for dialogue, or eye for detail. Their rough drafts show they had to work at these things like anyone else. When they succeeded it was the result of lots of hidden labor, support from others, relentless revision, and often simply throwing whole books out. Very often, these immortal geniuses had struggled, despaired, and completely given up. They had to be both persistent and resilient in ways that I had never understood before.

This, I finally began to see, was the real secret to genius: it's a façade. It's a beautiful one, but still, it covers over so much that is far more interesting.

When we first encounter great art, it seems both inevitable and impossible. We wonder how such a masterpiece could have been made by human hands. Whether it is an architectural marvel of a skyscraper, or a majestic symphony written for eighty instruments, or an Oscar-winning film, we experience profound awe. It feels like magic—and it *is* magic. But it's magic that depends on the careful obscuring of the intricate construction and revision processes.

We experience a great novel flowing gracefully from line to line, creating an uninterrupted dream in the mind of the reader, so impressive in its ultimate unity that it can feel sacrilegious to then try to break it back down into its constituent parts. If we disassemble a cathedral, stone by stone, doesn't that make it less beautiful?

But someone needs to look inside if anyone is ever going to make another. When we at last understand the mortal strategy of its assembly, we do not dispel the magic, but enhance it.

Any novel we buy in a bookstore or take out from a library is a finished work of art—only on rare occasions will we ever know much about what it was like in its larval or imago stages along the way. A curious reader might listen to an interview with a writer on a podcast or radio show, in which a host presses them on how many drafts they produced, or how long it took to write, or what continents they had to travel to research the lives of the characters. But even if a writer swears to the interviewer that their first draft was a disaster, we have trouble believing it once we're sitting with the perfect finished product in our hands.

Even if that writer tells us they owe so much to their editor or their spouse or their agent, we'll never know specifically what these others did to bring it all into being.

To really understand the actual evolution that a book takes, one must go further.

For many years, as I've written the popular "Unfinished Business" series for the digital magazine *Electric Literature*, I've traveled the United States, rooting around in university archives to dig up the lost, abandoned, and incomplete manuscripts of genius authors from Patricia Highsmith and James Baldwin to Octavia Butler and David Foster Wallace. I've seen how messes metamorphosize into masterpieces. These often lesser-known works range from a few dozen pages to thousands and thousands. But each presents us with the rare chance to examine a creative work in a raw, or semiraw, form. These works stuck in progress give us a chance to look behind the processes of those great authors.

An unfinished manuscript becomes a parting gift and a glimpse at what might have been. The discoveries I've made in reading them have shaped the way I write and the way I teach writing ever since. I've reconsidered my entire idea of literary merit—genius is not something bestowed upon a select few through gifts or talents, but something built up, over much time and effort, by those resilient enough to never stop testing new ways of creating.

What I've found, time and time again, is that these works show that every genius is also merely human, and subject to the same stumbles, flaws, blocks, and total failures as any first-time writer. To read these incomplete novels and to understand the stories behind them is to expose creativity as something far more interesting and accessible, even if in doing so we must dismantle the very notion of genius.

Geniuses Write Bad Drafts

F. Scott Fitzgerald

L et me begin by saying that I still believe F. Scott Fitzgerald was a genius. It's just that now instead of being awed by his "ear" or his "eye," I'm amazed by the *work* he put into developing these abilities. I'm captivated by the author's relentless planning and outlining, his systematic revising, and his thorough researching. He laboriously constructed systems that would help him produce a brilliant novel, systems that are both fascinating and useful to any writer. His genius was bigger than him alone and did not come from some divine or genetic source.

To get a clearer sense of F. Scott Fitzgerald's last novel, I wanted to see more than what Bruccoli included in the 1993 reprinting we'd read in school. So I took a trip to Princeton University, where the original manuscript pages of *The Last Tycoon* are kept at the Firestone Library, along with the full collection of the associated notes and letters and outlines. These are free for anyone to access after making a request to the special collections librarians—which is remarkable, considering that these literary artifacts are global treasures and irreplaceable. Any of these documents might easily be held in a vault in some billionaire's mansion, hidden from view like an auctioned Vermeer or Van Gogh. If you peruse the books and manuscripts department at Sotheby's you'll find similar items priced there at tens of thousands of dollars.

And at the archive you aren't admiring these works through a glass plate—no, you can *touch* (albeit gently) the *actual pieces of paper that F. Scott Fitzgerald held in his hands, perhaps on the very day of his death.* They are there to be studied, to allow us to get closer than ever to the genius himself.

Box 27 contains the actual manuscript of *The Last Tycoon.*

Inside it are five folders. The first contains a corrected typescript, covered in margin notes and copy edits. Folders 2, 3, and 4 contain hundreds of papers, everything from first draft pages written in longhand to typed-up versions of these pages that are heavily edited. In more than one case there is a note from Fitzgerald to keep only the parts underlined in red crayon, which leaves single lines, often only certain phrases, and very rarely an entire paragraph. "Unpleasant as hell except the end," he writes to himself. "Break up. Copy the red." On one page he simply notes in the margin, "all awful."

But was it so awful? Or was it just not yet great? To understand the whole story, we must rewind to the catastrophes preceding the final year of F. Scott Fitzgerald's life, and the way this novel almost saved him.

"Evolves Away from This": F. Scott Fitzgerald's *The (Love of the) Last Tycoon*

By the end of 1939, F. Scott Fitzgerald was mostly broke, in debt to his friends and editors, having earned only $13.13 in royalties on the sales of forty copies—*total*—of all his books that year. He'd made $4,600 selling stories, only keeping the lights on by freelancing for MGM as a screenwriter, which he hated. He had also recently survived tuberculosis, and his lungs remained damaged, worsened by heavy alcohol use. Even when sober, while working on set he was known to drink eight bottles of Coca-Cola back to back. According to biographer Jeffrey Meyers, Fitzgerald was also taking "potentially lethal doses of barbiturates and forty-eight drips of digitalis to keep his heart working overnight." He experienced debilitating panic attacks, and at one point suffered a nervous breakdown that his doctors told him had come close to permanently paralyzing both his arms—though this was a lie, told to scare him off drinking. In truth, the injuries to his limbs had occurred while Fitzgerald, drunk and blacked out, got twisted up in his own bed sheets.

His many benders had already strained his relationships with almost everyone he knew, including his wife, Zelda, and their daughter, Frances, known as Scottie. He'd been abusive, even violent toward his new companion, Sheilah Graham, and had humiliated himself professionally on multiple occasions.

But in January 1940, Fitzgerald cleaned himself up one last time.

He had a big idea for a new novel about a Hollywood producer modeled on Irving Thalberg, whom he had briefly known, the "boy genius" who headed MGM from 1924 to 1936. He was calling the novel *The Last Tycoon*.

Some of what we know about Fitzgerald's vision for *Tycoon* comes from a long letter that he sent to *Collier's* magazine a year before his death, outlining the plot and asking for a $15,000 advance so that he could get out of his screenwriting obligations and focus entirely on the book. The letter begins confidently, assuring the editor that he has everything about the novel completely worked out and there is "nothing that worries me in the novel, nothing that seems uncertain." But by the end of his long pitch, he turns desperate, essentially begging for a big advance. (His requested sum would be more than $300,000 in today's dollars.)

The *Collier's* editors asked to see a sample and Fitzgerald sent them around half of what they requested. They declined his request, declaring the opening chapters "cryptic" and "disappointing," though they said they'd take another look if he was able to press on.

Instead of becoming discouraged, Fitzgerald did his best to make progress and the work stabilized him. By mid-October, he wrote to Zelda to declare that he might finish soon, and that his walls were covered in charts just as when he'd written *Tender Is the Night*. He said he was "deep" in the novel and that it was making him happy.

He saw *Tycoon* as his chance to reestablish himself in American literature at long last, adding, "I am sure that I am far enough ahead to have some small immortality if I can keep well."

But then, on December 21, 1940, while at Graham's apartment off Sunset Boulevard, F. Scott Fitzgerald died at the age of forty-four from his third heart attack in three months. As it happened, he was listening to Bach on the record player and, according to Meyers, "sitting in a green armchair, finishing a chocolate bar and making notes on an article in the *Princeton Alumni Weekly*." His heart gave way at last. The bereaved Graham had to dig through his belongings to find the money to ship his body back east for a funeral, which, like that of his famous character Jay Gatsby, was poorly attended.

Not long after, Fitzgerald's lifelong friend, the literary critic Edmund Wilson, began to sort through the writer's papers—the very same ones now residing in Princeton.

What existed of *The Last Tycoon* was not even a final draft, but a "latest working draft." It must have been unclear if it could ever be published in the state Fitzgerald had left things, but Wilson began to work on the pages anyway. He uncovered outlines, charts to track daily word counts, lists of characters, summaries of character histories, and hundreds of notes.

The novel was still nowhere near finished, but thanks to Fitzgerald's careful creative designs, the shape of it in the writer's mind was much clearer than before.

According to Fitzgerald's notes and letters, the events of the novel would span a few months in 1935 and revolve around a love affair between producer Monroe Stahr and a woman named Thalia Taylor. Stahr would be an idealistic melding of art and commerce, an anti-Gatsby whose success resulted from hard work, bottomless confidence, and a deep creative sensibility. He runs his movie studio like a dream factory, bringing stories to life. As with *The Great Gatsby* and Dick Diver in *Tender Is the Night*, Stahr is first glimpsed through the eyes of an awed outsider—a young woman named Cecelia (sometimes Cecilia) Brady, whom Fitzgerald describes as "a pretty, modern girl neither good nor bad, tremendously human." The daughter of a rival producer, she starts out "a princess . . . a snob" but then crucially "evolves *away from this*," the evolution made evident as she looks back on her interactions with Stahr in the narration from many years later.

The narrative voice would be tinged with Cecelia's unrequited love for Stahr, and the plot would involve an interstudio rivalry between Stahr and Cecelia's father involving mobsters and murder for hire. It would all conclude with Stahr's death in a plane crash, representing the impending end of Hollywood's Golden Age. Most of this is knowable only through Fitzgerald's notes, since he was only about a third of the way through the "working draft" when he died.

Would the novel have been any good if Fitzgerald had finished it? In a letter to his daughter, Fitzgerald spoke of himself as a "a has-been" but felt his creative powers had not been entirely extinguished. His lifelong friend and rival Ernest Hemingway said in his own letters that he felt Fitzgerald was getting better and better with each new novel. He saw that Fitzgerald was falling apart, but also that he was attempting to get better, to "evolve away" from what he'd been before.

Stahr was to be a less-flawed hero, a sober stalwart, his "only true professional" who embodied the hardworking writer Fitzgerald had always been behind his Jazz Age partygoing. The love interest, Thalia, was not to be another beautiful, cold Daisy, or generous, wounded Nicole Diver, but "the most glamorous and sympathetic" of his heroines—a twenty-six-year-old widow who he wanted to "dower . . . with a little misfortune."

The shift to the West Coast, the focus on filmmaking, and the backdrop of the Great Depression all similarly would have been fresh territory for Fitzgerald, still widely regarded as a writer tied up in the Roaring Twenties, chronicling a world of elite Manhattanites and Ivy League expats in Europe. There's something remarkable in how he was branching out, exploring, trying what hadn't worked before to see what might work now.

As it stands, *Tycoon* consists of seventeen "episodes" out of an outlined thirty. These would have added up to a little more than five of nine chapters. Fitzgerald projected that he'd need to write about 60,000 words to trim to 50,000—around the length of *Gatsby*. At the time of his death, he'd written about 44,000 words, about two-thirds of what he hoped the final first draft might be.

The perspective remains a tangle in the hundred pages he'd drafted before his death, switching from a first-person limited to a more omniscient third-person point of view without warning. As I mentioned earlier, there are other plot holes, characters whose names change, and spelling and grammatical inconsistencies. These flaws are what depressed me as a young writer.

But now I know that such glitches are to be expected in the early stages of a novel in progress. Books often get rewritten in new perspectives, character names change, and punctuation is not always a forethought—for a genius like Fitzgerald or any writer.

Wilson fixed some of these issues and tried to bridge other gaps in the narrative before arranging for it to be published in 1941 by Fitzgerald's longtime partner Maxwell Perkins at Charles Scribner's Sons.

The manuscript's only surviving title page declared it to be *Stahr: A Romance*. Wilson and Perkins went with another option Fitzgerald had listed, *The Last Tycoon*.

That title stood until 1993, when Simon and Schuster reissued the novel along with many of the notes and outlines that Bruccoli had gone through and included. One of the many discoveries he made was that Sheilah Graham had written to Perkins back in 1940 to explain that three weeks before his passing, Fitzgerald had decided to change the name to *The Love of the Last Tycoon*. Bruccoli changed the title to reflect Graham's claims but decided to expose the uncertainty by reproducing a page from Fitzgerald's notes: a page marked "Title" at the top.

Beneath this are some cringeworthy options, all crossed out, including *The State of Metro* and *The Lumiere Man*.

The Last Tycoon is there but scribbled out.

Over *The Love of the Last Tycoon* there's a checkmark, though it could also be a slash.

Nearby, a note: "This is the familiar Fitzgerald formula but the boy grows tired."

That's crossed out too.

In the end there is no title to the novel, or no *one* title to the novel—it has many titles, including, I like to imagine, a dozen more that poor Fitzgerald never got a chance to stumble onto before the end.

Looking through the folders in the Princeton library, touching the same pages as Fitzgerald, and Perkins, and Bruccoli, and so many others in between, I am in awe of the energy this "tired boy" still possessed. In the folders there are numerous unlined pages covered in freehand penciled writing. These are the first rough drafts of the episodes, each spanning a thousand words or two over the course of ten or so pages. These then are hand-marked and edited, often very heavily, with whole sections crossed out at a time, and new things inserted in smaller writing.

At some point, these pages are typed up, either by Fitzgerald himself or by a typist he paid named Frances Kroll (referred to in one letter I saw as "Mrs. Typewriter"). These typed pages now could be reedited, by hand.

There are dozens of pages of outlines and other materials used to organize these fragments—first handwritten, then typed, then retyped.

Fitzgerald wrote out miniature biographies for each character. On another page he collected the names of everyone in the book, which he added to as he went, despite a note to self in the header: "MUST REDUCE CHARACTERS." He created a detailed schedule for Monroe Stahr's workday, beginning at eleven a.m. and going until nine p.m., broken up by the half hour. None of this would be in the novel explicitly, but all of it was important to work out so the rest could be written.

In addition to doing an intense amount of background work on his characters and the world of Hollywood, Fitzgerald also meticulously measured his writing, assigning himself deadlines and word count targets, just as I advise my own students to do today.

For his outlines, Fitzgerald began with a series of what he called "Episodes" and noted the characters introduced, the major plot events, the dates and times, the locations, themes, and even a target length for each. He then outlined how several of these episodes would be knitted together into a chapter. He intended there to be nine chapters, like in *Gatsby*, and he numbered them all in a second column on the outline. He then grouped the nine chapters into five acts using a third column, to chart the larger dramatic rising and falling of the book.

He wrote by hand, typed, then revised each typed page, ultimately moving things from chapter to chapter with the use of a red crayon. He polished dialogue by reading scenes out loud to himself. If he ever felt that his rhythm was off, he would ask Kroll to read aloud from the King James Bible until he found the proper tempo again. In fourteen months, he accumulated 1,100 draft pages of seventeen episodes, plus 200 pages of background notes. None of these, Bruccoli notes, were yet considered to be final, not even the only completely assembled chapter, the first, which Fitzgerald had left marked, "Rewrite from mood. Has become stilted with rewriting. Don't look rewrite from mood."

It stunned me to see the carefully wrought structuring, the mechanics of it all, laid out in such clean little boxes and orderly lines. It is a genius of another kind: a remarkably simple and efficient way of outlining the novel overall, and one that is easily replicable by any writer embarking on the journey themselves. Clearly, concisely, it organizes the story and holds it to a shape. Fitzgerald made himself a blueprint that could be followed, altered, adjusted as the process continued, and as the novel's form revealed itself more fully.

Take this as evidence: there are no shortcuts to greatness. Even in a time when Fitzgerald was hustling to meet his financial obligations, he exerted an enormous amount of his energy in off-the-page materials. He took the time to move through multiple drafts of each page. And at the same time, he pushed himself to stick to a rigid schedule.

For all that, the book is still a mess. There was so much more work to be done, and it remains tragic that he would not get a chance to do it. But looking over his schemas and summaries, it is not hard to believe he would have eventually found his way to another work of great brilliance just as he'd hoped.

FAIL LIKE A GENIUS

F. Scott Fitzgerald

Filed with Fitzgerald's unfinished novel is a folder marked "Stories Scavenged for Tycoon" containing various short pieces that he'd never published. Fitzgerald hunted through them, underlining phrases with red crayon—"the blue-green unalterable dream," for instance, or "she first discovered love in her throat." He typed those phrases out on a new page and later found places to drop these lines into *Tycoon*.

It's a great reminder that no failure is ever wasted. Try keeping a "Scavenge" folder near your work in progress, physically or digitally, and fill it with scenes or sections that you cut along the way. Toss in older projects, or abandoned works that connect thematically or in terms of setting or characters. When you find yourself having a slow writing day, open one of those pieces and run over them with your own red crayon (or change the font to red).

When you're finished, type them into a new document. Keep this sheet handy, and when you find a good spot in your work in progress to deploy a red phrase, make a note so you don't accidentally use the same bit twice.

Fitzgerald's older drafts outnumbered his "working draft" almost *five to one* in the materials I reviewed, but all that extra writing wasn't wasted time, and cutting that weaker material isn't a sign of failure. If you can pull even a few phrases out with your red crayon, then you too can turn any scrapped page into a success.

Geniuses Lack Confidence

Franz Kafka

$\left(2 \right)$

One reason so many of us badly misunderstand the creative process is that authors go to great lengths to cover up the trail of imperfections leading up to their finished work. I, as much as any writer, am tempted to set fire to the dozens of awkward fits and starts, and every terrible draft that it took me to get to the final one. By the end of the process, it is hard enough to feel much confidence in the achievement. When I look over the proof pages all I can see are hundreds of diverging alternate realities—what if I'd left that other bit in? What if I had not moved that paragraph over there? Even once the book is up there, sitting on a bookstore's shelf, and people are letting me know they're enjoying it, there is some imp of the perverse in me that *still* wants to say, "Oh, you should have seen it before. You can't believe what a mess it was!" This, I think, is why so many writers cringe at the idea of their drafts going up on display. We're barely faking the confidence to stand behind our finished work as it is.

But when we get the chance to see the deep insecurity our idols also experienced along the way, we realize that self-doubt isn't necessarily the mark of a lesser work, or a lesser writer. It's part of the process. This can be shocking, possibly a little heartbreaking, but in the end it leaves us less critical of our own fumblings.

There is no better case study that I've found for the crisis of confidence that surrounds literary life than one of the most famous writers of the twentieth century. Franz Kafka's work was hugely influential on the course of literary history, and continues to be a model for writers today—his irony, his dark worldview, his irrepressible humor all feel perfect and unalterable now. But the reality is that Kafka felt no confidence at all in almost anything he left behind, to the point that his final wishes were that his best friend burn of the bulk of it, including three novels that Kafka never managed to finish.

Great writers aren't any surer of themselves than you or I, and knowing that can be a great gift.

"An Infinite Difficulty": Franz Kafka's Unfinished Novels

At the time of Kafka's death from tuberculosis in 1924, the forty-one-year-old writer was scarcely known outside of the Prague literary community to which he belonged, and even within that circle, he was far from its shiniest star. In his lifetime Kafka had only published a handful of short stories in literary periodicals, including some like "The Metamorphosis" that were later printed in small stand-alone volumes. And he had published only two full-length books: the first a set of prose poems, *Meditation*, and the second a collection of stories, *A Country Doctor*, both to scant acclaim and popularity. Neither contains the works for which he is best known today.

Though Kafka had worked for more than ten years on three novels, *The Trial*, *Amerika* (previously *The Man Who Disappeared*), and *The Castle*, he never considered any of these books finished. None were published until after his death—and if he'd gotten his way, they never would have been published at all.

In a handwritten letter to his longtime friend and literary executor, Max Brod, the ailing Kafka willed that all his unpublished work be incinerated, including his letters and diaries.

A second note, written a few years later, specified only six stories that Kafka felt worthy of saving from the flames: "The Judgment," "The Stoker," "The Metamorphosis," "In the Penal Colony," "A Country Doctor," and "A Hunger Artist." Kafka again begged his friend to destroy the rest "as soon as possible."

But Brod ignored Kafka's requests and, instead of burning the stories, quickly set about editing and publishing them.

The greatest betrayal in modern literature, or the greatest miracle? Quite possibly it is both.

Max Brod met Franz Kafka at Charles University in Prague when Brod was eighteen and Kafka was nineteen, after a lecture Brod had given. The gregarious Brod later wrote that had Kafka not come up afterward to debate a minor point about Schopenhauer, he'd likely have never noticed the "inconspicuous and reserved" fellow, despite the elegant blue suits he wore.

Brod was several inches shorter than the six-foot Kafka and had a severe curvature in his spine that caused him to hunch over as the pair continued their chat during what Brod called an "endless walk home." The two were inseparable for ages after. Brod described their friendship as a "collision of souls." Together they devoured thinkers and writers from Plato to Flaubert, and passed hours together at the cinema and the cabaret. Even after their university days ended, they remained extremely close, vacationing together in Italy, Switzerland, and twice in Paris, all while keeping and trading travel diaries. When they journeyed apart, they sent each other postcards and wrote about each other in their private notebooks.

"We completed each other," Brod wrote, "and had so much to give each other."

The pair saw eye-to-eye on much about literature, but there were big differences in their outlooks on life itself. Brod was generous, loud, charismatic, and confident. He was eager to take the literary world by storm. Meanwhile, Kafka was neurotic and obsessive, often hypochondriac, and Brod lamented his friend's constant "hopelessness" even as he compared their time together as being like that of "merry children."

Brod could not understand why his friend was totally disinterested in the artistic fame and fortune that he himself craved. Brod wrote everything, and all at once: novels, stories, songs, plays, manifestos, essays, translations . . . from "ghost stories to Zionist poetry," as Kafka's biographer Reiner Stach put it. And writing was just one of Brod's pursuits. With similar zeal, he dined, drank, romanced society women, frequented brothels, experienced the rich Viennese musical world, and engaged in hoary philosophical and religious debates with others. Brod made a business of knowing everyone of any artistic importance in Prague, and elsewhere in Europe whenever possible. At one point he even performed a violin sonata with Albert Einstein, while the scientist was a young physics professor in Prague.

But for Kafka there was nothing but writing. He was reclusive, avoiding all distractions from his work other than time spent with Brod. "I am made of literature," he wrote in one diary entry. "I am nothing else and cannot be anything else. . . . Everything that is not literature bores me."

After Brod got engaged in 1913, Kafka wrote miserably that he felt Brod was "being separated from me." Kafka, instead, imagined he might live like his idol Gustave Flaubert, a bachelor to the very end. From early on, Kafka was convinced that any happy domestic life would be a hopeless distraction from his writing. He sensed romantic love could overpower him, and attempted to avoid what Brod embraced.

Amidst this near-monastic dedication, Kafka was working slowly on at least one novel, *The Trial*, about a man named Josef K. who is arrested unexpectedly for an unknown crime. Josef K. spends the entire novel trying to ascertain what it is that he's being accused of and by whom, getting no answers despite all his searching, only more questions.

After Kafka read two chapters of the work in progress to Brod, his longtime friend gushed in one diary entry that Kafka was "the greatest writer of our time."

Kafka felt overwhelmed by Brod's prolific output—already he had written and published several books, which Kafka admired. "How can I, as I am today, come up to it?" he lamented. His diaries reveal intense self-doubt and criticism: "I haven't managed a single line I'd care to acknowledge . . . the sentences literally crumble in my hands; I see their insides and have to stop quickly." Meanwhile Brod took it upon himself to talk Kafka up throughout Prague, and even reported on his friend's genius in a literary newsletter—all before Kafka had yet published a word.

He would soon see to it that his friend's work did go to print, first in a journal called *Hyperion* and later through a publisher named Kurt Wolff. Thanks to Brod, the slim volume of Kafka's prose poems, *Meditations*, was put out in 1912, even as Wolff lamented publicly that he was unable to get Kafka's novel due to his "idiosyncratic need to polish . . . again and again."

I've never found Kafka quite as relatable as I have while reading about his insecurities over his work. "Don't let the perfect be the enemy of the good," I've said to numerous students over the years, after they've emailed me at five in the morning on the day an assignment is due, to tell me they are miserable and hate everything they've ever written, but especially this thing they've revised thirty times now.

And yet I find myself feeling the same way when I stare at my own work, revised again and again, still not *quite* right. I have found myself frantically slashing things out of a finished copy of my own novel seconds before going up to do a reading at a bookstore—months or years after it hit shelves.

Perfection is impossible, but it is also what's expected—or at least, it's what we tend to expect of ourselves, because it's what we think great writers have achieved. Like Kafka looking enviously at his friend's output, we read the many-times-revised, polished end products of genius and wonder how we can measure up.

Ultimately, though, we have to find a way to say "This will have to do." If we can't do that, then we'll end up like Kafka, stuck in an eternal loop of endless revision, moving from initial pride to deeper and deeper dissatisfaction as we go.

When Kafka's *Meditations* was published, Brod reviewed it in glowing and rapturous terms, declaring his friend to be a major new voice in literature. Instead of being warmed by this confidence, Kafka felt overwhelming humiliation at what he perceived to be Brod's exaggerations, saying that he did not deserve the praise and wished he had "a hole to hide in."

Kafka took a "bread job" with the Worker's Accident Insurance Institute as a civil servant, reviewing claims and determining the payouts for various on-the-job injuries, a growing concern in the new industrial age. This demoralizing and dehumanizing work ate into his writing time and frustrated Kafka further.

Without a finished novel, he also could not afford to move out of his parents' apartment to find a solitary working space as he longed for—his diaries and letters are filled with complaints about his family's interruptions of his precious writing time. Even a stray cough or creak of the floor outside his room could derail Kafka's focus completely. Spells of depression left him feeling "hollow as a shell at the beach" and "incapable in every regard—completely."

As the First World War began, Kafka found himself even more unsteady, with the continent around him in perpetual upheaval and the once-bustling publishing landscape in Prague beginning to fall apart in the face of global calamity. He felt he could not complete his work on *The Trial* so long as the war went on and was helpless to do much beyond waiting out the uncertainty and chaos.

Kafka's uncertainty and indecision was not limited to his creative life. He proposed to a woman, Felice Bauer, only to break off their engagement a few weeks later. He continued to fear that he could not give himself to a lifelong relationship without pulling attention away from his work. Starting a family and building a home would be costly, and he'd need to earn more money and become stretched even thinner when it came to writing. Kafka was ironically paralyzed by the very freedoms that this literary step forward might have permitted him. In any case he avoided these attachments and yet still also managed to avoid finishing his novel.

Of course, if he *could* have finished his novel and allowed Brod to help him publish it, Kafka might have earned the money and literary bona fides he needed to support a life with Bauer—but Kafka could not manage it. He was reticent to even show his work to Brod and secretive about his progress, for fear that it wasn't good enough, despite the fact that Brod had already proved himself to be Kafka's most ardent cheerleader.

Frustrated, Brod scolded Kafka over his "overpowering will to perfection" and could not understand why his friend was so rigid about everything. Kafka tried the patience of everyone around him. The ever-plagued writer would frequently declare some task to be "impossible" before going on to complete it satisfactorily, and yet this would still not encourage him to believe the next impossible thing could be done.

Brod understood how Kafka's pessimism and anxiety was integral to his unique literary voice and to the powerful themes in his work. It was his impossible point of view on life that made his writing so compelling and special—as slowly and painfully as it was produced. Decades later, in the introduction to Kafka's *Collected Stories*, the author John Updike would observe that Kafka's great insight into the modern mindset was "a sensation of anxiety and shame whose center cannot be located and therefore cannot be placated; a sense of an infinite difficulty within things, impeding every step; a sensitivity acute beyond usefulness." Of course, the same list could be read as a list of reasons that Kafka found it so impossible to complete his creative work. As Updike put it, "rarely can an artist have struggled against greater inner resistance and more sincere diffidence as to the worth of his art."

Much of the bleakness that Kafka saw in humanity would indeed soon come to pass. His sisters would all be murdered in concentration camps; Prague would be occupied by Nazis. A young writer once asked Kafka if his work was not a "mirror of tomorrow" and this question reportedly made Kafka cover his eyes and rock back and forth as he answered, "You are right. You are certainly right. Probably that's why I can't finish anything. I am afraid of the truth. . . . One must be silent, if one can't give any help . . . for that reason all my scribbling is to be destroyed." By the latter part of the twentieth century, Kafka would be viewed as something like a prophet, presaging a certain ironic hopelessness and twisted humor that defines our culture to this day. But in Kafka's own lifetime, this same dark awareness of the twisted aspects of life, which would someday be widely known as "Kafkaesque," made Kafka's own experience of the world uniquely lonely, frequently harrowing, and inconducive to creative progress.

Like any protagonist in his works, the closer Kafka got to his goal of successfully establishing a writerly life, the farther he felt from it. He wrote in his diaries and in letters to Brod that his progress was "feeble" and the work "wretched" or "dead" or "inert."

But feeble progress is still progress, and while the novels remained undone, Kafka did complete several shorter fiction pieces, which thanks to Wolff and Brod were published: "The Judgment" and later "The Metamorphosis." In the latter, Gregor Samsa is transformed into a giant bug (or vermin, depending on the translation) and after a long struggle to right himself is finally killed by an infected wound after his sister throws an apple at him in horror. In the end the whole family turns out to be much better off with Gregor gone.

Today "The Metamorphosis" is regarded as one of the most influential and important stories ever written, but to Kafka's mind at the time, it was "woefully flawed." He specifically felt that the ending was "imperfect to its very marrow" and regretted that he had not been able to make further changes before it was published in a magazine called *Die Weißen Blätter*, as they never sent him the proof pages for final approval. Even then he did still eagerly make several edits before the story was republished as a slim stand-alone novella—but regretted the publisher there had rushed him (quite possibly intentionally, so that Kafka could not change his mind any further.)

Could anything other than Brod's relentless pressuring break through Kafka's indecisiveness and anxiety? It turned out that, yes, something else could.

In 1917, Kafka developed tuberculosis and initially seemed to find it to be some mixture of punishment and a blessing. On the one hand, he saw it as a fateful judgment of his cowardly indecisions, particularly with Felice Bauer. At the same time, it meant he had to leave Prague to spend time in the country, and this gave him an excuse at last to step away from his writing, to escape his family, and to break off his (second) engagement to Bauer.

During Kafka's time in the countryside, he did not attempt to work on *The Trial* or any other novel, but instead began writing fragments and scraps of stories in a series of octavo (pocket-sized) notebooks with no eye toward completion or publication purely for his own amusement and interest. He was away from his inhibiting family, and from Prague. His job at the insurance company continued to pay him while he was recovering, and he did not have to do any work. Even though he had to adapt to a new environment, and it forced the upheaval of his precious routines, Kafka described this period as one of the best in his life.

By 1920, Kafka had gotten well enough to assemble a dozen short works into a second volume, titled *The Country Doctor*, thanks to Brod's urgings, but the book was not widely circulated and received only a single review. Allegedly, a fellow dinner party guest would soon ask if he was the same Kafka who'd written the book, and Kafka tried to deny it.

Spooked by his fragile and at times still deteriorating health, it was in this period that Kafka wrote the first letter asking Brod to burn everything in the event of his death. He did not send the note but left it in his desk for Brod to find, should the worst happen.

Ironically, as Kafka faced the possible end of his life and the failure of his literary career, he'd begun making steady steps back toward his old creative life. The fragmented work in the octavo notebooks had led him in new directions. He wrote in the style of brief parables and what might today be thought of as flash fictions.

Meanwhile his work was beginning to become more widely recognized, as writers (aside from Brod) began to discover it and talk him up.

After surviving two nervous breakdowns, Kafka concluded that his "long fallow period" had led him in its way closer to his narrative ideal, and he resumed writing with never-before-seen bursts of productivity.

Rather than return to his still-unfinished books, Kafka began a third novel called *The Castle*. As in his first, *The Castle* begins with a man arriving in an unknown village, intent on finding his way into the castle that governs over it, without ever succeeding. Overtaken by a "new sense of strength" Kafka discovered a "possibly dangerous, possibly redemptive comfort" in writing. He saw his work reaching a new height of observation and deed: "the higher it is . . . the more independent it becomes, the more obedient to its own laws of motion, the more incalculable, joyful, ascendant its path."

In Kafka's case, a radical change of scenery and pace, along with a stark confrontation with his mortality, helped him overcome some anxieties. He short-circuited his drive to perfectionism with what today in my classes I'd call "low stakes" writing—by working in fragments and parables, and by escaping the novels that he'd become so bogged down with, Kafka found a way to reinvent his process and reclaim a lost joy in the process.

But what happens when the scenery changes back? What happens when the pressure of a long project returns? It begins to take a lot of work to keep up new habits, especially back in old circumstances. Poor Kafka soon returned to his former hesitancy and became "increasingly undecided" about the way he would develop the novel further. He pushed and pushed but could not work it out to his satisfaction. "The plot begins to unravel," Reiner Stach writes, of *The Castle* and its many disparate drafts, "various attempts and variants compete with one another, the deletions get longer and more complicated, and it is obvious Kafka is working against strong resistance, as though he were rolling an ever-growing mass uphill."

Though his notes showed that he had settled on a specific conclusion, Kafka remained lost in the middle. In the same way that he had once continually set aside *The Trial* to work on shorter pieces, he finally began to drift away from *The Castle* so that he could complete other things, including the short story, "A Hunger Artist," about a man who lives in a cage and fasts in full view of the town audience, who are largely disinterested in his performance. As the man gradually starves to death, he laments that his art form is unappreciated in his time. Only when his near-lifeless body is found does he confess that his fasting was never a matter of artistic integrity, but merely that he didn't like the food he was offered. In the end he dies and is replaced by a panther, which everyone enjoys, especially as it takes great joy in eating.

It was at this point that Kafka wrote his second note to Brod, perhaps seeking to override his earlier urging that everything be burned (though he left the first note as well). This time he allowed that a small handful of his shorter works might be worth saving, but none of the unfinished novels, including *The Castle*. He regretfully recognized that the works that had been published already were out of his control at this point, saying however that "if they should disappear completely it would be accordance with my real wish. But since they're there, I'm not preventing anyone from keeping them if he wants to." He went so far as to ask that Brod go around Prague to all the recipients of all his letters and urge everyone to burn them.

It seems ludicrous that Kafka might have expected Brod to do this. And knowing how Brod deeply admired his work, it is also hard to believe Kafka thought Brod would follow his simpler request to destroy those unfinished novels. Had Kafka really wanted his works destroyed he might have asked almost anyone *other* than Brod, one of the only people in his life he knew would be eager to see it all finally published.

Stach argues, on the other hand, that no one else, including Kafka's family, would have had access to the papers besides Brod. And no one else would have known what they were looking for, in order to destroy it. He speculates that Kafka might have hoped Brod would have an investment in destroying the letters in which they'd discussed Brod's marital affairs.

But Brod later claimed that he told Kafka in no uncertain terms back in 1921 that he would "burn nothing" and that in his own lifetime he "never once threw away the smallest scrap of paper that came from [Kafka], no not even a post card."

Even if Kafka had felt that his past works, including the three novels, were imperfect and unfinishable, it says something that he continued to work on those other stories as his health got rapidly and painfully worse. In the weeks before his disease finally overtook him, he wrote new stories, including "The Burrow" and "Josephine the Singer," and urged Brod to get these published as quickly as possible. He claimed that he simply needed the money to afford treatment for his illness, but he also asked Brod to hurry the publisher along with the final proofs of "A Hunger Artist" so that he could check them over before it was too late. Brod did so, and Kafka got to approve the final changes the day before he died.

According to all their letters to one another and their own diaries, Brod knew and accepted early on in their friendship that Kafka was a "genius," far surpassing his own abilities. Remarkably, this did not result in a jealousy that destroyed their friendship; on the contrary, it drew them closer together. For Brod also knew that Kafka needed him.

Left to his own devices, an anxious genius like Kafka would

never produce his best work, and even if he did no one would ever see it. Brod had the confidence in Kafka that Kafka never had in himself, and Brod understood that this truly was the most important thing he could contribute. From the start, their relationship was a steady collaboration. Not in the sense that they would write something together (they did attempt to do this once early on and never came back to it). But a collaboration in the sense that we now see commonly between an agent and an author—Brod was part publicist, part life coach, part business advisor, part advocate, part salesman. As busily as Brod churned out his own books (at least ninety in his whole career) he worked just as busily to push Kafka forward, even as Kafka tried to hide in the shadows.

Brod knew and accepted that Kafka's best work did come when he was not focused on publication or success, but when he simply felt free to explore his ideas without any ultimate aim, just having fun in his little notebooks, which Brod also carefully organized and preserved, later publishing them as *The Blue Octavo Notebooks*. The versions of those unfinished novels we read today are the versions that Brod dutifully edited, taking enormous liberties in arranging sections and chapters in his own order—making all the decisions that Kafka had never been able to. To some it is a violation, but without Brod's confidence in him there might be no Kafka, or not so much as we know him—especially through those letters and the diaries, a new translation of which has just been published.

Mostly, when we read Kafka today, we are reading Kafka-via-Brod. Brod's Kafka. Arguably this was the nature of their relationship since the day they met, an oddly healthy collaboration between two otherwise profoundly unhealthy people. Still, it was to much excitement that translator Ross Benjamin, in 2023, put out a new Schocken Library translation of Kafka's diaries, now at last liberated from the "heavy-handed" interference of Brod—who,

Benjamin contends, "took considerable liberties in refashioning the disorderly mass of material that Kafka had left behind into structurally coherent, smoothly readable editions."

Brod had long ago declared that he considered Kafka to be "a saint of literature," and according to Benjamin, Brod's editorial work on those books is in keeping with his own "pious myth of Kafka as a pure, saintly martyr to literature."

But then, sainthood only comes after death, when a lifetime of contributions can be judged after being presented by those like Brod who understood them to be miracles already.

There is a final story, almost a tangent in Stach's immense and beautiful biography, that comes briefly before the end of Kafka's life. It pertains to a fourth novel of Kafka's—this one truly lost. I think it reveals something, or reinforces something, about the conditions Kafka needed to escape his perfectionist tendencies.

During his last years, Kafka had fallen in love with a woman named Dora Diamant. He tried to marry her, though this time it was she who called it off and not him. But while the two of them were traveling together, Diamant and Kafka one day ran across a small girl who was in tears over the loss of her doll. Kafka kindly interceded and told the girl that her doll was not lost, only on a journey, and that it planned to send back letters along the way.

Over the course of several weeks, Diamant claims, Kafka wrote a flurry of letters to the girl, enough to amount to an epistolary novel, documenting the doll's incredible picaresque adventures, ending finally with the doll falling in love and deciding to happily marry. Kafka did not keep copies of the letters, and the girl's identity is unknown. No one knows who she was, or if she saved the letters, or even if she knew that she was getting them from one of the twentieth century's most important fiction writers.

Perhaps the story is too good to be true, invented posthumously by Diamant, but Stach finds it credible and I'm happy to do so as well. For it underlines Kafka's unique conditions for genius: again we see him coming alive in a collaboration, of sorts—with the situation, with the form required, with the exigency of getting a new letter out each day and letting the plot of the doll's journey push along as impulsively as it needed to. Because Kafka was not writing for the ages, or writing for any audience beyond the little girl, he did not find himself crushed by his own lack of confidence along the way.

With the pressure eased away, Kafka did his best work. It is fitting to think of him writing happily while on vacation, distracting himself from his growing lung pains, all for the amusement of one small child. Stach writes that his aim was not to protect her innocence, but to guide her more gradually to an acceptance of her loss.

But the gift that Kafka allegedly gave to the girl in that story is not so dissimilar to the gift given to the rest of us by Kafka, thanks to Brod. Though Kafka himself never felt any confidence in his abilities, he's given lots of it to us. So much of what we've faced in the century since, we've faced at least with his language and his ironies ready in our minds.

When confronted with the possibility that his horror-filled work might be a "mirror of tomorrow," Kafka said that he saw his "scribblings" as coming up short: diagnosis without cure. He didn't feel certain that his writing was saying what it needed to say—that it was able to help anyone in the end. But this misses the real impact of that work on all of us who came after. By so well naming the anxieties of the twentieth century, he illuminated our passage through it, and even allowed us a dose of dark laughter about it. He gave us confidence to proceed, and gives us even more when we see how insecure he was in doing so.

Most of us don't have a Brod to cheerlead us all along the way. We might get lucky and find ourselves blessed with a few mini-Brods though; we should listen to them more often. We should believe in ourselves more than we do. And, when we don't, we should look back on dear Kafka and remember that feeling uncertain about anything and everything is something we share with even the greatest minds.

Fail like a Genius

Franz Kafka

Kafka's trip to the countryside restarted his creative life. He was free of his job and his family for the first time in his life, but also free of his own expectations and the pressure he felt in facing his pile of unfinished work. His small notebooks could be carried anywhere, and smaller pages lent themselves to smaller scales. He turned to the form of the parable, brief but layered and highly symbolic, to be read as written: in one sitting. The practice helped Kafka recover his career and to discover what would become his "late" style.

If you feel pressure from some important work in progress, take a page from Kafka's book and get away from it for a while—literally. Grab a little notebook and a pen and spend some time in a new environment where you won't feel that looming pressure. Go to the woods, if you're a city-dweller, or to the city if you're out in the suburbs. Even visiting a new park, or a new neighborhood, can shake things loose. Watch people or describe the natural world. Jot down whatever comes to mind. Nobody ever has to see these, so you don't need to worry about what anyone will think of them. Your goal isn't to fill the notebook, or to write for any specific amount of time. Some of Kafka's octavo entries are one sentence long, others span several pages. Maybe some of it will be useful when you do go back to that gnarly work in progress, but don't focus on that. Just take the time to write for its own sake again.

Geniuses Get Off to a Bad Start

Louisa May Alcott

(3)

When I was still a new father, I often passed a local daycare center called Mozarts and Einsteins with little cartoon child versions of the two geniuses on the sign, urging parents like myself to hurry in with our infant-savants and get on the waitlist for a playgroup that could be all the difference between a lifetime of brilliant achievements and a plain old ordinary one. In those days practically every parenting book or internet article I read was stressing the critical importance to the developing brain of everything from proper diet and vocabulary exposure to specific paint colors and periodic "tummy time." The broad implication was that if wanted your child to grow up to be a genius, you had until about age five to get them eating omega-3s and mastering chromatic musical scales, or you were out of luck.

We're told that Mozart wrote his first symphony at the age of eight, that Picasso was creating his first genius sketches by nine, that Pascal was discovering mathematical principles of triangles at twelve, and so on. (I'm betting none of them had a diet rich in salmon and avocados, though.) Slow starters used to have Einstein to look up to, who allegedly did quite badly in school as a child—but since the mid-'80s when I was taught this, his biographers have changed that around, holding up academic records found in the

Swiss Literary Archives that show an eleven-year-old Albert conversant in high school level physics and already masterful on the violin.

So much for that!

As a parent I know the loving impulse to believe my children must surely be prodigies in the making, and to save every doodle and scribbled sentence, on the off chance that someday these juvenile projects will be considered museum-worthy historical artifacts. And do I still have all those things saved in storage? Next question, please.

There's nothing wrong with parents seeing the best in their children, but this can be another troubling way of misunderstanding the nature of genius—that our greatest thinkers and artists either were born that way or had some extraordinarily fortunate (but replicable, for a small fee!) experiences in childhood that made their natural potential blossom before it was too late.

We have the notion that some of us are simply blessed with genius, while others aren't, but thanks to Mozart and Picasso we also may believe that this blessing should be plainly obvious before we've lost our baby teeth.

Juvenilia is an understandable curiosity for biographers and literary fans. We want to believe that such early writings can reveal those first youthful sparks of creative power, and even show origins of an author's later themes and techniques. Scholars and publishers have gone back further, into volumes of Jane Austen's childhood notebooks, mining these for stories and poems written when she was as young as eleven or twelve, trying to show that the seeds of her greatness were present even then. Hermione Lee's biography of Virginia Woolf delves into a collection of homemade family newspapers, some written when Virginia was as young as ten, called *Hyde Park Gate News*. Lee suggests that one can detect seeds of genius in the little news articles written with her siblings. There are stories written by eighteen-year-old Charlotte Brontë under the pseudonym "Lord Charles Albert Florian Wellesley" that supposedly contain early models for characters in *Jane Eyre*. Recent publications have been issued of stories written by Truman Capote at age eight, F. Scott Fitzgerald's "secret boyhood diary," poems Faulkner wrote for the *Mississippian* at sixteen, and so on.

On principle, I object to publishers claiming they've got the *long-lost masterpiece* of a ten-year-old Ernest Hemingway, when the story isn't much better than any fourth grader might write. But I do find that reading the lost juvenilia of writers can be a helpful thing. When you take away all the bluster, juvenilia usually shows the opposite of what the marketing claims: that great authors start out more or less like anybody else, and that just because we weren't publishing brilliant gems in our middle school newspaper doesn't mean we'll never amount to much artistically as adults. Maybe sometimes there is some glimmer of talent somewhere, some shine of promise—but for that to become anything, a whole lot more needs to happen, and I don't mean a $25,000 a year preschool or daily doses of vitamin B_{12}.

Sentimental Education: Louisa May Alcott's "Aunt Nellie's Diary"

In the summer of 2020, an unfinished and previously unknown work by American writer Louisa May Alcott was published in the *Strand* magazine, a small literary quarterly based in Birmingham, Michigan. The publication of the "impressive" lost story, "Aunt Nellie's Diary" was written about in the *New York Times* and *Harper's Bazaar* and *Smithsonian* magazine. It was not part of another sequel about Jo and the other *Little Women*—in her lifetime Alcott published four follow-ups on the March sisters. No, the *Strand* magazine had published a half-finished story, not from the end of Alcott's writing career, but from the beginning—a work of juvenilia.

And it wasn't particularly good.

Discovered in Harvard University's Houghton Library, "Aunt Nellie's Diary" was handwritten by Alcott in an 1848 journal, when she was seventeen years old. In the *Strand* magazine's introduction to the story, Professor Daniel Shealy, a professor at the University of North Carolina at Charlotte, claims that "Aunt Nellie's Diary" shows readers "an emerging talent on the cusp of a promising career." It had already been long understood that Alcott was a prolific early story writer just like one of her literary idols, Jane Austen.

The story is unfinished, but hardly a fragment—it comes in at 9,400 words, which is quite long compared to the stories published in the magazines Alcott admired, like *Godey's Lady's Book*. But "Aunt Nellie's Diary" is incomplete not because the ending was lost or damaged, but because Alcott never finished it. She simply stopped writing partway through a sentence.

Did she get stuck? Bored? Distracted? We don't know.

What we do know is that at seventeen, Alcott was already an ambitious writer. According to biographer Katharine Anthony, at this point Alcott "could write melodramatic fiction with extreme fluency and prolificness." She'd grown up writing plays with her siblings, which were often performed at family events. By the end of the next year, she'd finish her first novel, *The Inheritance*—though her first publication, in 1852, would come with a poem called "Sunlight" (under the pseudonym Flora Fairfield) in *Peterson's* magazine, and for which Alcott was paid $5.

Alcott's diaries show that she modeled her early work on the stories that dominated popular magazines at the time. She hoped that commercial success would allow her to make an independent living as a writer. Alcott closely studied the wildly beloved *Sketches of Everyday Life* written by Fredrika Bremer, sometimes called the "Swedish Jane Austen." Bremer published stories of independent women traveling through Europe and the Americas and describing the tangled marriage plots of others. But these were not insubstantial works at all—Bremer is regarded as an early activist for gender equality and radical for her view that fiction should center more often on female characters. Alcott thought these stories were important, and in a memorable scene in *Little Women*, Alcott depicts Mrs. March reading Bremer's book to her four daughters.

Critics categorize stories like Bremer's as *sentimental* works, focusing on high emotions and feelings to manipulate the reader's sympathies. The term originated with a class of respected eighteenth-century novels, like Goethe's *Sorrows of Young Werther* and Samuel Richardson's *Pamela*, but by Alcott's time it had become synonymous with terms such as *women's fiction* and *domestic fiction*, and viewed as frivolous entertainments. One of Alcott's biographers, Harrier Reisen, described these stories as the "chick lit of the day."

However, the seventeen-year-old Alcott enjoyed these stories, and wanted to write some of her own, like "Aunt Nellie's Diary." But in her diaries Alcott confessed she secretly preferred more "lurid things" like the *Twice-Told Tales* of Nathaniel Hawthorne, as long as they were "true and strong also."

Alcott knew Hawthorne as an associate of her father, Bronson Alcott, who had also worked closely with Henry David Thoreau and Ralph Waldo Emerson in Concord. Hawthorne's stories depicted a turn toward darker allegories like "The Minister's Black Veil" and complex psychological realism like "Wakefield," and for

Alcott these impulses clashed with the more uplifting sentimentality and melodrama she was writing.

Shealy argues that "Aunt Nellie's Diary" reflects Alcott's struggle between these two diverging literary paths, and that her abandonment of the story could be a sign that, at seventeen, she was not yet able to reconcile these strands as she eventually would, to great success, in later stories like "The Masked Marriage" and "The Lady and the Woman," and ultimately in her enduring masterpiece, *Little Women*.

As the title suggests, "Aunt Nellie's Diary" is written in the form of the actual diary of "Aunt" Nellie, beginning on her fortieth birthday. (Unmarried and quite content, Nellie is a classic Bremeresque narrator.) The day is marked by the arrival of Nellie's eighteen-year-old orphan niece Annie and Annie's friend Isabel Loving. Alcott describes Annie as "gentle" and "full of quiet happiness" even as a "solitary childhood and lonely life have thrown a shade of sadness over her." Meanwhile, a few days into the visit, Aunt Nellie has had enough of the friend, Isabel: "How often are we deceived by a bright exterior, little dreaming of the darkness within. Isabel is not what I thought her. I fear under a fine gay manner of a light laughing face she conceals a cold, unfeeling heart, bent only on the accomplishment of her wishes. There is something not quite true about her." Nellie believes that Annie's harder upbringing has left her with "frank simplicity" while Isabel has been spoiled by a "selfish worldly" father who, in raising Isabel, "allowed her will in everything." Alcott describes Annie as "simple, loving, and sunny-haired," while Isabel is "beautiful" and "dark-haired" just to drive home the contrast.

The plot quickly comes to revolve around the girls' shared interest in Edward Clifford, a sickly young man who has also lost his mother, and who blends a "gentle heart" with the "calm and noble mind of his father." Once a "pale, slender boy" weeping at his mother's deathbed, Edward is now a "tall noble-looking young man" with a "low musical voice." Understandably, Aunt Nellie and Annie and Isabel are more than happy to nurse him back to health. Scenes ensue that drive home the difference between sweet and sunny Annie and darker-minded Isabel—there's a fancy ball, for instance, where Isabel wears a black Night costume covered in silver stars, and Annie wears all white and a "rose-coloured veil" and a wreath of "dewy half blown buds" so as to be Morning. You get the idea.

It's far from the quality of Alcott's later works. Still, lovers of *Little Women* will find much to compare in the sisterly tug-of-war between Jo and Amy over Laurie—though with less shading and complexity. Here, the descriptive writing is already lush and impressive, but the symbolism is a little on the nose, the characters more like caricatures, and the plot stalls for pages and pages. It feels as if Alcott got all the initial pieces in place but couldn't quite decide what to do with them.

Will the lovely (but blander) Annie win over Edward? That would make for a suitable, sentimental story ending. But Alcott pulls repeatedly away from this first-order choice, in favor of spending more time with the more interesting (selfish, jealous, secretive) Isabel. In a proper *Godey's Lady's Book* story, Isabel should not triumph without being morally redeemed. Over and over in the story, Alcott sets up moments that could make this happen, then stops short.

To try to resolve this tension, Alcott adds (quite late in the story) a stately "Mr. Ainslie" to the mix. Ainslie, a friend of Edward's, arrives at the costume party dressed as "Saint Guy." Seeing Ainslie makes Isabel turn "very pale" and hastily drop her veil. She claims she doesn't know him, but rushes away, making Aunt Nellie suspicious that there is some secret between them. Nellie later witnesses Ainslie in the cloak room with Isabel, begging her to see him, saying that he forgives her "for all that has passed" but that she should not "try" his love again.

Annie later confesses to Nellie that when she and Isabel were at school together, her friend had been engaged to "high-born rich and handsome" Herbert Ainslie, but that she did not love him. Annie simply can't understand how her friend "could be cold and careless when she had won so true and fond a heart."

And Alcott could not either, because a few lines later, she abandoned the story in midsentence: "Well not many days ago she told me she had written to Mr. Ainslie, breaking off the engagement, that she no longer loved him and would not be fettered by any bonds. I begged and prayed she would . . ."

Here, the *Strand* magazine urges its readers to submit their own endings to the story, as part of a contest in which winning final scenes would be published in some later issue. One challenge in doing this would be reconciling the many inconsistencies in the story: Did Isabel only *just* call off this engagement? If so, why has purehearted Annie been so generously encouraging her friend's competing interest in Edward the whole time? Perhaps Alcott would have dealt with these issues in a second draft, in which she'd also have needed to trim a lot of wheel-spinning in the middle, to get the story to publishable length. But she never did.

Why did young Alcott never finish the story? Possibly she saw the sentimental ending coming, found it unsatisfying, and so opted to walk away. She later would succeed at layering Hawthornian surprise and depth in romantic characters like the March sisters, but perhaps at seventeen she was not yet capable of it.

It is also possible that Alcott abandoned the story not because she was stuck, or lacked interest, but simply because life got in the way.

In 1848, Alcott's father, Bronson, had spent his wife's inheritance on an idyllic farmland in Concord he called "Hillside," leaving nothing for living expenses. The solution was to rent out the house and move everyone to a tiny basement apartment in Boston's South End, where Bronson wanted to give a series of intellectual lectures called "Conversations on West Street" based on his transcendentalist work with Emerson and Thoreau.

Biographer Susan Cheever notes that Alcott was stretched thin at this time, taking care of her siblings and their household while their mother was busy working. As a result of the potato famine in Ireland, the city of Boston had recently become flooded with starving Irish immigrants—Alcott's mother, Abigail (Abba) Alcott, was running a charity project to care for them, even as the Alcotts themselves were falling into poverty.

At one point everyone in the Alcott household got smallpox from an Irish family that Abba had been feeding at their home. Alcott wrote a series of "Hospital Sketches" during this time, describing the grotesque scenes of illness and death that she witnessed while helping her mother in her charity efforts, and these are notably quite different in tone from "Aunt Nellie's Diary." But she had little time for writing at all in that year.

Alcott was running the household, on top of teaching: her mother brought Alcott to help run a series of reading classes for Black families in their neighborhood. Both women were active in the abolitionist and feminist protest movements of the day. Meanwhile, the nation was lurching toward the Civil War, and Bronson Alcott's ambitions as a street philosopher weren't paying the bills. During this period her father was also "experiencing mental states and visions that suggest a frighteningly disturbed mind." According to Cheever, "he began working on a series of arcane charts showing invisible forces. He refused to sleep or eat. He thought he was God."

It was one of the darkest and most difficult chapters in Alcott's life. It is almost amazing then that none of this considerable weight is reflected in stories like "Aunt Nellie's Diary." Instead, Alcott relied on her scant writing and reading time as an escape from all the uncertainty and horror around her. Remarkably, she'd later look back on this same time in life as her "sentimental period." Even as her father was turning into a character in a Hawthorne story, Alcott was reading as much "Charles Dickens, Sir Walter Scott, and Charlotte Brontë" as she could get her hands on, and found lots of "tenderness and compassion" in all the exploitation of "high emotions and feelings."

Shortly after abandoning "Aunt Nellie's Diary" Alcott began working on her first novel, *The Inheritance*, which Cheever describes as a "short romantic Cinderella story written in girlish, sentimental prose" that is "weirdly enlivened by the desperate feelings of its author." This novel revolves around a young orphan named Edith Adelon, who works tirelessly for the wealthy Hamilton family only to discover that she is the true heir to their fortune. When a will is finally discovered that proves she should get the inheritance, angelic Edith rips it up and says she doesn't want the Hamilton family's riches, but only their love. (But she does then marry a wealthy prince and so ends up prosperous anyway).

Harriet Reisen noted the novel was escapism for the overworked, struggling, impoverished Alcott, its pages "furnished with the fine things she coveted." The novel "imitated the kind she devoured like plumcakes." Crucially, Reisen notes that "Louisa never attempted to publish *The Inheritance*. She had written it only for practice, and as an exercise it is impressive."

It was not published until 1997, when editors at Dutton announced *The Inheritance* as a "lost novel" of Alcott's and compared it to the work of Jane Austen. A review in *Publishers Weekly* called the novel "charming" but noted it does not rise to the "smart dialogue or lived-in characters" seen in Austen's works.

But so what if it isn't Austen—or even Austen at age seventeen? *The Inheritance* was a crucial step on a journey that Alcott was still taking. She couldn't get to *Little Women* without it. Interestingly, biographers contend that *The Inheritance* is the novel that Jo March is meant to have written (and Amy burned) in *Little Women*—another sign that Alcott always saw it plainly as a journeyman effort.

Scholars argue that juvenilia provides insight into the early training of great writers, and I agree that these early stories reveal a lot that can be useful to us today. Yes, the writing in "Aunt Nellie's Diary" isn't particularly great, and the social dynamics aren't as complex or realistic as we'd see in her later, more mature work. But that's no slight against Alcott, who we shouldn't expect to be writing masterpieces at age seventeen in the first place. What's important here is that she was writing. She was nurturing a passion for reading and mimicking the styles of stories she liked, trying to find her voice, and trying to figure out what sort of writer she wanted to be. What's admirable here is her ambition, her persistence in the face of familial hardships, and even her willingness to push beyond formulaic work that would have more likely brought commercial success. The remarkable thing about "Aunt Nellie's Diary" is that it is unfinished. It shows Alcott becoming bored with a work that wasn't challenging her artistically anymore.

The *Strand* magazine has, as part of its stated mission, published a slew of previously unpublished stories similar to "Aunt Nellie's Diary," including work by Raymond Chandler, Agatha Christie, Joseph Heller, John Steinbeck, Mark Twain, Tennessee Williams, and H. G. Wells. In some cases, these stories may have been better left resting in the university archives, though just as there's something to be gained from reading late unfinished work, we can still learn a lot from the early, awkward attempts of the authors whose mature work is widely hailed as genius.

In the end, I think more people should see that someone like Louisa May Alcott could get 9,400 words into a story and walk away unsatisfied. This didn't doom her to never succeed. In fact, it's the strongest sign that she eventually would.

We shouldn't expect masterpieces from middle schoolers, or anyone starting out at any age. If the universe does occasionally spit out a Mozart or an Einstein, that shouldn't be anyone's expectation. Genius isn't inborn; you aren't doomed if you haven't shown signs of it by five, or fifteen, or fifty-five. True genius comes with practice, with challenge, and with a whole hell of a lot of failure.

FAIL LIKE A GENIUS

Louisa May Alcott

If Louisa May Alcott's "Aunt Nellie's Diary" is not an example of great writing, it is a great example of how we learn to be better writers. Imitating the work of magazine writers didn't lead Alcott to become a copycat of their styles, but ultimately helped Alcott to locate her own. How better to learn how to write like yourself than by writing like someone else whose writing speaks to you?

Take one page of writing from something you love and put it next to you on the desk. Write it out, sentence by sentence. Pause after each line and consider what you've written. Why did they put the commas where they put them? Why did they use this word and not that one? What does it feel like to write that sentence yourself? Does it look impressive still in your own handwriting? Can you begin to imagine writing a line as good?

When you're done with that page, move to a blank document and start writing something new. It can be a continuation of what you were just writing if you like—change the details later. Take it in your own direction now. And think about the choices *you* make, and how they're different from the ones you were making on the first page. Do you go darker? Lighter? Do your sentences go longer? Do you choose different words or images? Ease into your own style again and recognize where it overlaps with your inspiration and where it is all you.

Geniuses Don't Measure Up

Vladimir Nabokov

There is only one perfect novel. It has no flaws, makes no wrong moves, contains no mistakes of any kind. Every word in it is the best word possible. Every sentence is exactly the correct length. Every paragraph, every page, every chapter—completely ideal.

The problem is that this novel only exists in one place—inside the head of a fan who's waiting for their favorite author's next book. When readership turns from appreciation to idolization, our hopes spike for anything new by the object of our worship. If we need to wait a decade, it doesn't diminish our ardor. We reread their previous work and dream about what's coming. How will they top what has already amazed us?

We put the same pressure on ourselves when we start a new creative project. (Does that imply we're our own biggest fans? It would be nice to think so!) A book or other undertaking is at its most unassailably perfect when it doesn't exist yet—and it stays potentially perfect as long as you don't start. As soon as you begin to write, the flaws are there, and things begin going downhill. This becomes, quickly, another way in which we thwart ourselves—the better our new ideas are, the more disappointed we likely are when we begin scribbling them out. It helps me, in these times, to look back at my shelf at those books by other writers that I'd idealized and to remember the ways in which the perfectionism I projected onto them turned out to be a bad idea. If I can forgive Donna Tartt or Haruki Murakami for writing a long-anticipated book that doesn't *quite* live up to the perfect image in my head, can I preemptively forgive myself as well?

The posthumous publication of Vladimir Nabokov's lost novel *The Original of Laura* is an especially stark example of the gulf between the ideal potential novel and the sometimes disappointing reality. Hailed as the "literary event of 2009"—thirty-two years after Nabokov died—*Laura* was published amid eager speculation about the great man's final work. People were desperate for one more novel from that brilliant mind. As it turned out, the whole literary community learned what, on some level, they probably already knew from their own creative struggles: no real book is ever as good as the one you dreamed up.

"Skidmarks and Broken Glass": Vladimir Nabokov's *The Original of Laura*

Nabokov's final wish, on his literal deathbed, to his wife, Véra, had been that his unfinished book, *The Original of Laura*, should be burned. Véra Nabokov, his wife of fifty-five years, was something of the Max Brod in Nabokov's life, and "silent partner" to his works. As Judith Thurman writes in the *New Yorker*, "She was his first reader, his agent, his typist, his archivist, his translator, his dresser, his money manager, his mouthpiece, his muse, his teaching assistant, his driver, his bodyguard (she carried a pistol in her handbag), the mother of his child, and, after he died, the implacable guardian of his legacy. Vladimir dedicated nearly all his books to her, and Véra famously saved *Lolita* from incineration in a trash can when he wanted to destroy it."

In similar spirits, Véra decided to keep the manuscript of *The Original of Laura* intact, despite her dying husband's wishes. Instead of publishing it, she locked the book away in a Swiss bank vault. Faithfully she kept it preserved there for fourteen years. Only when she passed in 1991 did the partially written novel become the responsibility of their son.

Dmitri Nabokov remained unsure of what to do for eighteen years. Should he respect his father's wishes, or his mother's hesitations? Hadn't his father once lectured his students that it was "fortunate" Max Brod had not gone ahead with the command to burn Kafka's papers?

At one point, Dmitri told scholars that he *might* have already burned the papers, though we know now that he hadn't. In an interview with BBC2's *Newsnight*, Dmitri speculated that his father "would have reacted in a sober and less dramatic way if he didn't see death staring him in the face. He certainly would not have wanted it destroyed. He would have finished it." He went on to explain that his father had once told him that *Laura* was among his most important books and then concluded that "one doesn't name a book one intends to destroy."

Meanwhile, the literary world could only speculate about what the novel could be—there were rumors that it was highly erotic, which would have been unusual for Nabokov. At one point Dmitri read a few portions of *Laura* out loud to a centennial gathering of scholars at Cornell, where it was enthusiastically received. Others would later claim to have privately been permitted to read the entire, utterly brilliant manuscript. When the literary journal the *Nabokovian* held a contest to see who could write the best replication of Nabokov's style, they published the winners alongside what they claimed to be two real fragments from *Laura*. Which were real? Which were the imitations?

In 1998, an essay on *The Original of Laura* by a Swiss scholar named Michel Desommelier was published on the Nabokov fan website Zembla, containing more excerpts from the novel. These were then verified as authentic by other scholars and even Dmitri himself.

Only later it would be revealed they had been faked—the whole thing a loving and elaborate prank concocted by the site's editor, Jeff Edmunds.

As long as the book remained unpublished, it lived excitingly in the minds of Nabokov's eager fans. They could project onto it all their hopes, speculations, and expectations. Nabokov's fans had the thing that they, and Nabokov, wanted most—an everlasting puzzle. A perfect novel that could never be read.

If it all feels like a plot lifted from a Nabokov novel, it isn't far off. In *The Real Life of Sebastian Knight*, the character V. broods over the literary works of his deceased half brother, trying to figure out which parts were real. *Pale Fire* is a not-quite-finished poem by the character John Shade, as annotated by his unhinged biographer, Charles Kinbote. (This is the origin of "Zembla," a fictional kingdom that Kinbote invents in his footnotes.) And Nabokov's final published novel, *Look at the Harlequins!* is the fictional autobiography of a Russian-émigré writer named Vadim Vadimovich N., whose life is almost identical to that of Vladimir Vladimirovich Nabokov and who publishes a series of novels that, though differently titled, align perfectly with Nabokov's own works.

Unfinished and nonexistent books, unanswerable questions, games of uncertainty and imagination . . . these were the very things that Nabokov most liked to engage with on the page. In a bizarre case of life imitating art, then, *The Original of Laura* began to become another of these metamysteries.

Nabokov fooled even himself into thinking the book was a master-piece before he knew what it was. In the year before his death, Nabokov said that the book was "not quite finished," but had been "completed in his mind." He spoke of it majestically: "I must have gone through it some 50 times, and in my diurnal delirium kept reading it aloud to a small dream audience in a walled garden. My audience consisted of peacocks, pigeons, my long dead parents, two cypresses, several young nurses crouching around, and a family doctor so old as to be almost invisible. Perhaps because of my stumblings and fits of coughing, the story of my poor Laura had less success with my listeners than it will have, I hope, with intelligent reviewers when properly published."

It's heartening to see that a genius like Nabokov was subject to the very same delusions that any of us might feel as we mentally kick around a novel we haven't written yet. Lying in bed at night, thinking about the next book I plan to write, I will conjure up my own imaginary audiences at imaginary *New Yorker* Festivals and National Book Award parties and think about what my own "intelligent reviewers" will make of it. There's nothing wrong with that—it's far healthier than beginning from a place of hopelessness and dread.

But either way, those fantasies must be dispersed before any real work can begin.

When, in 2009, thirty-two years after his father's death, Dmitri finally did release the novel to this expectant audience, it was revealed that the manuscript was very far from "not quite finished." It was not even a manuscript at all, but 138 handwritten notecards, and not in any particular order.

Nabokov often wrote his books this way, beginning in pencil, on cards that he would later arrange and have Véra type up for him. But in this case only the first sixty cards even form a linear narrative. Altogether, the text would have totaled around thirty typed pages. The story revolves around a scholar named Philip Wild who marries a woman named Flora partially because she reminds him of a previous lover named Aurora—the novel is meant to be the *real* story behind a novel that the narrator has written called *My Laura,* which has become a best seller. What we have of the book mostly revolves around Philip's preoccupation with his own death—of his long-standing fantasies of being able to erase himself like a figure on a chalk board, a wish for "self-deletion."

That, unfortunately, is all there is of the book—the rest was utterly lost in the imagination of the author when he passed. If Nabokov had hoped to get further along in his final year, to win over those ardent fans and "intelligent reviewers" he'd fantasized about, he simply was not able.

Misled and frustrated after decades of patience, the reviewers and fans did not react well. The *Wall Street Journal* compared reading the book to watching Lou Gehrig try to play baseball after his illness in 1939. A German reviewer called it a "labyrinthine, overgrown garden without a gazebo in its center." Martin Amis, in the *Guardian*, felt that it was a disaster. "When a writer starts to come off the rails," he wrote, "you expect skidmarks and broken glass; with Nabokov, naturally, the eruption is on the scale of a nuclear accident."

Very quickly the mood had soured. All the fun of anticipating and speculating about the lost book was over, and the "book" itself was nowhere near living up to the hype—which, worst of all, now seemed to have been based on a number of exaggerations and misrepresentations. Even Dmitri's judgment that "one doesn't name a book one intends to destroy" is odd, given that Nabokov had changed the novel's title at least three times, from *Dying Is Fun*, to *The Opposite of Laura*, and then finally to *The Original of Laura*.

I vividly recall receiving the book for Christmas that year, and eagerly flipping through in the family room, surrounded by discarded wrapping paper, my excitement rapidly becoming disbelief.

This was it?

To stretch 138 notecards into something resembling a finished novel, Knopf published the book on heavy stock, with a color reproduction on each page of the original card, complete with scribbles and cross-outs, with the cleaned-up text typed below. The whole thing would take about an hour to flip through.

But as with many of my feelings about these works, my thoughts have changed over the years I've spent with them. I now think of *The Original of Laura* as something of a treasure, and only with great care do I take it out to show my students sometimes—as if my mass-produced copy is itself something that has been kept in a vault for thirty-two years.

There's simply nothing else I've ever seen quite like it. Each image is perforated so that it can be punched out and then reshuffled in whatever order the reader pleases. There is no way to read the book without being reminded of its incompleteness. It vanishes in your hands even as you flip the simple, smudgy cards. You see Nabokov's scribblings-out, his uncertainty, his sudden flashes of inspiration—an entire emotional roller coaster of creative life is there, captured in bad penmanship like a bug in amber. And what a gift, actually, to show us all that even one of the twentieth century's greatest writers started his eighteenth novel as a lot of scribbles on a stack of index cards!

How glorious to be able to see the work *as* work—not a masterpiece but a process.

Despite what Dmitri might believe about the novel's academic importance, he must have realized it was no tour de force. According to the *Guardian*, his cousin Ivan, a publisher in France, had urged him to go ahead and destroy it. He had read *Laura* years earlier, as had Dmitri, and said, "We were all of the same opinion. It was just a torso, and not a glorious torso." The real motivating factor, according to Ivan, was that Dmitri was not well, in his seventies and facing steep medical bills and a poor prognosis. Publishing the manuscript was more a financial decision than anything else.

In his foreword to *The Original of Laura*, Dmitri owns up to some of this, describing the book as an "embryonic masterpiece" at best, and saying that while he could no longer conceive of destroying the index cards, he was still not sure if he ought to share them.

"Should I be damned or thanked?" he asks. "'But why, Mr. Nabokov, why did you *really* decide to publish *Laura*?' Well, I am a nice guy, and, having noticed that people the world over find themselves on a first-name basis with me as they empathize with 'Dmitri's dilemma,' I felt it would be kind to alleviate their sufferings."

It is a bequest, then, to us—the readers and the puzzle-solvers. Even if it was not the literary event of the year, I'm left believing that the cards should not have been burned—just as they should never have been described as anything they weren't.

I also believe that Nabokov was being sincere when he described hosting imaginary readings to peacocks and dead parents, and when he said, in that context, that the book was "nearly finished."

Because it *can* seem that way, even if it isn't true outside of your own mind. The perfect novel is always imaginary, but perhaps one key to genius is being able to keep hold of that vision even once you start to create its mundane, flawed mirror.

While *The Original of Laura* is *not* a great novel, or even a novel at all, it is a fantastic record of the creative process of one of my literary heroes, and an enduring reminder that he was never perfect, and that none of us are.

Every novel begins as a fantasy and then becomes a frustrating, fabulous pile of fragments: rough, resistant, and full of human flaws. They are, mostly, what is not there—our job is to find the gaps between the perfect novel in our minds and the imperfect one on the page and do our best to bridge them—knowing that we never really will.

FAIL LIKE A GENIUS

Vladimir Nabokov

You can slow down the moment when your ideal potential novel becomes a real and imperfect one by playing with form. Instead of writing in one big, intimidating document, take a page—or actually a card—from Nabokov's book and write a paragraph at a time (or a few lines of dialogue, even a handful of words or a single image) on an index card.

With index cards you aren't married to any order, and you also don't have to worry about leaving your notebook in the wrong pocket or bag. You can put a dozen blank cards in the pocket of each of your coats, purses, or bags, so one is always handy. At the end of the day, add the ones you've used to a pile on your desk. After a few weeks you'll be measuring your progress in inches.

Whenever you want they can be sorted, moved around, laid out on the floor, or tacked up on the corkboard.

Eventually the moment will arrive when you (or your Véra if you've got one) will begin typing them up and testing more permanent positions. But don't throw out the cards—you might keep them in a vault for thirty years and never look at them again, but you may want to go back and try new combinations. Take a card you deemed useless and put it in with your next pile.

Geniuses Get Blocked

Octavia Butler

Some people will tell you that writer's block is a myth, an excuse invented by writers who have simply fallen into complacency, boredom, or depression—not something any "real" writer would ever allow to stop them from productivity. We define a writer as someone who writes. Not only that, but we also very often describe a great writer's drive as compulsive, superhuman. A real writer is someone who cannot be stopped from writing, who would rather write than do anything else at all.

In *Letters to a Young Poet*, Ranier Maria Rilke advises, "Find out the reason that commands you to write; see whether it has spread its roots into the very depths of your heart; confess to yourself whether you would have to die if you were forbidden to write. This most of all: ask yourself in the most silent hour of your night: must I write?"

The implication here is clear—if you *musn't* write . . . if you simply *might* write or *like* to write, then, sorry, you are not a "real" writer, but more of a hobbyist. If for you writing is not essential, then it is no different than knitting, or bird-watching, or doodling in the margins of some other real, true calling.

Sadly, this attitude prevails despite all evidence that it is totally wrong.

Take a close look at the life of nearly any writer you can think of—and, I'm willing to bet, the real lives of many of those writers who claim writer's block is all a figment of the imagination of the unmotivated—and you will find that they experienced stretches of blockage. While we may picture a block as a total inability to write at all, often it is more accurately a sudden disinterest in writing, or a displeasure with anything you happen to be writing. But whatever we call it, there are always times in the life of any writer when they slow down, or pause, or simply don't feel they *must*.

In an article in the *New Yorker* called "How to Beat Writer's Block," researcher Maria Konnikova reviews two scientific studies on the subject that found that the condition can be subdivided into four different types of blocks, each stemming from different psychological causes. One writer might be blocked because they are paralyzed by insecurity and fear criticism by others, while a second writer might be under the arrogant delusion that their work is *too* good and therefore won't be appreciated by others—or will cause them to become the unhappy subject of others' envy. Another writer might be convinced, through the course of ordinary depression, that there's simply no *point* to them writing anymore—that it won't do anybody any good anyway. Still a fourth kind of writer, struggling from narcissism, withholds their work from the world in frustration over not being properly externally rewarded already.

Interestingly, the studies determined that the solutions to these blocks were similar, regardless of the differences in cause: a change of scene, doing more "low stakes" writing, or maybe just good old-fashioned therapy. Konnikova describes at one point how the writer Graham Greene overcame a long block, brought on by fear of his critics, by keeping a dream journal. Eventually Greene wrote about a bad dream in which T. S. Eliot had been viciously ripping one of his poems apart, and this cured him. In the end, Greene's subconscious found a way to sneak up and confront the blockage and, quite playfully, defeat it.

Even if the ghost of T. S. Eliot doesn't show up in your dreams to cure your writer's block, the message should be clear: experiencing a fallow period is never a sign that you are not a real writer. Not only have lots of geniuses had blocks and overcome them throughout their lives, but some have even faced blocks that proved insurmountable.

And even in this case, it isn't the end of the road, not at all.

"Acknowledge the Difficulty": Octavia Butler's *Parable of the Trickster*

In 1989, Octavia Butler set out to write *Parable of the Sower*, the first in a planned trilogy of novels about humanity's uncertain future. Her many earlier novels had already established her as a titan of science fiction. She'd written awesomely weird books about telepaths and time travel and aliens and psionic vampires. She was an anomaly in the sci-fi world. In interviews, Butler often described herself by saying, "I'm black, I'm solitary, I've always been an outsider." She had already upended a genre that had long been both very male and very white. And she wanted to do something even bigger.

As she later discussed in a lecture at MIT titled "'Devil Girl from Mars': Why I Write Science Fiction," Robert Heinlein had once delineated three kinds of science fiction stories: "The what-if category; the if-only category; and the if-this-goes-on category."

She had mastered the first two categories and had long been intrigued by the third. It was this category she set out to explore in *Parable of the Sower*. She envisioned a starkly realist novel about where America might carry itself in a few short decades—if things went on the way they were going on.

To do this, she amalgamated her own memories of growing up in racially integrated Pasadena in the 1950s with contemporaneous news reports about rises in global warming, racism, violence, prison populations, and megacorporations. In this way, she created the shattered America described by Lauren Oya Olamina, a Black fifteen-year-old with "hyperempathy" living in a walled-up town outside of Los Angeles in 2024.

Told through Lauren's diaries, the novel envisions the crises facing America thirty-some years later with eerie accuracy. Clean water is getting scarcer. Whole towns are being privatized by individual companies. Literacy is deteriorating, and all the while there's a charismatic president promising to make the country great again. Sound familiar? As Gloria Steinem wrote in a 2016 essay celebrating the novel's twenty-fifth anniversary, "If there is one thing scarier than a dystopian novel about the future, it's one written in the past that has already begun to come true."

Parable of the Sower was published in 1993 and became a *New York Times* Notable Book the following year. Already a Hugo and Nebula Award–winning writer, Butler soon became the first science fiction writer to ever receive the MacArthur Foundation "Genius Grant," which she hoped would help her to complete her work on the trilogy.

A year later Butler published a sequel, *Parable of the Talents*, in which a religion based on Lauren's diaries, called "Earthseed," struggles against Christian fundamentalism.

At the time, Butler spoke in interviews about her ideas for the third book, *Parable of the Trickster*, in which adherents of Earthseed would attempt to build a new, better society on another planet.

But after struggling for years with depression and writer's block, Butler never finished the trilogy as she planned.

She eventually turned her energies elsewhere and was able to complete several new stories and a novel, *Fledgling*, about a race of vampires trying to coexist with humans. But the Earthseed trilogy remained unfinished.

In 2006, Butler died of a stroke outside her home in Lake Forest Park, Washington. Her many papers now reside at the Huntington, a private library in San Marino, California. Curator Natalie Russell describes the collection as including "8,000 manuscripts, letters and photographs and an additional 80 boxes of ephemera." On display there now are numerous treasures, including working manuscript pages from *Parable of the Sower* covered in her brightly colored notes, urging herself onward: "More Sharing; More Sickness; More Death; More Racism; . . . More High Tech."

There are the beautiful, bold affirmations that recently went viral online, which she wrote to frame her motives for writing: "Tell Stories Filled with Facts. Make People Touch and Taste and KNOW. Make People FEEL! FEEL! FEEL!" On one page of her journals she wrote personal affirmations visualizing the success that she desired. "I am a Bestselling Writer. I write Bestselling Books And Excellent Short Stories. Both Books and Short Stories win prizes and awards."

But what is not on public view are the drafts—the things she had hoped to write someday and now, would not, including *Parable of the Trickster*.

Scholar Gerry Canavan described getting a look at that work in progress for the *Los Angeles Review of Books* in 2014:

Last December I had the improbable privilege to be
the very first scholar to open the boxes at the
Huntington that contain what Butler had written of
Trickster before her death. What I found were dozens
upon dozens of false starts for the novel, some
petering out after twenty or thirty pages, others
after just two or three; this cycle of narrative
failure is recorded over hundreds of pages of discarded drafts. Frustrated by writer's block, frustrated by blood pressure medication that she felt
inhibited her creativity and vitality, and frustrated
by the sense that she had no story for *Trickster*,
only a "situation," Butler started and stopped the
novel over and over again from 1989 until her death,
never getting far from the beginning.

The colorful affirmations that Butler used are all shared widely
on the internet today, and I have brought them in to show my own
students many times before because I think it is heartening on
some level to know that even a genius (certified, in this case!)
author needs to pump themselves up sometimes. I like that her
goals are so specific, even financial, and about wanting to be on
lists and win prizes—desires that most authors must surely share,
but often want to pretend they are in some way "above" or that
such honors are irrelevant.

But I think it is important that we also know the other side of
the story. That someone as brilliant and unique as Butler, with
every well-deserved accolade, can get completely stuck in a "cycle
of narrative failure" that sadly, in this case, she never was able to
break free from.

The novel's many abandoned openings revolve around another

woman, Imara, living on an Earthseed colony in the future on a planet called Bow, far from Earth. It is not the heaven that was hoped for, but "gray, dank, and utterly miserable." The people of Bow cannot return to Earth. Butler wrote in a note to herself, "Think of our homesickness as a phantom-limb pain—a somehow neurologically incomplete amputation. Think of problems with the new world as graft-versus-host disease—a mutual attempt at rejection."

From there Butler became hopelessly blocked.

But it is important to say, too, that her block was not at all the commonly held image of writer's block: staring day after day at a blank page, lacking inspiration and confidence, hurling crumpled pages into an overflowing wastepaper basket.

As Canavan describes, her "dozens upon dozens" of drafts represent a wide range of ambitious ideas. In some versions, the colonists struggle with a creeping blindness. In others, they develop telepathy. There are versions where Imara must solve a murder and versions where Imara is murdered but becomes a ghost. Canavan writes: "Sometimes Imara is an Earthseed skeptic; other times she is a true believer; sometimes she is, like Olamina, a hyperempath. . . . Sometimes Bow is inhabited by small animals, other times by dinosaur-like giant sauropods, and still other times by just moss and lichens; sometimes the colonists seem to encounter intelligent aliens who might be real, but might just be tokens of their escalating collective madness; and on and on and on."

What's fascinating here is that for Butler this writer's block was both frustrating *and* generative. While she couldn't land on the right idea to move forward with, she managed to produce dozens of incredible *new* ideas in the process. Rather than standing in front of a wall with nowhere to go, Butler's block was, in a sense, more like standing at a ten-way crossroads, unsure of which path to travel down. And the longer she tried to work it out, the more potential emerged.

Canavan reveals that Butler eventually hoped for this book to be only the middle of a *seven-part* series. *Trickster* was to be the first of four new novels about life on Bow and the colonists' struggle to build a better humanity.

Four more books. That was how long it would take, in her estimation, for the human beings of the future to move past their homesickness, their biology, and their history and truly become capable of working toward a common decency.

She saw hope, but only a long way off. I can't help but think that at least some part of her block stemmed from how much she saw riding on these books—how much she believed in the crucial importance of using writing to make people care, and how hard it can be to know whether that project will succeed. Looking back on her work today from a distance of many decades, it is easier for us to see the impact her novels have had on a whole generation of readers. But to see all that, and believe in it, from the writing desk before you've even begun? It's got to be one of the hardest things there is.

In 2001, during a speech to the UN's World Conference Against Racism, Butler explained that before embarking on the first *Parable* novel she had dreamed about writing a novel about a utopian civilization where everyone possessed hyperempathy. If only in fiction, she could create a world where "people were inclined either to accept one another's differences or at least to behave as though they accepted them since any act of resentment they commit would be punished immediately, personally, inevitably."

But soon she realized this would never work. "Popular, painful sports like boxing and football convinced me that the threat of shared pain wouldn't necessarily make people behave better toward one another. And it might cause trouble. For instance, it might stop people from entering the health care professions. Nursing would become very unpopular. And who would want to be a dentist in such a society? So much for fiction."

Instead, she created Lauren, a lone hyperempathic girl in a society of the empathy-deficient. Empathy was, Butler realized, not the solution but an affliction.

So much for fiction? I don't know about that. Butler may have ended up writing a dystopia instead of a utopia, but what she wrote gets right to the heart of our crises. It was not, she said, intended to be a prophecy, but a cautionary tale.

The rest of her speech to the UN that day is a clear outline of what she wanted the rest of the Parable books to be about—a way out, even if it was one she did not live to illuminate herself. Fortunately, what she did leave us influenced a generation of writers from every margin in society to continue her work.

"Whatever is the source of our intolerance, what can we do about it?" Butler asked. "Of course, we can resist acting on our nastier hierarchical tendencies. Most of us do that most of the time already. . . . Will this work? Well, it hasn't so far. Too many people will not, perhaps cannot, do it. There is, unfortunately, satisfaction to be enjoyed in feeling superior to other people."

Butler lists the basic human traits that catalyze our nasty tendencies into nasty behavior: ignorance, fear, disease, hunger, suspicion, hatred, war, greed, and vengeance. "Amid all this, does tolerance have a chance? Only if we want it to. Only when we want it to. Tolerance, like any aspect of peace, is forever a work in progress, never completed, and, if we're as intelligent as we like to think we are, never abandoned."

Butler sought to use her fiction as a way of addressing some of the hugest problems facing our society. If she got stuck, it was not for any lack of trying or lack of ideas—if anything, quite the opposite. Though her Parable saga would never be completed, Butler's work continued—she wrote several other unrelated novels and short stories in the years after *Parable of the Talents*. She also abandoned two other novels that we know about. But she did not despair.

In 2005, three months before her death, Octavia Butler gave an interview in which she was asked what advice she had for young people who might want to write.

"Oh, definitely that they should," Butler replied. "It's difficult, and sometimes impossible. I mean, here I am coming off a very long writer's block, so I can acknowledge the difficulty."

Asked to clarify, Butler added, "Seven years," and then laughed. "It didn't mean that I wasn't writing. Writer's block is not when I'm not writing. It's when I'm not writing anything worthwhile."

Pressed for advice for those stuck in a block as she had been, Butler was firm: "Keep writing. Keep writing. It's the old idea that behavior that gets rewarded tends to get repeated. If you stop writing, then you're kind of rewarding yourself with not writing. If you keep writing, after a while your brain gets the idea. I'm not sure I said that very clearly, but I hope you know what I mean. Just that if you are a writer, you can't stop writing. I used to have a teacher who said, 'If anything can prevent you being a writer, don't be one.'"

If a seven-year block didn't prevent Butler from being a writer, then you or I can make it through another day, or another week. Understanding blocks as part of a natural ebb and flow to creativity can help them feel less dooming. If the scientific studies Konnikova cited are correct, then it may be a sign that we have more work to do off the page for a while. Some low-stakes writing, some dream journaling, some therapy. In any case, writer's block is not as simple as most believe. The term can mean many things—from a complete inability to work to an abiding frustration with all that you are producing. This may be one reason that writers disagree about it even existing. It's a term that covers a range of symptoms and appears to have different roots in different writers.

What it *isn't*, however, is the result of laziness or unseriousness. It is not an affliction only experienced by imposters. It doesn't mean you give up too easily, or don't have the passion, or will never write again. It just means you're not writing right now.

Butler began writing stories as young as ten years old, hiding out in the Pasadena Central Library after school with a "big pink notebook." As a young woman she worked as a telemarketer and a dishwasher, writing all the while, even when it meant waking up at two a.m. before a shift as a potato chip inspector. When Rilke asks his young poets to ask themselves "must I write?" this is what he is really talking about—would you give up sleep or put up with a crummy job if that's what it takes to write? But I'm not sure writing relies on that level of sacrifice. It's OK to like writing, but still not want it more than you want sleep. It's OK to spend long periods of time not writing at all. I think the big question is this: whatever you do to keep writing, would you still do it knowing that there will be many days when the words won't come?

Would you show up again the next day, and keep waiting?

Just because we *must* doesn't mean we always *can*. But if we show up to work every day then any day might be the one when our blocks crumble at last.

Fail like a Genius

Octavia Butler

How do we write when we can't write? Octavia Butler believed in working each day no matter if she felt like it or not. "Screw inspiration," she said to one interviewer. Her job was to write, no matter how inspired she happened to feel. Butler described times in her life when she would routinely get up at two or three a.m. to write before putting in a long day's work at a warehouse or dialing numbers as a telemarketer. But we don't need to take Butler's case as proof that we all must pass feats of strength and constant exhaustion to write well. Forcing ourselves to write when our hearts aren't in it can make our blocks even larger. After so much labor we look at what dribbled out and wind up feeling like it was all just a waste of time.

As much as I sometimes love the idea of getting up to write in the dark at four a.m., I also know that if I do that, I'm going to be failing all day long as both a teacher and a parent. For me that's not an acceptable trade-off, so I find other times when I can work—and sometimes that work does not involve doing any writing at all.

Create a designated time to sit at your desk, or in a specific chair, or on the couch, where you can be alone with your project. Maybe that means writing it, but maybe it means reading other things for inspiration. Maybe it just means sitting and thinking about it. Maybe jotting down some stray notes or ideas. The key thing is to make this a regular part of your day. Be in that same place, at that same time, on some kind of daily or semidaily schedule. You may like the "morning pages" approach, or you may prefer a quiet half hour before tucking into bed at night. Maybe you need to slot in your creative time during your bus ride to work each day.

There's no right time for everyone—but consistency is the key.

Think of this time as your "office hours"—your job is to be there for whatever comes to your door. You may not write a word in that time, but that does not mean the time has been wasted. Ritualize the process. Drink a cup of coffee from the same mug, put on the same music—some writers I know like to wear the same slippers or light the same incense. Try a few things and see what sticks. The specifics should be personal, but the mechanism is the same: you're sending a signal to your creative mind that this is its time, and you are ready to get to work.

Geniuses Don't Get It Right the First Time

Flannery O'Connor

Back in my college writing classes, my professors would sometimes say things like, "There's no such thing as good writing, only good rewriting." Then they'd have us read works by meticulous prose writers like Flannery O'Connor, and spend hours marveling over her wording, which was clean to the bone. Here was a writer, they said, who truly considered each syllable, each punctuation mark. It's probably no wonder, then, that I always assumed "rewriting" meant paring down—that a genius's process involved generating a draft with all its basic parts in place, and then polishing it until there were no rough edges left.

If you're inclined to think of genius as an innate gift, it's easy to assume that this also applies to the editing process. Sure, geniuses rewrite, but for them—unlike for you!—rewriting means gradually making a good draft smoother, cleaner, and more economical. But what I've learned from looking at geniuses' real-life first drafts is that rewriting isn't usually just a matter of cutting away at something. It can just as easily be about expanding—even for the always-intentional Flannery O'Conner. One of the last stories she published, "Judgement Day," is actually a revision of one of her very first stories, "The Geranium"—and it is almost double the original length.

Less isn't always more. And revision isn't something you only need to do when you've done something wrong in the first place. It is a natural part of the *middle* of the process, not merely a final step. It is not just how a writer refines and reduces, but also how they explore and expand. It's not a chore, or a burden—it can often be a whole lot of fun. As a student I wondered what would possess someone like Flannery O'Connor to go back and revise an early story she'd already published. Today I find myself wishing I could do the same with my own older work. Because we get better, we grow, and each time we revise our work, we see new possibilities. What could be better than that?

It's notable that a similar misunderstanding about the nature of revision led scholars to dismiss a final unfinished novel by Flannery O'Connor, *Why Do the Heathen Rage?*, for decades after her death from lupus in 1964. When scholars first came across the manuscript pages of her final work, they saw O'Connor had written and rewritten the existing parts of the book dozens of times, and believed that this meant she had been badly blocked and that the novel was bound to be a lesser work.

But Dr. Jessica Hooten Wilson, author of *Flannery O'Connor's* Why Do the Heathen Rage?: *A Behind-the-Scenes Look at a Work in Progress*, has recently cast doubt on those assessments and brought about a reconsideration of O'Connor's final creative years. And in making her case, Dr. Wilson has reminded us that all writing—even the best—relies on revision.

"Like a Squirrel on a Treadmill": Flannery O'Connor's *Why Do the Heathen Rage?*

Most Flannery O'Connor fans know "Why Do the Heathen Rage?" as a brief, four-page story tucked into the back of her 550-page *Complete Stories*. The collection contains thirty-one short stories, making up the bulk of the work she published before she died at just thirty-nine years old. Though O'Connor published two novels, *Wise Blood* and *The Violent Bear It Away*, it is her short fiction for which she is best known: classics like "A Good Man Is Hard to Find" and "Everything That Rises Must Converge" that remain widely read and anthologized today.

"Why Do the Heathen Rage?" is not one of these classics. It is by far the shortest story in the collection, and rather unsatisfying. This is because it is not a short story at all, but an excerpt of her last novel, which O'Connor published in *Esquire* nine months before her death.

When researchers first began going through O'Connor's papers ten years later, in 1974, they found her novel in progress but determined it was insubstantial. One reported: "Of the 378 pages of material, it's a lot of repetitive episodes. There's no trajectory. There's no structure here." Seven years later, another scholar confirmed that assessment: "There's nothing approaching a proper novel in the unfinished papers. It is an untidy jumble of ideas and aborted starts. Full scenes written and rewritten many times."

The consensus was that Flannery O'Connor had run into a bad case of writer's block while working on the project, resulting in all those written and rewritten scenes. This fit another theory at the time, that O'Connor was in over her head with the project because she was using it to explore what, for her, were new and challenging ideas.

Why Do the Heathen Rage? was to deal more directly than O'Connor had before with the civil rights movement in the South, events that she had not personally fully come to terms with by 1963. She had worried that it "wasn't her material" and struggled to describe romantic relationships between Black and white characters. Scholars today largely agree that O'Connor's views on race evolved during her lifetime. When she revised "The Geranium" and republished it as "Judgement Day," one change she made was removing many, many instances of the N-word (though not nearly all of them). It is still very much being debated whether O'Connor's views on racial segregation evolved, and if so, how far.

Ironically, the once-dismissed *Why Do the Heathen Rage?* is some of the best evidence that O'Connor was attempting to revise her own thinking on race and equality.

Dr. Jessica Hooten Wilson argues that O'Connor was not stuck creatively, with themes she couldn't handle, but rather that she died in the midst of making a big leap forward. Her findings have the potential to change the way one of the South's greatest authors is understood today. In one view, O'Connor's late attempts to be more progressive in her fiction had backfired. In the other, she faced no such quandary at all, and was evolving through her work to the very end.

Wilson has dedicated more than a decade now to the painstaking process of piecing together the fragments and drafts of *Why Do the Heathen Rage?* so that it might finally be published in a form that shows its real scope and significance. During a 2020 lecture on her research for the Dallas Institute of Humanities and Culture, Wilson acknowledged that this was an "audacious task" and one fraught with ethical considerations, especially because O'Connor *was* such a relentless revisionist, thoughtful about the placement of every word. On the other hand, she noted that "the majority of O'Connor's work was published after she died." This list includes the collection *Everything That Rises Must Converge,* all her journals and letters, and even the popular collection of craft essays *Mystery and Manners*, which was produced by editors using "scissors and connective brackets," to combine numerous lectures

O'Connor that had delivered over the years. Even *The Complete Stories* includes pieces that O'Connor did not want to be published in her lifetime.

According to Wilson, the excerpt of *Why Do the Heathen Rage?* that is included in *The Complete Stories* bears only slim connection to the rest of the drafted work. O'Connor published those four and a half pages in *Esquire* in response to a request for some work in progress. The story (misprinted as "Why Do the Heathens Rage?") features tropes common in O'Connor's previous stories. After a debilitating stroke, Tilman, an elderly farmer, is brought home by his wife and two children, Walter and young Mary Maude. The provincial mother tries to convince her disinterested son to step up and take over some of the farming responsibilities since his father can no longer do so. But Walter is a modern-minded would-be intellectual who enjoys reading philosophy and writing letters to the newspaper in the voices of imagined characters. He tells his mother he can't be a farmer and wouldn't even know *how* to do such a thing. Mary Maude rudely chimes in from the background. Nothing is resolved in the end. (Remember, it's an excerpt, a fragment, still quite raw.)

The piece feels very similar to other work, particularly "Everything That Rises Must Converge," in which a young white man, Julian, berates his mother about her backwards views on race while they ride together on a recently integrated bus. Desiring to show her how evolved he is compared to her, he picks on her so much that she eventually has a heart attack, and Julian is left in distress and guilt.

Wilson explains that *Why Do the Heathen Rage?* would have continued this type of dynamic, but as the starting point of the novel rather than its end. O'Connor intended to connect it with another earlier story, "The Enduring Chill," in which another grumpy son, Asbury, returns to the South from New York City in poor health, believing that he is dying. He hates his mother and in flashbacks we find out that when he was home previously he spent much of his time trying to get the two Black farmhands to rise up and disobey her rules—he gave them cigarettes to smoke on the job and tried to persuade them to drink milk straight from the cow, going so far as showing them how he does it.

As with Julian in the other story, Asbury's real aim in all of this is not genuinely to advocate for the equality or even the fundamental humanity of the Black farmhands, but simply to irritate his mother. When Asbury becomes gravely ill, it is his same superiority that compels him to dismiss his mother's attempts to get him to see a local doctor. Asbury declares that what's happening to him is *spiritual* and can only be addressed by a priest. One soon comes, but he yells at Asbury for not knowing his catechisms or anything about the Holy Spirit. In the end it is the humble local doctor who realizes Asbury has developed an illness from drinking the unpasteurized cow's milk months before. As the story ends, Asbury believes he's being visited by the Holy Spirit—a very typical O'Connor ending, where a character is humbled, sometimes violently, but still receives a spiritual revelation.

According to Wilson, a revised version of this story (swapping in Walter for Asbury) would only have been the *first* chapter of *Why Do the Heathen Rage?* in its book form. Instead of having the book conclude in a discovery of faith, O'Connor envisioned her new book taking what for her would have been a "novel" shape. *Begin* with Walter's visitation by the Holy Spirit, and then proceed into his "comic" journey to adjust his former life as an agnostic to his newfound beliefs.

In "The Enduring Chill," Asbury flashes back at one point to a frustrating encounter in New York City with a Buddhist woman in a sari who dismisses any concept of salvation as "meaningless" during a discussion with a priest named Ignatius Vogle. According to Wilson, in *Why Do the Heathen Rage?* O'Connor had intended to combine these secondary characters, Vogle and the Buddhist woman, into a love interest for Walter: Oona, a secular civil rights activist. The middle of the novel would be epistolary—another challenge for O'Connor, with an emphasis on colloquial style—comprising letters between "Yankee" Oona in the city and Walter on the farm. But Walter would write pretending to be a Black man, testing Oona's claim that she does not judge people based on race.

Wilson acknowledges that all of this would have been quite challenging and different for O'Connor, but that the writer had always challenged herself in this way with new projects.

With all this new material and big challenges, we can begin to see why scholars originally leaped to the conclusion that O'Connor had gotten blocked. When they saw those piles of scenes, written and rewritten dozens of times, they assumed she was doing so out of frustration and creative blockage. But Wilson points out that O'Connor said she was writing "like a squirrel on a treadmill," and that her "jumble of ideas and abortive starts" was no different than the way that O'Connor had written her earlier novels. To get back into the mood of a longer work, O'Connor would routinely rewrite several pages from the previous day, sometimes making minor adjustments along the way, before charging ahead into new material.

This isn't uncommon. Many other writers use similar strategies to jump-start their creative momentum at the start of a new day. In a late interview for the *Paris Review*, Ernest Hemingway described his process along these same lines—ending each day with some idea of where the story will go the next day, and then beginning by rewriting the earlier work and charging ahead. Especially for those working on typewriters, or going from handwritten pages to typed ones, some amount of backtracking and retyping is a key part of the process.

Wilson's new book on O'Connor's unfinished work expands on her Dallas lecture. After years of working with editors and representatives of the O'Connor estate to find the best possible way to present the work, Wilson aims to interest both O'Connor scholars and everyday readers alike. Her research revises our understanding of the ways that this great American writer was processing and adapting to the changing South.

In doing so, she may also help more readers to see how nonlinear the revision process can sometimes be. Our misunderstandings of revision not only skew our understanding of geniuses like O'Connor, but they misinform writers attempting to follow in her footsteps.

We see struggle in places where there may have only been searching; we see someone lost when they were only exploring. We see agony where there may have been considerable fun. We see blockage when, really, we are all always squirrels on our treadmills, going on at our own pace, even when it means taking a step backward in order to take two forward.

FAIL LIKE A GENIUS

Flannery O'Connor

We tend to think of revision as a process of compression and refinement, but it can also be an expansive process. A genius isn't someone who produces a masterpiece on their first try, but it may be someone willing to push ahead, through dozens of tries.

Here's something I call the "Goldilocks Revision," adapted from a marvelous book called *The Art of Revision*, by Peter Ho Davies.

Take something you've written that you're pretty happy with already, but that you know isn't quite perfect. Now, rewrite it bigger. Look for places to *expand*. Let it get woolly and wild. Double it in length, if you can.

Then take the new version of the story and cut it way down. Take out as much as you can—more than you need to take out. Cut it to the bone. Be relentless. Make it a quarter of the length, or half as long as it was *originally*.

At this point you can triangulate between the "too small" draft and the "too big" one to find the "just right" version. When you're finished, compare it to that original draft. They might be the same length, but the new version is going to be quite different, and much better.

Flannery O'Connor wrote 378 pages just to work out the first quarter of her novel. So don't look at revision as a chore or a sign of weakness. See it as a key part of the work—and even as a huge part of the fun.

Geniuses Often Quit

Jane Austen

Growing up in central New Jersey, I, like most other Garden State schoolchildren, learned an inordinate amount about Thomas Edison, the Wizard of Menlo Park, an area of what's now known as Edison Township, on the other side of Middlesex County, neighbor to my own. It was there, in his sprawling laboratory, that the great genius perfected many inventions that changed the shape of the twentieth century: the phonograph, the kinetoscope, the automatic telegraph machine, and, of course, the light bulb. Reputedly, this last invention came only after Edison made thousands of failed prototypes.

Edison's friend and biographer Walter Mallory recounted this anecdote of coming into his workshop as Edison was trying to develop the alkaline battery:

I said: 'Isn't it a shame that with the tremendous amount of work you have done you haven't been able to get any results?' Edison turned on me like a flash, and with a smile replied: 'Results! Why, man, I have gotten a lot of results! I know several thousand things that won't work.'

It was this line, "several thousand things that won't work," that became glued in my young mind and came back to me later in life as I plugged away for months and years on novels and short stories that still weren't fully successful. I didn't want to let them go. I revised endlessly, even when I felt like many of the changes were only causing the pieces to become worse. As I grew as both a writer and a person, I remained stubbornly tethered to my oldest work. The story of Edison reassured me that there was truth in an adage which my parents often trotted out: *Quitters never win, and winners never quit.*

What if Edison had thrown in the towel just *one* failed prototype before success? Would we all still be living in darkness?

We imagine that a genius like Edison has the special gift of *perseverance*, and that if we are not successful in our own endeavors then it must be because we've sold ourselves short. In previous chapters we've lauded writers like Butler and O'Connor for fighting through seven-year writer's blocks and revising their work repeatedly to get it right. It took Michael Crichton twenty years to write *Sphere*, my father has often reminded me. Seventeen for J. R. R. Tolkien to write *The Lord of the Rings*. Ten years for Margaret Mitchell to finish *Gone with the Wind*, and the same for J. D. Salinger to finish *The Catcher in the Rye*. The list goes on and on.

One quality of geniuses is that they outlast the rest. They refuse to abandon ship when others would be heading for the lifeboats.

But as my time with unfinished novels has shown me, the opposite is often also true.

A real genius *also* knows when it is time to walk away and give up on a project that isn't working, no matter how much they want it to pan out.

We praise Octavia Butler for struggling through her epic writer's block, continuing to write habitually, even when the writing coming out wasn't to her liking. But doing so also meant accepting a move away from the Parable trilogy/saga into other ideas that she thought might lead her forward.

Perseverance is one important key to success. But we hear a lot less about the great benefit that a writer may find in walking away from a project that isn't working, or doesn't feel right, thus liberating them to tackle something else, or discover something new. I think of this trait of genius as *resilience*—similar to perseverance but at times its very opposite. When pressing ahead won't work anymore, we need something else: an ability to bounce back, to face failure and rejection without blinking—or without blinking much.

"Too Clever, Too Bold": Jane Austen's *Lady Susan* and *The Watsons*

In 1811, Jane Austen published her first novel, *Sense and Sensibility*, at the age of thirty-five, after commissioning it on her own through publisher Thomas Egerton. She published the book anonymously, the author on the title page stating simply, "A Lady"—this after *sixteen* years of work on the book. *Sense and Sensibility* started out as an epistolary novel, *Elinor and Marianne*, which Austen had written in 1795, when she was only nineteen. But she wasn't happy with it. After two years she would rewrite the entire novel into the third person, and then revise it even further before its publication fourteen years later. At first glance, Austen would seem to be a perfect example of the importance of Edison levels of perseverance. How many others would have given up, at any point along the way?

But what's left out of that story is another story—of abandoning an earlier novel, *Lady Susan*, a year before beginning *Elinor and Marianne*, in 1794.

Lady Susan, written when Austen was only eighteen, is told by the eponymous character, in a similar epistolary style. But Susan is a character unlike any to be found in Austen's later works, "the most accomplished coquette in England" who is the recently widowed "glamorous, shrewd and calculating" daughter of an earl. Lady Susan boldly seduces and manipulates the men around her, both single and married, in a naked bid to regain her former financial security.

Scholars speculate that the young Austen was inspired by her cousin Eliza de Feuillide (who would later become her sister-in-law) and by the popular, scandalous novel *Les Liaisons Dangereuses*, to which Eliza most likely introduced to Austen. While being a "bad mother" and a "dazzling female Don Juan," Lady Susan outwits the "dullards" who seek to undo her—always with perfect sweetness and impeccably polite manners, inverting all the usual moral tropes of a romantic novel of her time.

It wouldn't be so strange for a young novelist to abandon a juvenile work in progress to focus instead on more ambitious adult work, but this isn't the case with *Lady Susan*. For one thing, the novel is complete, and also of especially high quality, even in comparison to Austen's later works. Biographer Claire Tomalin describes the novel as "polished, sophisticated in its analysis of behavior, and quite unlike anything she had yet written or was ever to write again: an altogether extraordinary piece of work to come from the pen of a country clergyman's daughter." As a teenager, Austen successfully embodied the voice and character of the thirty-five-year-old protagonist, a woman who bears a mature intelligence and forcefulness, who "knows herself to be wasted on the dull world in which she is obliged to live."

So why, then, did Austen walk away from the book?

Tomalin speculates that Austen, rather than becoming discouraged by her struggles to pull off such a challenging experiment may have been alarmed by its success: "The experiment is brilliant. So brilliant, that Austen may have frightened herself, and felt she had written herself into a dangerous corner, and been too clever, too bold, too black." By setting *Lady Susan* aside and never seeking to publish it, not even later in life, Austen opted to instead "censor the part of her imagination that interested itself in women's wickedness, and particularly sexual wickedness." Austen moved off these overt themes after *Lady Susan*, beginning those long sixteen years in search of the more mature but still subversive style she'd locate at last in *Sense and Sensibility*. Tomalin argues that this spark would eventually be enflamed in *Mansfield Park* in the character of Mary Crawford, but significantly "banked down."

With all her successful later work, *Lady Susan* was largely forgotten until 2016 when auteur director Whit Stillman adapted it the film *Love and Friendship* (the title of a different early Austen novel, written when she was only fourteen), starring Kate Beckinsale as Lady Susan.

I said already that Austen jettisoned *Lady Susan* to embark on the sixteen-year journey toward *Sense and Sensibility*, completing *Elinor and Marianne* by 1795 and then rewriting it into the third person by 1797. But did she really spend those next fourteen years before 1811 stubbornly and faithfully rewriting that novel? Was she, like Edison, plugging away on several thousand things that wouldn't work, to find the one that would?

No. In fact, she set *Sense and Sensibility* aside for nearly twelve of those years, only returning to begin revisions of that book in 1809. The delay allowed Austen to, in the meantime, begin a number of other important works, including early versions of her later novels *Pride and Prejudice* and *Northanger Abbey*.

Additionally, during this pause on *Sense and Sensibility,* in 1803 Austen also began a novel called *The Watsons,* which she would never return to.

The Watsons was a novel about an ailing clergyman, whose youngest daughter, Emma, ends up in a marriage plot between neighboring Lord Osborn and the local vicar, Mr. Howard. The manuscript is thought to be only about a sixth of the way finished, abandoned by Austen at a length of around 7,500 words, about two years after she'd begun writing it. We know that Austen worked on *The Watsons* while living in Bath, and then shelved it after the death of her own father in 1805. Tomalin speculates that "her personal circumstances resembled those of her characters too closely for her comfort." Just as *Lady Susan* may not have fit the tone that Austen ultimately sought, *The Watsons* may have proved to be too pessimistic, written in a period of deep unhappiness.

Still, the fragment of the book she wrote was compelling, according to editor Margaret Drabble, who introduced a recent republication of the work as "tantalizing, delightful and highly accomplished," and asserting that it "must surely have proved the equal of her other six novels, had she finished it." The novel would have stood out as being one of the only books of Austen's to focus primarily on a humble and unaffluent family. However, Drabble argues that the Watson family's struggles are not unrefined but quite charming, and that there is something uplifting about the novel that supersedes the sadness surrounding it.

Austen worked hard on *The Watsons*, taking the time to strike out and rewrite the incomplete manuscript, and if you look closely at the pages you can even see small pinholes in the pages where she tacked rewrites of some sections directly over the old pages to see how they would flow.

Both *Lady Susan* and the fragments of *The Watsons* were only published posthumously, first in 1871 by a nephew of Austen's named James Edward Austen-Leigh, as part of his own memoir about the life of his aunt.

Scandalized by the idea of a novel about common folk, Austen-Leigh blamed the novel's abandonment on Austen's becoming "aware of the evil of having placed her heroine too low, in such a position of poverty and obscurity as, though not necessarily connected with vulgarity, has a sad tendency to degenerate into it: and therefore, like a singer who has begun on too low a note, she discontinued the strain."

It may be telling that Austen-Leigh found *Lady Susan* to be the "least satisfactory" of the unfinished novels, due to the "slightly melodramatic nature of its plot and the excessive wickedness of its heroine, Lady Susan herself" and cited a lack of balance between Susan and the other characters, a hallmark of the sophistication of Austen's later novels.

Later in this book, I'll return to Austen to discuss the last of her three unfinished novels, *Sanditon*, which was left incomplete not because Austen abandoned it but because of her death in 1817. But with *Lady Susan* and *The Watsons*, the choice to end her work on those projects was entirely her own, and nothing she regretted. In both cases Austen was trying something slightly different, and for separate reasons decided to not pursue it further. If she stepped away from the rebellious impulses of *Lady Susan*, it was only to find more subtle and subversive ways to dissect society in her later writings. Setting one novel aside allowed her to discover *Sense and Sensibility*—which itself had to be put on pause for many years.

Austen left those early books behind because she sensed she was capable of better things, bigger things. But even a genius writer may walk away from a project for the opposite reason just as easily: recognizing that the project is, for whatever reason, going to be too challenging, too difficult, and that they may simply not be capable of doing it justice.

Surely, though we hear less about it, the workshop at Menlo Park must have been filled with plenty of dead-end ideas, shelved so that more work could be done on kinetoscopes and light bulbs. We should remember, then, that giving up on any particular idea, and setting it aside for a few years, or even forever, is in and of itself a secret to creative success.

Geniuses quit all the time. The truth is that winners often quit, and quitters often win.

Fail like a Genius

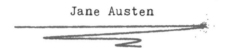

Jane Austen

Jane Austen wrote her books entirely by hand, using a quill pen made from goose feathers. Without the option to backspace or even use Wite-Out, authors of the time had to either scribble out small mistakes or start the page over for bigger ones. But when Austen wanted to rewrite several sentences or a whole paragraph, she'd write the revised version on a new piece of paper and use a straight pin to affix the changes directly over the old.

It makes for a nifty way of tracking one's changes on a handwritten manuscript and can be a useful tool for writers today who work by hand before typing their work. Scotch Tape or paper clips can be used similarly even on a typed and printed manuscript. There's something gratifyingly tactile about editing with literal pins, a feeling of assembling something, physically, that often gets lost in the wash of computer screens.

Modern word processing software can do a lot, but it can also be a pain to keep track of changes over many months, across multiple files and versions of files. With Austen's method you have an easy visual way of seeing the changed areas, and can easily look beneath to see what you had two, or three, or thirty versions ago—something that could take ages in Microsoft Word or Google Docs.

Take a shorter project at first and see what comes of tacking your pages up and taking a pair of actual scissors to it. You may find the drudgery of editing lifts when you make it into an arts and crafts project. It can provide a great shift in perspective and inject fun back into the process. Above all, you may find it a welcome reminder that you're creating something real.

Geniuses Still Have to Do the Dishes

Sylvia Plath

We're familiar with the scene, a staple of the genre: The genius is wide awake. It is past four in the morning. They are working feverishly, ideally by the light of a spare, dangling bulb. Who knows how long since they've last slept? Eaten more than bags of chips? They make more coffee without looking away from their project, spilling dark fluid everywhere. Puddles form on the floor. Already, dishes are stacked high in the sink. There must (by law, I assume) be a wire wastepaper basket that is overflowing with crumpled pages. Our hero gnaws distractedly at a cuticle! Cuts a few words from one line! Stands up and dances about pensively as they review the change. *No! It's terrible.* They tear at their hair, and collapse. In solemn defeat, they stare out the window into the darkness. Oh! All is lost. But then—inspiration! This is it! They rush back, knocking everything over, grasping for the pen. Can it be? Has the muse spoken? Scribbling like a maniac, their smile deepens as they, at long last, nail it. And so, the music swells. Triumph!

Typically, in a movie about a great artist, we get around a twenty-second montage of hard work. Genius is evidenced by obsession, mess, and neglect. The mundane tasks of domestic life are blithely cast aside in order to allow the great breakthrough to occur. (If these geniuses do have partners or lovers, they must gaze on, either adoringly or in irritation, from a bed somewhere.) They don't have children, these geniuses, or if they do, someone else is going to deal with them in two hours when they wake up.

And that's because these geniuses are probably men, in these montages. They're pretty much always men.

We've seen, already, the conflicts that can arise between domestic and artistic lives. Kafka believed he could not get married and start a family without dashing his creative future, as he'd need to do more office work to support them. In other cases, we've seen male writers utterly reliant on their spouse's support and labor: Véra Nabokov typing her husband's work off the index cards he scribbled all morning. Zelda Fitzgerald gave F. Scott Fitzgerald not just inspiration but even whole passages from her own pages. Without her around (and later Sheilah Graham) he struggled to maintain himself and his productivity.

Meanwhile, Jane Austen, Louisa May Alcott, Octavia Butler, and Flannery O'Connor all have one thing in common beyond their genius: none of them ever married, nor did they have children. There could be many reasons for this, but they unarguably each also lived within some form of patriarchy, where women are expected to make either married life or motherhood, or both, their top priority, no matter how brilliant or creative they are.

Tough to be the messy genius having the four a.m. breakthrough. Even tougher to be the one also washing up all those piles of dishes and taking out the overfull trash and mopping up the coffee puddles and feeding the very-much-on-camera children (wide awake by six!) and buying the groceries and cooking the meals and doing the laundry and walking the dog and teaching three adjunct classes and on and on and on.

Plath would soon move, with Nicholas and her older daughter, Frieda, into a room in a London house where the poet William Butler Yeats had once lived. All of this turmoil had left Plath inspired to return to fiction, as she described in a letter to a friend, Olive Prouty, that November. She hoped to sell a novel to be adapted into a movie so that she could buy her house instead of renting it. She described how she would then rent the rooms out, and furnish it by writing more poetry, and that she wanted to proceed to new novels, which were inside her, "crying out to be written."

This would begin with *The Interminable Loaf,* by then already underway, though under a new name, *Doubletake.* The novel, which she called "semiautobiographical," was about a woman who'd been deserted by her cheating husband.

Friends who'd read excerpts described it as a dark comedy and Plath herself remarked to her brother that it was "hellishly funny" and that writing it often left her laughing.

In the novel Plath aimed to skewer her husband, and Wevill. "She'd given herself permission to hate Hughes," remarked Ronald Hayman, in his biography, *The Death and Life of Sylvia Plath,* "and the hatred apparently helped to fuel the fiction."

Hayman also claimed that Plath rated the novel more highly than *The Bell Jar* and that scholar Judith Kroll had seen a complete outline of the book—now called *Double Exposure,* its final title—on a series of index cards.

But with two children to care for and limited financial resources with Hughes gone, Plath struggled to find the time to work on *Double Exposure.* "I write at my novel now from about 5 a.m. when my sleeping pill wears off, till they wake up, and hope to finish it by mid-winter," she told Prouty.

Several letters during these months referenced an epic search for a nanny for the children so she could finish the book. Plath estimated that it would take "six weeks of daylong work" to reach the end. But without the money she hoped to get from the novel, it was hard to find a nanny; without the nanny, she could not finish the novel.

Double Exposure was almost surely never completed. December on the 1962 calendar is jammed with household chores and duties, including repeated notes on painting and repainting the floors and furniture in the new apartment, and appointments to get a phone installed. By January, Plath was suffering severe depression and insomnia.

On the twenty-second of that month, Plath wrote to Olive Prouty again, mentioning that she'd been prescribed sleeping pills and "tonics" to boost her appetite. She had, finally, found someone to watch the children six mornings and one evening a week. Still, she wrote, there was the novel, which she hadn't been able to work on. Plath repeated her plan to write a novel that would help her buy a house so she could earn income from renting out the rooms.

She spoke of her desire to write "resolutely" in the mornings over the coming years, despite the strain of dealing with frozen pipes and sick children, along with her feelings of loneliness without the company of Hughes, whom she'd loved for so long.

Three weeks later, on February 11, Sylvia Plath killed herself at the age of thirty.

After her death, Ted Hughes became the heir to Plath's estate, including all her papers. He sent out two more sets of Plath's poems to quarterlies the following month and marked these down by hand on her meticulous submission log. He also found a black spring binder on her desk containing the collection of *Ariel* poems, and arranged to have it published in 1965, though only after omitting several poems—it would not be until 2007 that a new

Restored Edition faithfully replicated Plath's original manuscript.

But what happened to the novel she was writing at the same time as these poems? Was *Double Exposure/Doubletake/The Interminable Loaf* there on her desk as well?

The novel that Plath hoped might save her financially has never been published, nor, as far as we know, has it been seen since her death by anyone other than Ted Hughes.

But in 1977, Hughes published a collection of Plath's short fiction and journals in a volume titled *Johnny Panic and the Bible of Dreams*. In his introduction to these previously uncollected works, Hughes remarked on that Plath had "typed some 130 pages of another novel, provisionally titled *Double Exposure*. That manuscript disappeared somewhere around 1970."

Plath's readers wanted to know how exactly a manuscript could "disappear" (seven years after her death). Given the purported subject matter of the novel, some were wary of Hughes's claims. These suspicions were amplified when, in the foreword to a 1982 collection of Plath's *Journals*, Hughes admitted to interfering with some of her other notebooks: "Two more notebooks survived for a while. . . . The last of these contained entries for several months, and I destroyed it because I did not want her children to have to read it. . . . The other disappeared." Hughes would later add that this first notebook "disappeared more recently (and may, presumably, still turn up)."

The notebook that "disappeared" is likely not *Double Exposure*, but an earlier journal that scholars have sought, describing Plath's and Hughes's return to England. Notably, Hughes distinguished between this journal and the other, which he specifically claimed to have "destroyed."

The destroyed notebook would likely be another journal, the one she kept after their separation and before her suicide. But if he destroyed the journals from those "several months," he may have destroyed the novel she was writing at the same time about his being a "deserter and a philanderer."

By 1995, in the *Paris Review*, Hughes revised his story a third time: "Her mother said she saw a whole novel, but I never knew about it. What I was aware of was sixty, seventy pages which disappeared. And to tell you the truth, I always assumed her mother took them all."

Was it one hundred thirty pages, a whole novel, or sixty, seventy pages? Did he destroy them, or did they disappear? Why would her mother have taken them? And if she had, wouldn't she have given them to Smith College along with the many other letters and childhood notebooks and possessions that she later donated?

We still have few answers to these questions, but there are a few new pieces to the puzzle—many stemming from discoveries of pieces of another novel entirely.

In the Smith College Library's special collections, there is a copy of the November 20, 1962, letter to Olive Prouty typed by Sylvia Plath, with some notations in the margins left by her mother, Aurelia, made when she gave the letters to Smith.

There is a circle around the place where Plath wrote, "I hope to really get into my second novel this winter" and a note scribbled in the left margin from Aurelia: "It would be her <u>third</u> novel, counting the burned ms as #2."

The "burned ms" she mentions here was Plath's *first* novel, called *Falcon Yard*. Plath had begun writing it years earlier, even before *The Bell Jar*, and some scholars even consider it a lost "prequel." Ironically, *Falcon Yard* also dealt with Sylvia Plath's marriage to Ted Hughes—not its grisly demise, but rather its passionate beginnings.

In 1956, the twenty-three-year-old poet Sylvia Plath attended a party at Falcon Yard, near Cambridge University, where she was studying, to celebrate the launch of the *St. Botolph's Review*. The first (and only) issue contained four poems by one of the founders, Ted Hughes. Prior to the party, Plath had taken care to memorize one of his poems, "Fallgrief's Girl-Friends" and when she met Hughes, she recited the poem back to him.

The following day, in her journal, Plath recounted this leading to their first kiss in a side room, and then to him tearing off her red headband. She, in turn, bit him on the cheek and she wrote that when they returned to the party, Hughes still had blood on his face.

Soon they began writing poems to one another. Less than four months later, they were married, on Bloomsday, June 16.

Plath and Hughes worked intimately together at first, sharing a writing desk and editing and guiding one another. Hughes would jot down lists of ideas for poems and Plath would dot the ones she thought were most interesting. They routinely wrote on the backs of each other's scrap paper. The following year, while living together in Massachusetts and teaching at Smith College, Plath began working on a novel based on her romance with Hughes. She planned to call it *Falcon Yard*, in reference to the place where they'd met.

In her journal, Plath described it as being autobiographical, and being set in Cambridge. The central character, at times in the third person as Jessica, or Jess, or Jill, or Sadie Peregrine, was to be, "kinetic, a voyager, no Penelope" (which is to say, not someone who sits at home waiting for a heroic husband).

On a pink sheet of Smith College memorandum paper, Plath kept a long list of character names to use in the novel, with one column, "Real People," that included several former boyfriends. She marked "Leonard," the character based on Hughes, as the "hero." In her notebooks she described him as "Pan-like, spermy,

Dionysiac, God-man." Later she wrote, "his voice. UnBritish. Refugee Pole rather, mixed with something of Dylan Thomas: rich and mellow-noted: half sung."

Plath wrote of the overall plot in her journal. There would be a series of brief love affairs with other men before the "big, blasting dangerous love" with Leonard. Her character would experience a profound depression, which would be then erased by their marriage. The central dilemma of the novel would be, she wrote, "How to lead Pan into world of toast and nappies?"

Her hope was that this "slick bestseller" might sell for enough money to allow her and Hughes to resume a life of writing poetry without also needing to teach.

Ultimately, Plath set the *Falcon Yard* project aside, convinced by Robert Lowell and Anne Sexton that she should instead focus on her poetry and try to write a more serious novel about her experiences with depression before Cambridge, which had led to her first suicide attempt. Plath soon assembled *Colossus,* her first collection of poetry, and began to work tirelessly on that new novel, which would become *The Bell Jar.*

Here again she hoped that this novel might bring in the money she needed to support their growing family—but publishers were not sold. Despite receiving a fellowship from Harper & Row to help her write the book, they rejected it as "disappointing, juvenile and overwrought." She would end up publishing it in the UK under a pseudonym, "Victoria Lucas," originally the name of the novel's protagonist before it was changed to "Esther Greenwood." But US editors remained uninterested. One, at Knopf, remarked on its "youthful American female brashness" but added "there certainly isn't enough genuine talent for us to take notice." They hoped, "maybe now that this book is out of her system, she will use her talent more effectively next time."

The Bell Jar would, many years after her death, indeed become a best seller and an enduring classic. Today, decades later, the novel thrives on high school and college reading lists and has sold over three million copies. But during the final months of Plath's life, this success remained elusive.

By the time *The Bell Jar* was finished in 1962, Plath and Hughes were living in England again and searching for more stable income. They did paid appearances on BBC programs. Plath sold bouquets of flowers from their garden. They moved to Devon and rented out their London apartment to a young couple—David and Assia Wevill.

Rubber nipples for Nicholas. Grocery lists. Ashcans, Wednesday. Keeping house and caring for the children. Plath's daily calendars show a growing number of these responsibilities and obligations, which at this point could be nominally supported by Hughes. It shows a classic clashing of worlds—just as Plath's career was beginning to take off and creative success felt near, if elusive, she found herself with less and less time available to pursue her craft. She wound up betting on *The Bell Jar* being a strong enough seller that she could begin to hire help and cut back on those paid appearances. But while the book earned strong reviews, this failed to translate into actual sales, and Plath found herself once again stuck.

Eventually Plath decided that the solution was to write another novel, and so she revisited her abandoned *Falcon Yard* manuscript. She set a goal to finish the novel by August 17, Hughes's birthday, as a present to him.

But when she learned of her husband's affair in July of that year, everything changed. It is hard to imagine how she could have finished the semi-autobiographical "romantic comedy" after Hughes's infidelity came to light. Distraught and angry, she

I've been a longtime member of a kind of support group called Pen Parentis that gives grants and other aid to writing parents, but this sort of assistance, especially for writing mothers, remains a rare thing today. The challenges faced would have only been greater back in Georgian England, or nineteenth-century Concord, or Georgia in the 1950s.

To gain an appreciation for this, one only needs to look at the life of Sylvia Plath (and, in the next chapter, Shirley Jackson). These writers' domestic lives presented enormous challenges to their creative success—and in both cases this is evidenced plainly by their unfinished novels.

"The World of Toast and Nappies": Sylvia Plath's *Falcon Yard* and *Double Exposure*

On a 1962 calendar, now archived in the Smith College Library's special collections, the poet Sylvia Plath kept careful track of the routine details of her daily life. She jotted grocery lists, planned the meals she'd cook, and noted when her husband, poet Ted Hughes, was going to be out of town. She noted how many bouquets of flowers from their garden sold each week, and when new rubber nipples would be needed for her infant son, Nicholas. Each Wednesday she left herself the same one-word reminder: "Ashcans."

Then, on August 10, she left herself the single writing-related note that I could find:

"Start Int. Loaf!!!"

From her journals, we know this note refers to a novel she planned to write, titled *The Interminable Loaf.*

Plath had recently finished *The Bell Jar* and was separating from Hughes after discovering his affair with his friend Assia Wevill.

confronted Hughes, who refused to end the affair. A few weeks later, Plath built a bonfire in her backyard. Then, while her mother watched, Plath burned the only known draft of *Falcon Yard*, a few pages at a time. In two subsequent bonfires, Plath would destroy nearly a thousand of her own letters and several boxes of Hughes's papers, acts which she described in a poem called "Burning the Letters."

By October of that year, she had thrown Hughes out of their house and begun work on the *new* "second" novel, *The Interminable Loaf.*

For decades it was believed that none of *Falcon Yard* had survived the bonfire. But in the 1990s, scholars at Smith College found something surprising in the collection of Plath's papers they'd been accumulating from her mother and from Hughes.

On the *back* of a page listing corrections to *The Bell Jar* was a single page, numbered 25, from something called "Venus in the Seventh"—a chapter of *Falcon Yard.*

The page describes a young woman on a train ride to Munich with a man named Winthrop (likely based on former boyfriend Gordon Lameyer). Though the prose is quite beautiful, and the later dialogue sparkling, it was probably an early draft. At one point, the narration shifts from the third person to the first, as Plath had not yet decided which point of view she'd use.

Subsequently, similar discoveries were made at the Ted Hughes archives at Emory University. Because Hughes and Plath had reused each other's scrap paper, a page of a chapter called "Hill of Leopards" was found on the reverse of some of Hughes's notes. Eventually, thirteen more pages from "Venus in the Seventh" resurfaced at Emory, continuing the story of Jess's European tour, though incompletely, going from page 35 to 42 and 43, then from

64 and 65 to 68, and so on.

In these pages, Jess travels to Venice and then St. Mark's Basilica in Rome. Ultimately, she leaves Winthrop to fly home to England. After the flight, on the bus ride to London, she meets a man named Michael Butcher, who convinces her to join him for dinner. (At one point she recalls a resolution she's made to stay sober after the *St. Botolph's* party, suggesting these scenes would take place sometime after that event.) While then leaving dinner in a rush, she refers to herself as "Cinderella Greenwood," a suggestion that the character's name was, at one point, Jess Greenwood, an early incarnation of the name Plath would eventually use for the heroine in *The Bell Jar*.

By pages 73, 76, and 79, Jess returns to campus and the arms of a man named Ian, described as reminiscent of Dylan Thomas. (According to later notes, "Ian" was changed to "Leonard," the character based on Ted Hughes.) The surviving fragments of "Venus in the Seventh" leave off with Jess and Ian in conversation about poetry.

According to Plath's mother, the novel would continue from this blossoming romance and into the first years of their marriage, ending with the birth of a daughter—with "Pan" having been successfully led into the world of "toast and nappies" after all.

If Plath got that far before she burned *Falcon Yard* on the lawn, we may never know. Unless more missing draft pages resurface, this is all we have to go on. Still, it is something, and it gives some hope that fragments of *Double Exposure*—if not all of it—may similarly resurface.

Unless, of course, it was deliberately destroyed.

Painstakingly written around Plath's domestic obligations, *Double Exposure* also revealed her resentment of the man who abandoned her to navigate "toast and nappies" alone. Did Ted Hughes destroy his wife's unfinished novel about the affair that ended their marriage, as he did to her final journal?

Perhaps not. For one thing, though Hughes claimed to have destroyed that journal (in order, he said, to protect their children), we don't know that he did.

In 2005, an exhibition on Hughes and Plath was presented at the Grolier Club by Karen Kukil, Associate Curator of Special Collections at Smith College, and Stephen Enniss, then Director of Special Collections and Archives at Emory University (and now Director of the Harry Ransom Center in Texas). Alongside many invaluable artifacts of the Hughes-Plath marriage was a draft of a letter Hughes wrote to biographer Jacqueline Rose after Plath's death, in which he stated that he secretly hid two months of entries in her last journal to protect "someone else." He then crossed this out and none of it was included in the finished letter.

Who is the "someone else"? Assia Wevill? And where might it have been hidden? Finally, if the journal was never destroyed, are there other "disappeared" and "destroyed" things that might also come to light?

Fortunately, in the world of Plath scholarship, things do keep emerging. Several journals that Hughes gave to Smith College were originally meant to be sealed until 2013, fifty years after her death, but they were released early by Plath's daughter, Frieda Hughes, and subsequently edited with Karen Kukil and published with the rest as *The Unabridged Journals of Sylvia Plath* in October 2000.

Then, in April 2017, the *Guardian* published a story describing a trove of never-before-seen letters, sent by Sylvia Plath to her former therapist, Dr. Ruth Barnhouse, between 1960 and 1963. Dr. Barnhouse was likely the model for the Dr. Nolan character in *The Bell Jar*, the therapist who helps Esther recover from her depression. Plath and Barnhouse remained in touch through letters after

Plath returned to England.

In these letters, Plath described how she felt upon first discovering Hughes's infidelity. She reflected on a miscarriage, before becoming pregnant with Nicholas, which occurred days after Hughes had physically abused her. She wrote that she felt Hughes "wanted her dead." These letters are now included in the new *Letters of Sylvia Plath, Volume 2*, co-edited by Karen Kukil and Peter Steinberg and published in late 2018.

In those letters, Plath also alleges that Hughes felt threatened by having a son, Nicholas, a "usurper," and that during their separation, he goaded Plath to kill herself.

Carol Hughes, the widow of Ted Hughes, has commented that these accusations are "as absurd as they are shocking to anyone who knew Ted well." Frieda Hughes also expressed her doubts, writing in the foreword to the new volume, "My father was not the wife-beater that some would wish to imagine he was." She noted that in earlier letters, her mother had mentioned the miscarriage, saying it had happened for "no apparent reason." During this period of betrayal and separation, Frieda asked, "what woman would want to paint her exiting husband in anything other than the darkest colours?"

If Plath's missing journals, or the manuscript of *Double Exposure*, similarly painted Hughes in "the darkest colours" then it is no wonder why he might have resisted their publication. If Plath's descriptions of physical and emotional abuse in the letters to Barnhouse are echoed in her journals, and in her novel, then this would only reinforce those charges.

Did *Double Exposure* disappear? Was it destroyed? Or was it hidden? Or could it remain under seal in one of the Plath collections, until some future date?

At the Smith College Library's special collections, I spoke with Karen Kukil, who told me that there's been a renewed interest in

Plath's unpublished works lately, a good sign that people are still excited for more from Plath.

Kukil remains hopeful that the missing journals, and the novel in progress, *Double Exposure*, will indeed resurface in the coming years.

We don't know what might have gone differently for Sylvia Plath if, say, *The Bell Jar* had rocketed to the top of the best-seller lists right away and she'd been in a better financial position in the last months of her life. We don't know if this would have allowed her to hire the nanny she was looking for, so that she could finish *Double Exposure*, and if any of this would have had any impact on her depression or suicide. Possibly nothing would have changed. But it is hard not to stare at those overcrowded calendar squares without wondering what those final weeks must have been like for her, straining to turn her husband's infidelity and absence into something artistic that might nurture her family and her future. It is hard not to think of how little has changed today for far too many creative women, far too many parents, and ultimately to wonder how many works of genius are going unwritten, or being left unfinished, every week and every year, because the toast and nappies must be attended to—because the rubber nipples must be sanitized and the ashcans must go out and so the four a.m. inspiration must be set aside for another day. At minimum, we shouldn't delude ourselves that only those unburdened by such things can ever become geniuses.

"Writing, teaching, family," a fellow author once advised me, "you can only do two at a time." She told me she'd heard this same advice from a mentor of hers. But it didn't sit with me then and it doesn't sit with me now. I love teaching, which gives me the opportunity to explore new literary ideas all the time. And don't my children, while sometimes exhausting and demanding, also inspire me? Bring immeasurable joy? Don't I get as many "four a.m. inspirations" from watching them play—freely and wildly—in ways I have largely forgotten how to do?

Anyone in any walk of life should be able to pursue art if they sincerely, deeply, want to. If you, like me, sometimes find yourself standing in front of a sink filled with dirty dishes, phone buzzing with messages from your friends asking about plans, knowing the check engine light is on in your car, and that your children are about to have pizza for the third night in a row . . . just know that plenty of other geniuses have been there before, with to-do lists just as long, and with crises lurking around every corner. It may not look like the movie image of the genius, but it looks a whole lot like many geniuses' real lives.

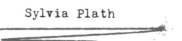

FAIL LIKE A GENIUS

Sylvia Plath

Plath had the right idea—get a calendar. If you are overwhelmed, write your responsibilities down. Start each new week by drawing up a list of what you need to do. Put all the ashcans and the rubber nipples on there, but also your social plans, your kids' orchestra concert, the trip you need to make to Target, the quizzes you need to grade on Monday, the chicken you'll marinate on Wednesday, the bills that need paying on Friday, the phone call to your sibling on Thursday night. Get it *all* on there.

Spread them out as best you can. Fight the urge to think that you can "knock them all out" on the first day and free yourself up to write nonstop for the rest of the week. You'll likely exhaust yourself, and more things always emerge to fill the open time.

Try and fit some pleasure reading in there, and also time to get some exercise—even walking for fifteen minutes a day can clear your head about your work in progress.

But most of all, get writing time on the calendar.

Sometimes I'll chart out twenty minutes a day when I'm going to write. Other times I'll set a daily word count. I often aim for 3,000 words a week. That can be six days with 500 words each day. But if I have a productive hour and get 1,000 words written on Tuesday, I can bank the extra words and sleep in on Saturday. If I'm still 1,000 words down on Friday, I know I'm going to need to skip the glass of wine, set my alarm for 5:30 and be ready to brew some extra coffee.

Five hundred words a day can seem insignificant, but over the course of three months, at that pace, you'll have written 36,000 words—that's a third of the way to a novel, or a handful of short stories.

Simply putting writing time down on the calendar gives it the same weight on the page as all the other stuff in your life.

It isn't "Teaching and family and then, if there's time and I'm not too burned out, I'll do some writing if nobody else needs anything."

Now it's an item on the list, as important to the whole as anything else.

Even that can be a radical act to start.

Geniuses Hold Grudges

Shirley Jackson

After publishing my first novel, I had a conversation with my mother-in-law that has stayed with me. She told me she enjoyed my book and said all the kind and supportive things any writer would ever wish to hear from their mother-in-law. But she also said, "I was surprised how *outraged* the character was sometimes! It didn't sound like you. I just want to say, if you ever need to let some of that anger out, we're here for you."

It was a kind thing to say, even if I'd thought the novel was pretty lighthearted. I thanked her. But maybe what I should have said was, "This *is* how I let it out!"

We often talk about making art as being an "outlet" for the artist, a place to express themselves freely without thought of judgment, and as the audience we prize that honesty—it's how we know we're being trusted by the artist, and what they're trusting us with is the truth, no matter how thorny or antisocial or enraging or terrifying.

We may feel sometimes like we shouldn't show these sides of ourselves publicly, that we ought to keep our grudges hidden away and off the page. But what feels petty to you might be quite powerful to others. And if I hypothetically model a character in my novel on a critic who wrote nasty things about my last one?

Well, it might not be the most mature thing in the world, I'll grant you, but it might just be the thing I need that day to propel me into the scene I'm writing. Most likely, no reader will ever know what prompted it, but I believe they'll feel the energy beneath it, and they'll know how true it is.

There is great pleasure to be found in hating, and as with friends, nothing bonds us quite so powerfully to a narrator as hating the same things. Think of poor Sylvia Plath, pushed by her anger at her philandering husband into wanting to write another novel, largely to spite him and his mistress. That's heavy stuff, to be sure. But according to her and those around her, the book was "hellishly funny" and made readers laugh out loud. If Plath ever finished the book, I imagine a lot of readers with interminable loafs of their own would have taken quite an enormous amount of pleasure in reading about hers. Great art can do real good in this way, even when it's hateful in spirit—maybe especially then.

Writer and critic William Gass, in a *Paris Review* interview in 1977, had this to say about the literature of spite: "I write because I hate. A lot. Hard. And if someone asks me the inevitable next dumb question, 'Why do you write the way you do?' I must answer that I wish to make my hatred acceptable because my hatred is much of me, if not the best part."

In an essay from the nineteenth century titled "On the Pleasure of Hating," William Hazlitt opined that "without something to hate, we should lose the very spring of thought and action." At length, and with pleasure, he describes how much he loves to hate various things: politics, history, foods, bugs, novels, even his friends: "Old friendships are like meats served up repeatedly, cold, comfortless, and distasteful."

Perhaps no writer better embodies this delicious amalgam of hate and love in their work better than Shirley Jackson, writer of horror and psychologically twisted novels, who throughout her career drew from all the things she feared and detested about small-town domestic life—not least of all her own husband, Stanley Hyman. Like Sylvia Plath, Jackson also passed away in the midst of writing a novel about the end of a marriage, though in the case of *Come Along with Me*, it is thanks to her husband that this "funny" and "happy" work was published, not destroyed—even though a lot of it seemed to be inspired by how much she wished he'd drop dead.

"Laughter Is Possible": Shirley Jackson's *Come Along with Me*

In the spring of 1965, author Shirley Jackson embarked on a cross-country college lecture tour in a new MG sedan. The cost of the car would be completely covered by the speaking fees she was earning for the five lectures she'd be delivering. After the tour, she settled back at home with intentions to rest and continue working on her latest novel, *Come Along with Me*. In one of her final diary entries, she described it as "a funny book. a happy book."

A few months later, in August 1965, Shirley Jackson passed away during an afternoon nap. Doctors would later give the official cause as "coronary occlusion due to arteriosclerosis, with hypertensive cardiovascular disease as a contributing factor." Her death was met by an outpouring of affection from readers and publishers. Her last two books, *The Haunting of Hill House* and *We Have Always Lived in the Castle*, had been great successes, though her most significant claim to fame was (and probably remains) a single short story, "The Lottery," published in the *New Yorker* in 1948, and present in American literary and political conversation ever since.

Come Along with Me was only about seventy-five manuscript pages at the time of her death—six brief, mostly connected episodes. Three years later, Stanley Hyman would publish it along with a selection of her essays and stories—including "Janice," the story that had made him fall in love with her twenty-seven years earlier.

In the collection, Hyman praised these shorter works effusively in his preface, but of *Come Along with Me* he wrote only that it was "the unfinished novel at which Shirley Jackson, my late wife, was at work at the time of her death in 1965. She rewrote the first three sections; the remaining three sections are in first draft."

In one of Jackson's final diary entries she wrote about finally feeling unblocked after a long depression following President Kennedy's assassination and Hyman's suspected affair. But beginning to work on *Come Along with Me* had brought her incredible joy—the novel is about a woman named Angela Motorman whose husband has just died, to her great delight, and about the excitement and freedom she feels in the wake of his death.

Jackson concluded her diary entry with these repeated words: "laughter is possible laughter is possible laughter is possible."

Shirley Jackson first fell in love with Stanley Hyman in 1938 at Syracuse University. Jackson had transferred from the University of Rochester to study journalism, but according to Ruth Franklin's biography, *Shirley Jackson: A Rather Haunted Life*, young Jackson dedicated much of her time and energy to writing poems and short stories, the first of which were soon published in a class magazine, *The Threshold*, put out by her professor, poet A. E. Johnson.

Jackson's 250-word story "Janice" opened the magazine. It begins with the narrator describing a casual phone call from a friend, Janice, who wants to tell them that her mother can't afford to send her back to school. Almost as an afterthought, Janice adds that, earlier in the afternoon, she tried to kill herself by sitting in the garage with the car motor going, but was thwarted by the man mowing the lawn, who came and got her out.

Hyman read the story and insisted he meet Jackson because he'd decided to marry her.

They soon became a couple. Hyman was a well-liked, self-styled bohemian who loved to debate the merits of Communism with his classmates. As his companion, Shirley Jackson initially flourished. Hyman encouraged her to keep writing fiction, something he had long desired to do himself, but after meeting Jackson he realized he would never be as good as she was. Instead, Hyman soon began to focus his efforts on becoming a literary critic, giving Jackson detailed pages of notes on her stories and, later, her novels.

The following year, Jackson was elected to the post of fiction editor of the long-running campus magazine *Syracusan*, but the magazine soon stopped running fiction altogether, leading Jackson and Hyman to start their own literary magazine, *Spectre*. With hand-drawn images and typewritten pages, *Spectre* had an edgy, homemade sensibility, as if it had been run off in secrecy behind enemy lines. From the start, Hyman and Jackson wanted their magazine to invite controversy. They commissioned a sketch of a male nude for the cover of the first issue and then cajoled an English department advisor into publicly criticizing it, so that they and *Spectre* could turn around and rail against the hypocrisy that only female nudes were of artistic value.

With Jackson as editor and Hyman as managing editor, *Spectre* soon became a conversation piece in the literary community on campus. Likely thanks to Hyman's influence, the magazine frequently criticized the politics of the university. In the first issue, Jackson and Hyman, writing together in an introduction called

"We the Editor," took on the topic of campus antisemitism. In the third issue, they wrote scathingly of the campus policy to house Black students separately from white students—pointing out that conveniently this allowed the university to admit fewer Black students since there was such limited housing available for them.

This third issue contained a poem of Hyman's, "Ill Fares the Land," and one short story of Jackson's, "Had We but World Enough"—the title suggested by Hyman. Jackson's three-and-a-half-page story is mostly dialogue between a "boy" and a "girl" sitting on a park bench on a snowy day watching children tobogganing. The young couple talk about how they'd like to get married, if only the boy can find a job, which the girl jokes might take years. The boy says he hopes they'll have children. She tells him off: "You think I'm going to have children and ruin my whole life?" He insists they'll have twenty boys, and she compromises: they'll have nineteen boys, one girl, and a yellow living room—even if he hates it.

In Jackson's hands, the story manages to have both a lightness and a foreboding air. Children would indeed eventually become a major source of friction between Jackson and Hyman—clearly a model for the couple in the story.

But as they neared graduation, the major obstacle to their future together was not money, or children, but the fact that both Hyman's parents were Jewish, while Jackson's were Presbyterian. Both sets of parents were very much opposed to the Stanley-Shirley relationship.

Friends of the couple, who called them "S & S," told Franklin of a tempestuous relationship, a "symbiosis" that "was always in danger of turning parasitic." S & S broke up several times, but always came back together in the end.

Often, they fought about politics: As Europe lurched into the Second World War, Hyman had become an ardent Communist. Meanwhile Jackson wrote in her diary that politics interested her "less than does Sanskrit." Hyman insisted that she write more politically, declaring that "you must show misery and starvation" to create lasting art.

Specifically, he pointed to "Janice"—the story that had made him want to marry her before they'd even met. Two years later he told her that it was "a finger exercise, well done, but meaningless." (It wasn't her fault, he conceded, that she'd had a "sheltered upbringing.")

At other times the issue was, according to Franklin, Hyman's "persistent interest in other women, which he saw no reason to hide." His interpretation of the teachings of Communism extended to a disavowal of monogamy, and in lurid detail, he wrote letters to Jackson about his attraction to other women he'd encountered, and once he even brought a girlfriend over and introduced her to Jackson. He insisted that she was welcome to see other boyfriends, but by and large she did not.

A friend told Franklin that at one point Hyman gave Jackson a "cheap engagement ring" but that it was soon lost during a fight, because she "bounced it off Stan's skull."

They graduated in 1940 and Hyman soon landed a summer job in New York City at the *New Republic*, for which he was paid twenty-five dollars a week. A few months later, Jackson married Hyman in a "brief three-minute" informal ceremony at a friend's apartment, attended by a "small, motley group of friends," and they began wedded life in Greenwich Village.

Hyman would soon end up working for the *New Yorker*, while Jackson wrote more stories, which he would meticulously critique. They yearned for a quieter life, outside of the city, and began to travel to New Hampshire to work, finding "country life suited productivity." But in the winter of 1942, their uninsulated cabin became too cold to work in, and so they returned to Syracuse together.

There, they saw old friends, and reminisced about the good old days working on *Spectre* together. Soon there was a daily salon of visitors, for whom Hyman would play jazz records and provoke political conversations and talk about involvement in the war in Europe.

During this period, a doctor told Jackson she was likely pregnant; she jokingly referred to the baby as "Simon Hyman."

But being back in Syracuse also "triggered a relapse" of Hyman's infidelity. Once, while Jackson was out of town, he immediately set off to seduce an ex-girlfriend. When Jackson returned home, Hyman happily showed her the diary entry he'd written describing how badly his attempted seduction had gone—the ex-girlfriend had gotten so drunk on Sauternes that she became ill and he'd had to throw her into a shower.

Jackson rebuked herself in a subsequent diary entry, saying that if she had married a "dog" she couldn't "expect him to be house-broken so quick." Of the ex-girlfriend, Jackson wrote that despite being "coarse and vulgar" she had "a beautiful body and after all i am too fat."

She had long struggled with anxiety and depression, but now she began to experience panic attacks, leading her to worry that she was psychopathic or insane. She eventually decided to sleep with a heartbroken friend of Hyman's to try to settle the score, only to end up feeling that it had just given Hyman more license to cheat.

Franklin cites one of Jackson's diary entries during this period as evidence that Hyman forced Jackson to have sex with him: "'If it is sex I can't do anything about it. . . . He forced me God help me and for so long I didn't dare say anything and only get out of it when I could and now I'm so afraid to have him touch me."

Later, Jackson wrote that she should never have married him at all: "Tantrums and hatred and disgust—what a married life—" But she was hopeful that motherhood would be better. "Maybe when I have my baby . . . I can talk to it and it will love me and won't grow up mean."

Jackson and Hyman eventually settled in North Bennington, Vermont, after he was hired as an instructor at Bennington College. They would have four children together, not twenty—two sons and two daughters (none of them, thankfully, named Simon).

Jackson kept the house and lived in relative anonymity in the town, known to most as "Mrs. Hyman," the quiet wife of the boisterous, quirky new professor.

It was an incredible struggle for Jackson to balance writing with the demands of raising the children. Meanwhile Hyman continued to insist on their marriage being "open" and carried on public affairs, including with his own students—one of whom even moved in with them for a time.

Just a few years into their life in North Bennington, Jackson wrote what would become her most famous short story, and probably her most famous work of any kind. "The Lottery" is about a group of residents in a small town gathering to stone a randomly selected citizen to death, as a way of ensuring a good harvest. The story kicked up a near-immediate furor within just a few days of being published in the *New Yorker*. Jackson received over three hundred letters from horrified readers that summer alone. Even her mother wrote of her distaste. "It does seem, dear, that this gloomy kind of story is what all you young people think about these days. Why don't you write something to cheer people up?" Jackson was most disturbed by several letters from people who believed "The Lottery" was real—and wanted to know if they could come up to watch.

Jackson was relieved that most people in North Bennington did not read the *New Yorker* and largely had no idea that "Mrs. Hyman" had stirred up such a national scandal, especially because Jackson had used real people in the community as models for the townspeople in her story. But after a few months, the story became so widely discussed that even her neighbors began to hear about it. The "general consensus" in town was that the "nasty story" made them look "bad and uncivilized." Jackson began to experience bouts of agoraphobia and began chain-smoking and rapidly gaining weight.

Hyman, meanwhile, had been effectively fired from his position at Bennington (others in the faculty found him to be "abrasive"). His first major book of criticism, *The Armed Vision*, was published without much impact, just as Jackson's story was becoming more and more celebrated in prize issues and anthologies. In 1949, she sold three stories to *Good Housekeeping* for $1,000 apiece. Hyman, meanwhile, was making only about $35 a week writing for the *New Yorker*. Though the money from Jackson's literary career continued to vastly outweigh Hyman's income, Hyman still controlled the family finances, and gave his wife money only as he saw fit.

As Jackson withdrew further from public life, her work returned to some of her favorite youthful fascinations, including witchcraft and the occult. Her turn to "gothic horror" was a huge success. In 1959, *The Haunting of Hill House* was nominated for a National Book Award and reviewed by the *New York Times* as evidence that Jackson was "the finest master currently practicing in the genre of the cryptic, haunted tale."

Three years later she published her final completed novel, *We Have Always Lived in the Castle*, centered on sisters Merricat and Constance Blackwood, who live alone in a gothic mansion with their doddering uncle after the mysterious poisoning of their parents. They are surrounded by a Bennington-esque town full of suspicious and hateful villagers, who eventually try to destroy them and their home.

As Jackson's literary successes mounted, she began exploring new methods of writing, including experimenting with automatic writing (writing in a trance state). She was busily generating new ideas for novels and stories before her death at forty-eight.

What might she have written, had she lived longer?

Thanks, in part, to Stanley Hyman, we have some idea.

Soon after Jackson's passing, Hyman began to respond to the outpouring of affection from readers and publishers with what Franklin calls "efforts on behalf of Shirley's reputation." He wanted people to see her as more than a writer of ghost and horror stories—to "dissipate some of the 'Virginia Werewoolf of seance-fiction' fog."

To this end, in 1968 Hyman agreed to publish a posthumous collection of Jackson's work that would include "Janice," as well as the only known pages of a novel in progress called *Come Along with Me.*

This unfinished project gives us a rare glimpse into the writer, and the woman, that Shirley Jackson was so close to finally becoming.

The novel begins with a nameless woman arriving in an unfamiliar city, shortly after the death of her husband, "Hughie." Of him, she adds quickly, "my God, he was a lousy painter."

About Hughie's sudden death she says she feels "a fine high gleefulness; I think you understand me; I have everything I want."

She happily recalls clearing all of Hughie's papers and books from their barn, including the half-finished canvas he was working on when he died: "It was just as lousy as all the rest; not even imminent glowing death could help that Hughie." She unloads everything, despite her fears that "Hughie might turn up someday asking, the way they sometimes do . . . knowing Hughie it would be the carbon copy of something back in 1946 he wanted." It takes "one thousand and three trips back and forth" but eventually she has sold all her old things to their disingenuous neighbors and is finally free to leave.

A series of random encounters leads her to take a room on Smith Street with a woman who has a disabled son. She decides to call herself "Mrs. Angela Motorman" almost arbitrarily, after chatting with a trolley car operator (a motorman) on the way there.

The chapter ends with an abrupt shift into third-person perspective: "So Mrs. Angela Motorman walked slowly and decently up the walk to the fine old house with the sign in the window saying ROOMS. . . . As she set her foot on the steps, she put her shoulders back and took a deep breath: Mrs. Angela Motorman, who never walked on earth before."

Her landlady, Mrs. Faun, is also recently widowed, and the two soon bond over burying their husbands, each confessing that they feel relieved.

Like much of Jackson's work, there is an eeriness to Angela Motorman's narration; she explains several times that she "dabbles in the supernatural." At the end of the third chapter, she sits alone in her room and looks outside at the place where she'd stood earlier, picking out her new name: "'It's all right, Angela,' I said very softly out the window, 'it's all right, you made it, you came in and it's all right; you got here after all.' And outside the dim nameless creature named herself Mrs. Angela Motorman and came steadily to the door."

In the fourth chapter the narrator describes her childhood, when she learned that she is a clairvoyant, able to see people everywhere that no one else can see. After marrying Hughie, the ability left her, but now that he's dead it has returned. Eventually, she gives a séance in the main room of the house for the other tenants, explaining that she can speak to their dead loved ones that way that others might take a long-distance call on the telephone. They all drink sherry and ask questions; Angela is dismayed at the end at how little they tip her and that all they want to talk about is "death and dying." Mrs. Faun says they all want someone to tell them what to do, and that they'll listen to any crackpot at all willing to tell them.

The final chapter shows Angela in a large department store where she goes shopping because the small boutique in town doesn't carry blouses in "my age and size—both forty-four, in case it's absolutely vital to know."

"I'm trying my hand at shoplifting," she tells the salesgirl in the department store—and they both laugh. Later she says it again and they enjoy another laugh, at which point Angela really does set off to shoplift a candle that she plans to give to Mrs. Faun. When the salesgirl sees her put the candle in her bag, she asks if she can help her, and Angela replies, "No, just trying my hand at shoplifting," and they laugh a third time before Angela puts the candle back and leaves the store.

The novel ends here, with myriad possibilities still unexplored, but the key themes already clear. While *We Have Always Lived in the Castle* examined the crushing agoraphobia of the Blackwood sisters trapped and isolated in a small town, *Come Along with Me* has an older female protagonist not isolated but unbound by death—not fearful of the villagers, but footloose and happy in the big city.

Franklin writes that the narrator sounds like the charming but isolated and vengeful sister, Merricat, from Jackson's previous novel, but "a Merricat who somehow managed to grow up, leave the house, and get married."

From her diaries, we know that Jackson had increasingly moved toward leaving Stanley Hyman in her final months. That with the help of friends and therapy, she'd embraced her rising popularity as a writer and left Bennington to tour colleges in her new MG sedan—bought by herself, with her own money—and that she felt she was heading into a new phase in her life at last. You can tell, reading the pages of *Come Along with Me,* that Jackson was, as Franklin notes, "thoroughly enjoying herself."

There is something of a vengeance, and a mirth, in Angela Motorman, of which we can only imagine the full power. With the netherworld communicating to her, she is alive and well, ready to wreak a bit of havoc on everyone as she passes through. "There is a comfort in largeness," Franklin adds, that "never appeared in Jackson's work." Angela Motorman is not anxious, or panicky. She is a laughing spirit, newly freed, and in full control of her supernatural powers for the first time in a long, long time.

Our work should be the place where we feel the most freedom—indeed, for many of us it may be the only place in our lives where we can truly be free. This isn't to say there aren't risks involved, of course. Writing "The Lottery" might have made life in North Bennington harder for Shirley Jackson than it was already. But would she have gotten to *We Have Always Lived in the Castle* without first taking that leap and risking some neighborly disfavor? One drawback of having an active imagination can be how easily we can spin up a mental maelstrom of resentment for simply speaking our minds honestly. It helps to remember that these same fears have been faced down by many others before us, and that the reason we still admire some of these geniuses today is that they not only allowed themselves grudges, spite, and frustration but also channeled those impulses into shaping their greatest work.

FAIL LIKE A GENIUS

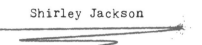

Shirley Jackson

Natalie Goldberg says in *Writing Down the Bones*, "Your obsessions elicit deeper emotions, deeper energy . . . they are what you will come back to in your writing over and over again. And you'll create new stories around them. So you might as well give in to them."

But what do you *hate*? We aren't only passionate about things we love. Make that list of obsessions, and then make a second list—this time of your biggest pet peeves: gum chewing, golf, *The Bachelor*, the music of Nickelback . . . whatever it is, embrace it. The weirder the better.

These are little things but they can add some dark fun to the page. They can also make you more comfortable when it does eventually come to addressing bigger topics (including, à la Shirley Jackson, bigger hatreds: your neighbors, say, or your spouse).

And sometimes the small things *are* the big things. Sitting in one of many endless committee meetings in which nothing of consequence is being debated as if it were a matter of life and death, I close my eyes and think of Shirley Jackson, walking out of some mundanely aggravating Bennington town meeting, ready to pull her own hair out . . . and then gradually smiling more and more, hurrying home so she could start jotting down the opening lines of "The Lottery."

Whatever it is for you, embrace it.

Geniuses Struggle (But Not Because They're Geniuses)

David Foster Wallace

Many years ago, I had lunch with a friend who was a big fan of the writer David Foster Wallace. I did not then know a lot about Wallace, or his work, but I was curious to hear about my friend's recent trip down to the Harry Ransom Center, where he'd spent a few days digging through Wallace's papers, which had gone to the University of Texas after the author's suicide in 2008. As we had lunch, my friend told me about the things he'd read there, particularly the boxes dedicated to Wallace's final, unfinished novel, which had been published in 2011. He was quite sad as he spoke, not just about the loss of Wallace, but about this last novel, *The Pale King*. I asked if he was upset that it would never be completed. "No," he said. "I wish he'd never written it. I mean, I think it killed him."

What he meant was that he suspected that the work on this final novel had unraveled Wallace's mental health to the point where he'd committed suicide—a disturbing thought, which haunted me for a long time afterward. It echoed in my mind with other impressions and worries I'd absorbed over the years. Why was it that so many of my favorite writers had struggled this way, even died this way? Does being a genius require a certain amount of madness? Or, worse, does genius actually *drive* you crazy? Does the mental pressure of being a David Foster Wallace (or, for that matter, a Sylvia Plath) weigh so heavily that even a towering mind can't handle it?

When it comes to mental health, we have two different, basically contradictory myths about genius. We imagine the mind of a genius as something irreplicable and unassailable, a very special kind of brain that works somehow *better* than yours or mine. At the same time, we have a persistent myth of the "tortured genius," whose own abilities drive them mad.

David Foster Wallace turns both those ideas on their head. Looking at his life, and the work he left undone, it's clear that he was a troubled man who often felt at odds with his own brain. The contours and effects of mental illness were also a frequent subject of his fiction. At the same time, he himself strongly disagreed with the idea that genius and mental illness must go hand in hand.

Misconceptions about the links between creative power and "madness" can be traced back to the Romantic era, or even as far back as Aristotle. The argument runs like this: an artistic temperament, or the achievement of extraordinary artistic goals, *depends* on some level of volatility and instability. Great geniuses are therefore inherently more prone to mental illness, more likely to die by suicide, and artists are driven to these conditions *because of* their artistic pursuits.

In this case, a common misunderstanding about the unique nature of genius is not just damaging to the work of those pursuing artistic goals, but may be damaging artists themselves.

In all the unfinished works I've read, and in finished ones too, I have never come across a situation in which an artist was truly "driven mad" by their art, or one where they committed suicide as a direct result of their artistic frustrations. Yes, it is true that there are many famous artists who have suffered from mental illness or died by suicide, several of whom are discussed in this book—but that doesn't mean their art was the cause of their turmoil.

If anything, it's most often the opposite. Engagement with artistic practices has been clinically understood since the mid-twentieth century as a reliable therapy for those suffering from mental illness. It's true that studies have shown an overrepresentation of mental illnesses among those in artistic occupations, but this does not mean the art has made them ill.

On the contrary, people already suffering from anxiety, bipolar disorders, and depression may be more attracted to artistic pursuits because they provide an outlet and because they have therapeutic effects. The correlation between creative work and mental struggle, in other words, may come about because the work makes you more *well*.

There are a lot of facets to this discussion, many of which are outside of my expertise—I wonder personally how the bigger picture might change if those pursuing art were better supported by our society financially, or if those pursuits were better understood by others in their lives, but I'll leave that to people more qualified than me to pick apart. For our purposes the most important thing to know is that while it is obviously good to monitor our mental health and to take care of ourselves as best we can (not uniquely important for artists), we shouldn't have to also shoulder the burden of believing that the work we love doing is harming us. If anything, it may be the thing keeping us going.

"The Long Thing": David Foster Wallace and *The Pale King*

On Friday, September 12, 2008, David Foster Wallace hung himself at his home in Claremont, California. In his forty-six years, he'd written two novels, three short story collections, two essay collections, and a mathematical treatise on the nature of infinity. A MacArthur "Genius Grant" recipient, Wallace was also a beloved professor who had struggled with a major depressive disorder for most of his life.

At the time of his death, Wallace was best known as the author of the 1996 postmodern epic, *Infinite Jest*. I came to it late, as I mentioned earlier, put off by the auras of masochism and machismo around it for many years, and by the stories I'd heard about Wallace's deeply troubled life, including his stalking and abuse of author Mary Karr. At a pre-college writing program, a friend insisted I read the short story "The Girl with Curious Hair," about a violent sociopath named "Sick Puppy" that set my skin crawling and probably scared me off Wallace for another decade.

But when I did finally read *Infinite Jest*, I enjoyed it far more than I expected to—it is as playful as it is weird, deeply sad as it is deeply funny, and in the end, I found it worth the struggle.

The doorstopper of a novel revolves around a dizzying cast of characters: Hal Incandenza and the other young stars at the elite Enfield Tennis Academy; recovering Demerol addict Don Gately and others at the Ennet House Drug and Alcohol Recovery House; a team of violent Québécois separatists called Les Assassins des Fauteuils Rollents (The Wheelchair Assassins). The plot threads are connected by a hunt for a videotape of such addictive, entertaining power that a viewer will die (isolated, absorbed) rather than stop watching it.

In the novel, Canada and North America have merged into a supernation known as ONAN. Most of New England is a toxic, irradiated no-man's-land referred to as the Great Concavity (on the American side, while on the Canadian side it is the Great Convexity). Time itself has been corporately subsidized, with most of the action of the novel taking place in the near future during the Year of the Depend Adult Undergarment.

Even this barely begins to describe the strangeness and scope of *Infinite Jest*.

Though Wallace would publish five shorter books in the years after the unexpected success of *Infinite Jest*, he felt an ongoing pressure to deliver another novel of similarly immense size and importance. Indeed, he had a new major project in the works, which he referred to as "The Long Thing," a few excerpts of which had been published already. One of these, called "Good People," ran in the *New Yorker* the year before his death. That story follows Lane A. Dean Jr. navigating a religious crisis with hard moral-searching and straightforward prayer, after impregnating his girlfriend.

Reading it, I was surprised by the story's earnest, technically uncomplicated prose, and by the spiritual subject matter. I wondered if this new novel would be a far cry from the zany convolutions of *Infinite Jest*. But then, shortly after Wallace's death, a second excerpt from the novel, this one called "Wiggle Room," was also published in the *New Yorker*. In "Wiggle Room," Dean returns as one of a number of IRS agents in an undecorated office, and over the course of the story processes 1040 forms and struggles to focus on the incredibly dull task until he has a hallucination in which a ghostly figure begins to lecture him on the nature of boredom. Long stretches of the prose concern themselves entirely with describing Dean examining forms, turning pages, and occasionally stretching for a moment.

This second excerpt reads much more like the strange, looping, challenging Wallace prose that *Infinite Jest* fans were used to. How would it work, I wondered, as part of the same novel? How could this even be the same character as the one in "Good People"?

The answers to these questions would not come until April 2011, when *The Pale King* was published posthumously by Little, Brown.

When I picked up this final work, I was wondering a million
things: How much of it had been finished by the time he'd died?
Had he set it in this order, or had that been done by his executors?
Was it a novel or just a bunch of . . . *stuff*? I thought back to the
glorious mess of *The Love of the Last Tycoon* and braced myself
for the worst. It occurred to me that for the first time I was reading
something that had been rendered unfinished during my own
lifetime. As long as I'd been alive, Fitzgerald's novel had always
been one-third completed. With *The Pale King* I held for the first
time a thing whose incompleteness had resulted from a loss I'd
experienced in real time, during one fissuring moment in September 2008.

For several months I lugged the huge tome around, eventually
reading it (guiltily) instead in a lightweight electronic format,
where its footnotes could be jumped to with the quick press of a
hyperlink. (Would Wallace have loved or hated this? I wished it
were possible to ask him.) And by the final pages of *The Pale King*,
I had few answers to my questions, other than a vague awareness
that parts of it ranked among the best things I'd ever read.

Each time I opened it, I thought about the words of my friend
after returning from the Harry Ransom Center, where he'd dug
through those same papers, and come away feeling like their
contents had driven their writer mad. Was that really the case?

As I would begin to understand in 2012, after reading the
touching and elegiac essay "Farther Away" by Wallace's longtime
friend Jonathan Franzen, Wallace's suicide had come at the end of
a long depression that itself had been instigated by a decision to
switch antidepressants. Returning to the original drugs had proved
ineffective, leaving Wallace in despair of regaining his former
stability.

There is more to that story, and it is entangled with Wallace's efforts to write *The Pale King*—but for now I'll say that my friend's assertion, that Wallace's novel killed him, missed a lot.

<hr>

According to D. T. Max's biography, *Every Love Story Is a Ghost Story*, ideas for a novel about the IRS were percolating in Wallace's mind as far back as the mid-'90s: "He had the idea . . . of the IRS as a secular church, a counterpart to Alcoholics Anonymous in *Infinite Jest*." If his second novel had been about our human addictions, to ambition, drugs, and pleasure, then "The Long Thing" was going to be about a counterpart and opposite to these things: boredom.

"I think in a country where we have it as easy as we do, one of our big dread vectors is boredom," Wallace said in a 2004 interview with Steve Paulson for *To the Best of Our Knowledge*. He talked about feeling this as a child while doing homework, or waiting through long stretches in the classroom. As he got older, he began to consider that people who can endure boredom are, in some respects, society's greatest heroes. Tedium-handlers are needed in all kinds of places in our modern world: in education, administration, government, and beyond. Indeed, the ability to withstand objectively boring work is often a skill worthy of greater compensation. Otherwise, why would anyone want to process tax returns all day long?

The centrality of boredom in modern life burned in Wallace's imagination. What does someone in a soul-crushingly boring job do to keep their soul from being crushed? Does it run counter to, or parallel with, our modern cravings for entertainment and diversion?

Furthermore, Wallace wondered about ideas in Eastern religion claiming that a greater happiness might follow boredom—a peace arrived by moving *through* boredom.

In a note left with the *Pale King* manuscript, Wallace had written, "Bliss—a second-by-second joy and gratitude at the gift of being alive, conscious—lies on the other side of crushing, crushing boredom. Pay close attention to the most tedious thing you can find (Tax Returns, Televised Golf) and, in waves, a boredom like you've never known will wash over you and just about kill you. Ride these out, and it's like stepping from black and white into color. Like water after days in the desert. Instant bliss in every atom."

Wallace had the idea that a novel about the tedium of IRS agents processing tax returns might provide some answer to the questions posed by *Infinite Jest*: rather than escape boredom through fevered pursuits of pleasure, what if we instead stared it down and locate a more potent and lasting ecstasy on the other side? Wallace spent years researching the history of boredom as a concept, and even as a word in the English language (the ghost in "Wiggle Room" observes that the word "boredom" may have existed even before the word "interesting" did.)

Wallace also dug into the history and structures of the Internal Revenue Service itself, collecting the terminologies and review procedures for his characters to employ. He sought knowledge about the kinds of blank Zen states attained by practiced meditators. He envisioned characters at the IRS who could become so immersed in their work that they floated above their seats as they processed their W-2s and 1040 forms. Another auditor would discover a string of numbers that, if he repeated them to himself, allowed him perfect focus on his task.

It's easy to see how some can be tempted to make a facile connection to his suicide here. Wallace was writing a big, difficult book about a big, difficult thing, that required tons and tons of big, difficult research. It isn't surprising that some may have jumped to the conclusion that spending years of his life picking apart the minutiae of IRS procedures ended up leading to a breakdown, but if anything, it appears Wallace truly enjoyed this study time, and this makes sense as well—why else would he want to build a book around it, unless some part of him thought that the topic of boredom was pretty interesting?

Still, by the early 2000s, Wallace was finding that making progress on the book was incredibly difficult. He had always had fluctuations in his mental health, and experienced periods of depression and anxiety that could get in the way of his work. At times he worried that, since *Infinite Jest*, he had lost his ability to write well. He reached out to friends about his crisis, lamenting to Franzen and others that much of his work was heading right into "the wastebasket." Wallace had always taught undergraduate writing classes while writing, back at his alma mater Amherst College, at Emerson College, and then at Illinois State University in Bloomington. He decided to take a break from teaching to see if that would help him get more work done on the new novel. Still, he struggled.

At some point, Max writes, Wallace traveled to Bordeaux, France, to attend a two-week meditation retreat with a Zen master, hoping that it would help him: "He found that writing about mindlessness and achieving it for oneself were two different things: he left early, blaming the food, and was home as soon as he could be."

Putting the novel aside, he worked on those other writing projects I mentioned earlier, his essays and stories, and the book about mathematical infinity. Still, Wallace hoped he'd eventually come back to "The Long Thing."

By the early 2000s, as Wallace remained stuck on this third novel, he moved to California and began teaching at Pomona College. He found himself unexpectedly happy in the "land of 1600 SAT scores." He began a relationship with a visual artist named Karen Green and settled into a comfortable and content life for the first time in a long while. Max writes of Wallace reading Tom Clancy novels by the pool and getting sunburned, collecting articles about shark attacks, and driving six hours each way to visit Green in Arizona. In 2002, Wallace shared two sections of "The Long Thing" at the *New Yorker* Festival to a warm reception there, and with his friend Franzen on the stage reading alongside him. Once again, the work was progressing.

One of the projects that Wallace took on during this period was the book I mentioned earlier about the mathematical nature of infinity, called *Everything and More*. He was interested in the idea of infinity, which had been one thematic focal point of *Infinite Jest*—as boredom now was in "The Long Thing." Now, Wallace delved into the life of nineteenth-century German mathematician Georg Cantor, whose work in infinite sets was of huge interest. Early in the book Wallace made space to dismiss a particular popular notion, that the manic-depressive illness Cantor suffered from was, in some way, *caused* by his work on the nature of the infinite: "Saying that ∞ drove Cantor mad is sort of like mourning St. George's loss to the dragon: it's not only wrong but insulting."

In an interview with Dave Eggers in the *Believer* in 2003, Wallace emphasized the importance of this understanding to Cantor and his work. He dismissed the "∞-drove-Cantor-mad stuff" as a "flabby, unconsidered pop version of . . . the 'mad genius syndrome.'" The "unsexy" truth was that Cantor suffered from a bipolar disorder, and that his hospitalizations for it occurred well after his mathematical achievements had been made. While it might be exciting to think of infinity as "some kind of intellectual Lost Ark that made Cantor's face melt off when he looked inside it," the reality was more mundane. Cantor had a neurological chemical imbalance, undiagnosable as such in his lifetime, and he suffered from it the same as anyone else with similar imbalances who weren't also staring at complicated equations on a whiteboard.

In the biography of Wallace, Max makes this point about Cantor as he begins considering *The Pale King* and Wallace's suicide. The parallels are clear: writing books, even gigantic and complicated ones about boredom, don't drive people insane any more than solving complicated mathematical problems.

Wallace finished his collection of stories, *Oblivion,* as well as the book about infinity, and yet critics were impatient for him to produce his follow-up to *Infinite Jest*, which was beginning to come up on its tenth anniversary. Even in positive reviews of his new books, critics wondered when "big novel number three" would "thump into the world" and hoped it would be even more generous and dig even deeper. Max writes that Wallace knew that "All roads led back to his . . . Long Thing, *The Pale King.*"

For twenty-two years Wallace had been taking the drug Nardil, an extremely strong antidepressant. Today, Nardil is prescribed typically in cases of bipolar depression when gentler drugs like Paxil, Prozac, Zoloft, etc., have already proven not to be effective. But those medications were not yet in common usage when Wallace first began to take Nardil, and he had never had the chance to see if they'd have helped him. Drugs like Nardil have interactions with certain foods, requiring the patient to maintain a strict diet, and come with side effects like insomnia, impotence, drowsiness, and dry mouth.

Max explains that while Wallace felt that the drug had saved his life, he also "had never been certain that being on Nardil was the right thing" and that whenever his work was not going well, he'd debate whether the medication "played a role."

Then, in 2007, Wallace experienced an attack while eating at a Persian restaurant with his visiting parents, maybe anxiety-related, but possibly hypertensive. In any case, it led Wallace to speak to a physician about finally getting off Nardil and trying out some of the newer, sleeker drugs that had fewer side effects. Green was supportive of the plan and knew that it was partially motivated by his suspicion that without the side effects of Nardil, he might be better able to focus on his writing, including "The Long Thing," which he felt was way "overdue" even though it was not under any contract.

Getting off Nardil after twenty-two years required months of steady stepping down from the medication, which Wallace likened to going through chemotherapy in its side effects. While the plan had always been to move over to another antidepressant once he was flushed of the Nardil, Wallace began to then fixate on the idea of remaining off the drugs entirely (something Max connects back to some "fundamentalist factions" within the AA groups Wallace had met with, who viewed any medication as a "crutch"). Green worried that Wallace was expecting a full-blown "Jungian re-birth."

But the attempt to go drug-free backfired, leaving Wallace more or less unable to write at all, plagued with depression and facing increased thoughts of suicide. By the following spring he was back on the newer drugs and stabilizing. But then he resumed his earlier deterioration and tried to kill himself by overdosing on pills. After this he underwent twelve sessions of electroconvulsive therapy. Still, he could not get back to the place he'd been before getting off Nardil. By the time he agreed to try going back on the drug again, "he was too agitated to give it the weeks it takes to work," writes

Max. Despite numerous interventions by Green and Franzen and others, Wallace ended up hanging himself that September.

Before doing so, Wallace wrote a two-page note to Green. He left all the lights on in the garage where he had left about two hundred pages of *The Pale King*, organized for her to find there. "Below it," Max wrote, "around it, inside his two computers, on old floppy disks in his drawers were hundreds of other pages—drafts, character sketches, notes to himself, fragments that had evaded his attempt to integrate them into the novel over the past decade."

It is this scene that Wallace's editor, Michael Pietsch, describes in the foreword to the final, published version of *The Pale King*. When he arrived at the author's home he found "hundreds and hundreds of pages of his novel in progress, designated with the title 'The Pale King.' Hard drives, file folders, three-ring binders, spiral-bound notebooks, and floppy disks contained printed chapters, sheaves of handwritten pages, notes, and more." Pietsch would then spend several months going over them. Aside from reading the excerpts of the novel that Wallace had shared or published elsewhere, Pietsch had not read "The Long Thing" before this point. There were the two hundred pages that Wallace had organized, likely the same arrangement that he'd considered submitting for an advance and a contract. But there were also other parts handwritten in "zero draft" freewritten form, and sections that did not connect in any direct way to the rest. Still, Pietsch said he discovered within all those pages, for the first time, "an astonishingly full novel, created with the superabundant originality and humor that were uniquely David's." On the other hand, he pointed out that "nowhere in all these pages was there an outline or other indication of what order David intended for these chapters." The full collection of Wallace's papers is now stored at the Harry Ransom Center at the University of Texas, and accessible to anyone interested in seeing them for themselves.

Asked by Green and Bonnie Nadell, Wallace's literary agent, to assemble the work into something publishable, Pietsch began to work through the material, eventually forging a "backbone" out of the chapters that followed the IRS agents through their orientation and into the job at the Regional Examination Center, intercut with other sections in a way similar to the organization that Wallace had used in *Infinite Jest*. Still, Pietsch admits, "The novel's central story does not have a clear ending, and the question inevitably arises: How unfinished is this novel? How much more might there have been?" Pietsch speculates that Wallace may not have intended there to be a lot more, based on several notes Wallace left, one of them claiming that the book would consist of "a series of setups for things to happen but nothing ever happens." In the end Pietsch could only present what Wallace left behind, and try his best to clean it up to the exacting standards of the "perfectionist of the highest order" that he'd long known Wallace to be.

David Foster Wallace's mental health decline and subsequent suicide left his final work in the hands of another person to complete. The arrangement of the "tidied up" manuscript in the garage and the leaving on of the lights indicated to D. T. Max that Wallace intended it to be found and even taken up by others after his death. Certainly, he did not burn it all, or ask someone else to burn it all, as Kafka did. Had he followed through on his earlier plan to submit the work for an advance, and to get it under contract, he might have ended up in a similar place—with the project suddenly open to editorial assistance and input from Pietsch and others. With their guidance, might he have been able to make some of the progress he hoped for, instead of trying to carry the burden of "The Long Thing" on his own?

These questions, like many revolving around suicide and mental illness, are hard to answer. But it's clear to me, from the accounts of those around him, that while Wallace may have taken a risk in changing medications because he thought it might help him finish "The Long Thing" at last, this isn't the same thing as saying that the work led to his suicide. He had struggled with these mental health issues for his whole life, after all. For decades, while his medication still kept him well, his genius and his chemical imbalances coexisted, though sometimes with awful friction. But this doesn't mean one caused the other. If anything, it is likely that creative work gave Wallace a powerful outlet for his considerable mental energies, and a reason to keep himself stable for as long as he did.

Reading Wallace will always be complicated for me. Because I only began reading him in earnest after he was gone, I can't always untangle his death from his work. There's still much in his work that makes my skin crawl, but this is also something I've learned to admire alongside a determined earnestness within nearly all of his writing. Wallace spoke in interviews about fiction existing to make us feel "unalone" in whatever we're struggling with in our own lives, which are otherwise so secluded and claustrophobic. Now I think about him when I am reading anything and feel that odd, warm unaloneness forming around me. I think about him and his cursed videotape when I am craving my cell phone or a quick hit on social media. And every year when I'm filing my taxes. Wallace reminds me not to shy away from the immense or the frightening, and in this way, he's become so much more to me than the particulars surrounding the way he died. But when I do think about that piece of his larger story, I no longer worry that it might have been the logical end to an ambitious, creative life. For every tragedy like Wallace's, I remind myself, there are thousands of others that end in thousands of other ways—that there's nothing inherently dangerous or mad-making in the pursuit of genius.

FAIL LIKE A GENIUS

David Foster Wallace

One challenge that editor Michael Pietsch faced as he assembled *The Pale King* from the piles that David Foster Wallace left behind in his garage was sifting through multiple drafts of the various pieces of the novel in progress, some handwritten, some typed on a typewriter, and others saved on a PC. Fortunately, Wallace was methodical about his drafting process, as he described in an interview for *Amherst* magazine entitled "Brief Interview with a Five Draft Man." Explaining his insistence on conducting the Q and A through the mail, he told the interviewer:

"I am a Five Draft man. I actually learned this at Amherst, in William Kennick's Philosophy 17 and 18, with their brutal paper-every-two-weeks schedules. I got down a little system of writing and two rewrites and two typed drafts. I've used it ever since."

In the archives of the Harry Ransom Center at the University of Texas in Austin, where the boxes containing *The Pale King* now are stored with Wallace's other work, curious readers can see firsthand how the Five Draft system worked. He routinely handwrote a draft of a story or essay or chapter, before revising it and handwriting it all a second time. At that point he'd move to the typewriter (and later, the PC) to type it, revise it again, then type it back over again a fourth time, before finalizing everything in the fifth draft.

It's an arduous process, but in some sense, the struggle is the point. Having to write by hand forces us to slow down, to economize, because it takes a physical toll that typing, especially on a computer keyboard, no longer requires. And if a bit of bad writing has to be rewritten five times, we're more likely to notice it. We're incentivized to work more cautiously, so we have less to copy.

Try it out—if not the full five drafts, then at least three: a handwritten draft first, making line edits, and then moving to a typed version. At that point, print it out and make another round of line edits before retyping the piece again (don't just open the file and edit it there). It will take longer and feel harder, but you will notice a real difference as you work through the stages.

Not only are the final results stronger in a technical sense, but the finished pieces will be more thoughtful than if you simply opened up a blank document and began typing.

Geniuses Get Lost
in the Weeds

Gustave Flaubert

While I was chasing my children around our local library one afternoon, my young daughter noticed a low shelf with all twenty-two volumes of the World Book Encyclopedia. Their spines, arranged neatly from A to Z, formed a super-image of an enormous bumblebee on a yellow flower. She asked me what they were, and I did my best to explain the concept of an encyclopedia—that inside each book was an entry about anything you might want to ever know about. I explained that when I was a child in the 1980s, before iPads and even the internet existed, my parents had owned a set of these and I'd spent hours poring over them, looking up random things. They had seemed then like an incredible key to understanding everything in the entire universe. By the time I graduated college, only ten years after my family got our first Encarta encyclopedia on CD-ROM, the internet had already made both digital and physical encyclopedias obsolete.

I recognize that instantaneous access to information is something of a miracle—but I am also the sort of person who sits in the aisle of my local library near weeping because my six-year-old daughter doesn't know what an encyclopedia is and will never need to know. I pulled out my phone and searched to see if they even still made them—then saw the $450 price tag and thought better of it. Nostalgia is a powerful force, but it does have limits.

Why would I want a set of World Books when I have Google? Because the internet is vast and boundless. If all we did was read it all day long, for our whole lives, we'd barely know a fraction of all it contained. (Nor would we want to—a boundless, uncurated repository of information contains, by definition, a lot of garbage.)

But an encyclopedia has a start and a finish, an A and a Z. With enough time, you could read it and know everything—maybe not everything in the world, but everything important enough to be in the encyclopedia, and that should be enough. For a bibliophile like me, there's something alluring in the idea that a book could contain everything worth knowing.

This spirit has been followed by writers for centuries, even before there were printing presses. A scholar could set out to collect *all* the information available on a particular subject—not just facts and data, but ideas and stories as well.

Here's one early example: in 1621, a fellow at Oxford named Robert Burton published *The Anatomy of Melancholy*, aiming to catalog absolutely everything known about melancholia (or what we today would call clinical depression).

The full title of the book is:

```
The Anatomy of Melancholy,
What it is: With all the Kinds, Causes, Symptomes,
Prognostickes, and Several Cures of it.
In Three Maine Partitions with their several
Sections, Members, and Subsections. Philosophically,
Medicinally, Historically, Opened and Cut Up
```

Because it compiles narratives and philosophies, and with no small amount of humor and style, Burton's book has long been beloved by fiction writers from O. Henry and Washington Irving to Jorge Luis Borges and Samuel Beckett, who consider it to be a work of literature in its own right.

Inspired by Burton's *Anatomy* and similar works, in 1957, literary critic Northrop Frye wrote his own *Anatomy of Criticism*, in which he proposed that the anatomy was one of four genres of fiction alongside the romance, the novel, and the confession. Frye defined a work of anatomical fiction as one "characterized by a great variety of subject-matter and a strong interest in ideas."

Another critic, Edward Mendelson, coined the phrase "Encyclopedic Novel" in 1976 to categorize books (like *The Divine Comedy,* or *Don Quixote,* or *Moby-Dick*) that "attempt to render the full range of knowledge and beliefs of a national culture, while identifying the ideological perspectives from which that culture shapes and interprets its knowledge." Joyce's *Ulysses* and Pynchon's *Gravity's Rainbow* were two more contemporary examples of fascination to Mendelson, and today we'd surely throw in books like David Foster Wallace's *Infinite Jest* or Roberto Bolaño's *2666* or Lucy Ellman's *Ducks, Newburyport.*

It is not simply that these are very, very long books. It is that they *are* so long because they attempt to be all-encompassing. They embrace that primal desire to get it *all* in, to leave nothing out: every fact, every facet, every angle, every opinion, every aspect of their chosen topic.

This epic, encyclopedic grand novel-of-everything has deep historical roots going back to the earliest novels (Laurence Sterne's *Tristam Shandy* is the prime example) and endures today. It drives great writers, grandly, impossibly, quixotically, excitingly. Something about the hugeness of these projects, the never-ending nature of the work, seems to forever attract the skills of great authors, because it seems as if only a rare genius could write one. So if you write one, then, ipso facto, you are a genius.

Reading the great doorstoppers discussed above can be a deeply satisfying journey to go on. Rather than move into a clearing, we enter a thick jungle. It becomes enveloping, absorbing, the sort of book we get to live inside of for weeks if not months.

But when it goes wrong? It goes really wrong. The problem with a book that seeks to smash the limits is, well, it has no limits. The encyclopedic aim has led more than a few geniuses into inescapable gardens of forking paths, where years or even *decades* are dedicated to works that, in the end, are never finished.

Flaubert's Final Fuck You: *Bouvard and Pécuchet*

Some time ago, I was dining with my French editor and his friend at an upscale brasserie in Paris, and I mentioned that I was doing some research for a column on Gustave Flaubert's famous unfinished novel, *Bouvard and Pécuchet*. I asked them what they thought the book was about.

"Everything," my editor replied. "Nothing. Everything is nothing."

"Very French," I joked.

"What is it about?" said the other. "It's . . ."

He paused, and I thought maybe he was searching for the proper English word for it—le mot juste, as Flaubert would have called it. He looked over his shoulder to be sure the nearby patrons were not watching. Then he stared at me, raised one hand between us, and flipped up his middle finger.

FUCK YOU, he mouthed, and broke into giggles.

Was this truly the final sentiment of the author of *A Sentimental Education* and *Madame Bovary*? A writer whose unparalleled prose changed everything about the way fiction was written? Even to Flaubert's most ardent admirers, the unfinished *Bouvard and Pécuchet* presents something of a challenge. He is praised as the father of modern realistic fiction because of his dedication to exactitude, to finding le mot juste. Draft pages of his manuscripts are filled with cross-outs and cuts and scribbled-over lines. It took Flaubert nearly six months to write a single thirty-page story, "A Simple Heart," because he was so intensely focused on making every word in it the perfect one. But his unfinished final novel about a pair of imbeciles who attempt to learn everything about everything in all of human history, is almost anti-realist—more akin to the satirical *Candide* or *Don Quixote* than it is to *Madame Bovary*.

"Economy and perfectionism in point of words would have been the last concern of the two losers featured here," Christopher Hitchens remarks in his review of Mark Polizzotti's translation of *Bouvard and Pécuchet*—entitled "I'm with Stupide."

At the time of the novel's publication in 1881, critic Émile Faguet remarked that the book should not be judged severely, as Flaubert surely would have improved on it had he lived, and that the existing book is the "result of one of his manias," summing the novel up as "the history of a Faust who was an idiot."

Even Flaubert thought that he was out of his mind, working on it. "One would have to be insane, completely deranged, to take on such a book!" he wrote to a friend early in the process.

But take it on he did—for eight years, reading a supposed 1,500 books in research and writing 4,000 manuscript pages, at a legendarily slow pace of five words an hour, until his death by cerebral hemorrhage in 1880.

Flaubert's niece pared down the voluminous manuscript into roughly 300 pages that were finally published the following year.

At one point titled *The Story of Two Nobodies*, the novel opens with the chance meeting of its protagonists, Bouvard and Pécuchet, two Parisian clerks who form a fast friendship over the fact that they have each written their name inside of their own hat, to prevent them being taken accidentally by someone else at the office.

They exchange pleasantries about the weather, and if things might be nicer in the countryside, and whether women are better than men, which they agree they often are, but sometimes aren't. Each enjoys the cavalcade of banality immensely and they make a plan to meet again to continue their conversations about politics, fossils, furniture . . . this and that. It never particularly matters.

They are a classic duo not unlike Bertie and Jeeves, Abbott and Costello, or Jerry and George on *Seinfeld*—knowledgeable but not very bright. *Bourgeois*, if not downright clownish. They are incapable of original thought, though they talk and talk, attend lectures, and discuss various important discoveries. They marvel at their good fortune in meeting and lament that they must spend time in their offices surrounded by "stupid" people.

Things change when Bouvard inherits a large family fortune, and the two men decide that they will move to the countryside (where things may or may not be better) and set about trying to grow vegetables. They speak to their country neighbors about how this should best be done, and set about on a project to study the science of agronomy in depth. They wind up reading dozens of books, hiring various farmhands, and trying to raise animals and make cider and so on—it all soon ends in disaster. After exhaustive efforts, they end up losing most of their crops, growing cantaloupes that taste terrible, wasting some thirty-three thousand francs, and insulting most of the townspeople at a disastrous dinner party. Having failed completely, and nearly blown themselves up in the kitchen, Pécuchet concludes, "Maybe we just don't know enough about chemistry!"

And as the next chapter begins, the two set about to learn

everything they can about chemistry. They read dozens of books, talk to various knowledgeable experts, attempt various kinds of experiments . . . and it all results in total failure. They conclude that what they really need is to better understand anatomy.

And on it goes, in cycles. Anatomy leads them to medicine, to biology, to geology. Then to archeology, architecture, history, mnemonics, literature, drama, grammar, aesthetics, politics, love, gymnastics, occultism, theology, philosophy . . . at this point they, despairingly, take an interest in suicide, which leads them to Christmas, religion, education, music, urban planning . . . each new attempt to learn everything about something is a comedic, disastrous failure.

Critics have viewed the book as a satire of Enlightenment thinking, and of the Rousseauian idea of humanity's progress through acquiring greater and greater knowledge. At every step Bouvard and Pécuchet are frustrated by the limitations of their grand ideas at the hands of reality. Without any actual intelligence, having all the knowledge in the world turns out to be, over and over again, utterly pointless.

"My goal," Flaubert wrote, "is nothing less than to conduct a review of all modern thinking." He described the novel as "a kind of encyclopedia made into a farce . . . I am contemplating something in which I'll vent all my anger. Yes, at last I shall rid myself of what is stifling me. I shall vomit back onto my contemporaries the disgust they inspire in me, even if it means ripping my chest open. . . . It will be big and violent."

To write this big, violent book, Flaubert claimed to have read over 1,500 volumes of research in all the various areas that his characters explore, often reading several books on a particular topic to ultimately yield a few useful details for the novel.

Faguet, in his review, noted the ridiculousness of this effort. "If one stubbornly insists on reading from the point of view of a man who reads without understanding, in a very short while one achieves the feat of understanding absolutely nothing and being obtuse oneself."

Stubborn, indeed. Flaubert worked on the book for nearly eight years continuously, at times describing it as a masterpiece that would exceed his earlier work, and at other times lamenting that it was killing him. Two years in, Flaubert wrote to friend George Sand that the novel was "leading me very quietly, or rather relentlessly, to the abode of the shades. It will be the death of me!"

The last finished chapter of *Bouvard and Pécuchet* leaves the main characters in a cliffhanger. Having run into conflict with their provincial neighbors, they decide that to set things right they must deliver a lecture about the "usefulness" of their project. Several more pages of notes, on what might have been two or so more chapters, describe what would have been the climax and conclusion of the novel.

The inflammatory lecture was to set the townspeople in an uproar, at which point Bouvard and Pécuchet would return to the farmhouse to discuss the future of humanity. Pécuchet takes a pessimistic view. "Modern man has been diminished and turned into a machine." Peace is impossible, barbarism is inevitable. Soon there will be no more ideals, religion, or morality. "America will conquer the earth. . . . Widespread boorishness. Everywhere you look will be carousing laborers. End of the world through the cessation of heat."

Bouvard takes the optimistic view: "Modern man is progressing." Europe and Asia will soon regenerate one another and their populations will "meld together." The future will see incredible scientific advances and inventions. "Underwater boats with windows . . . we will watch fish and landscapes parading by at the

bottom of the ocean. Trained animals. Everything cultivated."
After magnetic energy is harnessed, phosphorescent substances
will soon light people's homes and radiate the streets. "Disappearance of evil through the disappearance of need. Philosophy will be
religion. Communion of all peoples, public celebrations. We will
go to the stars—and when the earth is used up, humanity will
spread to other planets."

They would then be interrupted by the police and the townspeople, trying to have the men arrested for their inflammatory and
blasphemous lecture.

After a debate over whether or not they were insane and in need
of being committed, the two would leave town at last and, at a
special copydesk built for two, begin the work of assembling a
Dictionary of Accepted Ideas in which they would share at last all
the knowledge they had come to in the course of their studies.

Was my French editor correct? Did Flaubert write 4,000 pages,
while reading 1,500 books, about the antics of two clownish
characters, to prove that even if someone knew everything there
was to know about everything, they could still fail? Did he spend
eight years writing to prove that self-improvement is a waste of
time? That all the experts on all the knowledge in all of history do
little more than simply contradict one another until nothing means
anything?

In today's age of information overload, it is hard not to take
Flaubert's point—and his raised middle finger—to heart. With all
the knowledge democratized by the internet that resides at our
fingertips, are we making any progress? Have we only gotten
stupider? But for all the laboring that Bouvard and Pécuchet are
doing, they aren't unhappy. They keep hitting dead ends, but these
turn into jumping-off points for the next thing. Maybe we're

meant to think they're too stupid to quit like sensible people would. But what's so sensible about that?

I think Flaubert must have admired their passionate, futile seeking. He knew it well. Working at a famously glacial pace, obsessing over each sentence and word, he wrote for hours a day but could produce as little as two pages in a week. Still, he kept on writing. And when his masterpiece, *Madame Bovary*, got him sued for immorality, and cost him years of agony and strain? He kept on writing.

Which isn't to say he didn't love to complain about it, often in quite melodramatic terms: "Sometimes I don't understand why my arms don't drop from my body with fatigue, why my brain doesn't melt away," he wrote. "I am leading an austere life, stripped of all external pleasure, and am sustained only by a kind of permanent frenzy, which sometimes makes me weep tears of impotence but never abates."

We've all been there. But why keep doing it, then? Well, Flaubert adds: "I love my work with a love that is frantic and perverted, as an ascetic loves the hair shirt that scratches his belly." He may be in agony with writer's block, collapsing in frustration—but "a quarter of an hour later, everything has changed; my heart is pounding with joy." If *Bouvard and Pécuchet* is, as it seems to me, ultimately an optimistic book, perhaps this is why: by depicting, and indeed engaging in, the compulsion to create an encyclopedic catalog of everything, it celebrates both the futility and the pleasure of this great work.

Critic James Wood, in his book *How Fiction Works*, says that "novelists should thank Flaubert the way poets thank spring," but if I'm honest I often find myself resenting Flaubert for the impossible standards he created. Are we all supposed to read 1,500 books?

Must we all write so meticulously that we labor for hours a day just to find two satisfactory pages a week? In order to keep a roof over his head while he worked, Flaubert moved in with his mother for many years—and took full advantage, by the way, of her servants in the process.

I have a photocopy of one of his draft pages of *A Simple Heart* hanging on the wall in my office, so thickly covered in scribbles and cross-outs that it is hard to find anything that he didn't mark for deletion. I'm never sure if it is aspirational or a reminder that it can always be worse—perhaps it serves both ends nicely.

But if Flaubert is the father of modern realism, I love *Bouvard and Pécuchet* for its reminder that Flaubert dedicated his final years to blowing it all up. It is a novel about two idiots, yes, but in their simplemindedness they also embody in a magical sentimentality that his earlier works strived so hard to avoid.

Like Laurel and Hardy, or Jerry and George, Bouvard and Pécuchet love one another. To use a modern phrase that Flaubert probably would probably have abhorred (but maybe adored) the novel is a "bromance."

After a long week of arduous and discouraging writing, Gustave Flaubert reserved his Sundays for visits from his dear friend Louis Bouilhet. The two of them would read the new pages aloud to one another, with Bouilhet encouraging Flaubert until his confidence was finally restored. Bouilhet passed away in 1870, two years before Flaubert began to work in earnest on *Bouvard and Pécuchet*, and I wonder if he wasn't thinking fondly of his silent collaborator as he did.

There's something beautiful to me about Flaubert losing himself in this new work, even one he described as "deranged" and "violent"—for how else can we describe our grief when we lose someone we love? As Bouvard and Pécuchet discover, each thing we seek to encompass leads to something else.

In the ending that Flaubert never wrote, Bouvard and Pécuchet do not die, but go on copying their work into eternity—side by side, at a desk specially designed for two. It is a beautiful image, and one that I wish dearly that Flaubert had lived to set into perfect, economical prose.

Of all the things that they study and fail to understand, they never come close to solving the first mystery they are faced with that day when they met. Why do they become friends at all? What is the root of our affection for one another? Why do we, human beings, persist in our daily efforts to know, even when there is already too much to ever know, and when progress is elusive?

"We still know almost nothing," Flaubert wrote, "and we would wish to divine the final word that will never be revealed to us. The frenzy for reaching a conclusion is the most sterile and disastrous of manias."

There is a sincere moment late in the novel, where Bouvard comes to something of an awareness of the futility of their endless task. While stargazing, he says to his dear friend, "Science is based on data supplied by a small corpus of knowledge. Perhaps it doesn't apply to all the rest that we don't know about, which is much more vast, and which we can never understand."

He says this, and then, they go on.

Ordinarily we expect an artist to be a master of *selection*, not inclusion. Knowing what to leave out is a skill we usually begin teaching young writers in their very first creative writing classes. We talk about simple and direct language. We talk of Ernest Hemingway and his famous "iceberg theory" of literature, which proposed that a story or a novel should be like the small fraction of an iceberg that floats above the water; what gives it the power to "sink" us is the huge portion of the story that remains submerged, all that unwritten life of the characters that is nonetheless felt by a reader. We must understate, we must imply, we must suggest.

We often say of great prose that it is "economical," meaning that we get a lot out of a little, because things are tuned perfectly.

It is incredibly difficult to write in a simple, straightforward, earnest way—there is nowhere to hide in there, and we admire that nakedness.

But a marvelous thing about fiction is that whenever any rule or standard emerges, someone is bound to come along and break it. What if we don't want economy, but luxury? What if we want something ornate, awe-inspiring, complicated? Baroque, rococo, opulent?

What if we decide to go bigger and bigger and bigger, and get encyclopedic and anatomical? Can't we reverse the usual schema to allow room for *more, more, more*?

There's a fine line between being generous and being excessive, but I think the distinction is in who the excess is there for—keep the reader and their enjoyment in mind, and you'll find that the drive for more can be its own mark of genius.

Fail like a Genius

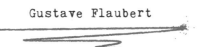

Gustave Flaubert

Flaubert's inspirations for his two clownish pals came from all the information he was collecting about history and science. We don't need to read 1,500 books to find inspiration, but like Flaubert, we may want to find ways to organize and collect the random interesting things we do come across.

In an article for *Lapham's Quarterly* called "Pale Ink," author Ed Park describes a method for collecting inspiring tidbits that may or may not become useful in future work, by creating a commonplace book where he jots down anything and everything that strikes him in whatever moment as interesting. "There are quotes from musicians, paragraphs clipped from the *New York Times*, passages from Sontag and Philip K. Dick, Wodehouse and Kim Jong II," Park explains, "attractively grandiose statements rub up against humbler fare."

This can be done in any empty journal, or electronically—you can cut and paste things you like or copy them over—play with colors and fonts if you like. This can become something between a mood board, a scrap heap, and a work of art depending on how you incorporate your material.

It ends up looking like Flaubert's *Dictionary of Accepted Ideas*, a wide-ranging catalog of knowledge, something between a journal and an encyclopedia—an anatomy of you.

The practice of keeping commonplace books goes back to antiquity, and they were used by Charles Darwin, John Locke, Isaac

Newton, Virginia Woolf, E. M. Forster, and many others.

Park describes his initial handwritten commonplace book evolving digitally, a gigantic open file where images and photographs and Facebook posts can be inserted, and which can be updated from a phone.

Instead of filling your cloud storage with hundreds of disparate "notes" and voice memos, the idea here is to gather them in one place so that you can easily look back at how things juxtapose and overlap. Your commonplace book can be appended or revised, entries can be sorted and organized or kept in loose chronological order. Just the act of writing these things down helps us commit them to memory, and the act of collecting the transient things that fly by us each day will help us to observe larger patterns and even forge meaningful links between moments of life.

And then, on slow writing days, as you sit like Flaubert feeling your brain turning to liquid, you can flip open your commonplace book and reencounter the things that fascinated you over the months and years, until something strikes you as a way forward.

Geniuses Bite Off More Than They Can Chew

Ralph Ellison

(12)

One fall, in college, I took a history course called "The Age of Tolstoy," where we learned about the nineteenth-century events that surrounded and inspired the great writer, along with Dostoevsky, Herzen, and many of their contemporaries. I'd been excited to finally have an excuse to read some of these classic novels, but by the end of the semester I found myself way behind. The night before the final exam I stacked up the reading I had not yet done and measured it at nearly nine inches high.

"Why did these Russians write such massive books?" I complained to anyone who would listen.

There was no way I was going to get through it, so I confessed my situation to my professor the next morning before the exam. He nodded sympathetically and offered me a life preserver. If I took the intersession break to read all those books, as well as *Anna Karenina*, and then took the exam and wrote an extra essay, he'd call it even.

So that winter I hunkered down and read the Russians. And in doing so, I realized why they were all so long—what better way to pass a long season of deep snow and frigid storms than buried deep inside a book?

Thinking of great novels as works of art, even masterpieces, it is easy to forget that they serve a more basic function: first and foremost, they are a means of escape. Just as my grade school teachers would tell us that books were our passport to the world, I remind myself today that what I'm writing is meant to be a mode of transportation, a bullet train heading into, of all improbable places, my imagination.

Part of the allure of an encyclopedic novel for a writer like Gustave Flaubert might be that it becomes, itself, a journey. While readers eventually enjoy a hearty diversion inside of an enormous book, an author gets to *live* inside of it, and for much longer. For all of Flaubert's moaning and groaning about his liquifying brain, when he sent off his *Madame Bovary* after five years of agonizing, he reflected on it gratefully.

"After all," he wrote, "work is still the best way of escaping life!"

But can this be taken too far? Might a project like this become *too* big? Too enveloping? So massive that it *cannot* be completed? And what if that is the whole point? A novel can become an escape route, a hiding place, an alternate reality that overrides the rest. After eight years of work, Flaubert's *Bouvard and Pécuchet* was still unfinished, but based on his outlines he wasn't *too* far from the end. But that's nothing compared to the story of Ralph Ellison's second novel, which he had worked on for *forty years* at the time of his death, and which was not even close to done.

Forty Years in the Making: Ralph Ellison's *Juneteenth*

The novel has got my attention now," Ralph Ellison said in an interview with the *New Yorker*'s David Remnick in early

1994. "I work every day, so there should be something very soon." Two months later, Ellison passed away of pancreatic cancer, and the novel, a long-awaited follow-up to 1953's *Invisible Man*, was at last uncovered by his executor, John Callahan.

In the introduction to *Juneteenth*, the version of that novel published in 1999, Callahan described the scene in Ellison's office on his first day: "As if to protest [Ellison's] absence, the teeming bookshelves had erupted in over his desk, chair, computer table, and copying machine, finally covering the floor like a blizzard of ash." There were over two thousand pages, some handwritten, some typewritten. Some had been collected in binders and filing cabinets since the 1970s, "painstakingly labelled according to character or episode." There were mimeographs and there were floppy disks. There were notes scribbled onto newspaper clippings and magazine subscription cards. There were print-outs, first dot matrix and then laser. The project had survived four decades of advances in word processing technology: Ellison's typewriter had been replaced by the Osborne Executive computer bought in 1983, which was then replaced by an IBM in 1988. Between them all, Callahan would find a range of overlapping narratives, some long enough to be novels unto themselves—but no finished book.

Callahan would ultimately publish the 366-page *Juneteenth* in 1999, and then in 2010, a new, fuller assemblage of excerpts and notes called *Three Days Before the Shooting . . .* , which clocked in around 1,100 pages—still just half of what Ellison had left behind. But neither of these books is *the* book that Ellison first began to envision back in 1951 when he optimistically wrote to his lifelong friend, Albert Murray, "I probably have enough stuff left over from [*Invisible Man*] if I can just find the form."

Ellison left all his papers in the care of the Library of Congress, where he had frequently worked. On a C-SPAN *BookTV* special in 1999, Alice Burney, of the library's manuscript division, described how the novel was first brought to them in "reams of chaotic scribbled papers . . . hundreds of cartons." Over the better part of two years, these were carefully sorted into "seventy-six acid-free banker's boxes" and "thirty-two additional flat containers." Deteriorating pages had to be specially preserved by conservators. It took another six months to then identify separate essays, stories, and various overlapping drafts of his second novel's many sections. Because Ellison had never settled on a title for the project, she explained, the project was referred to as Ellison himself most frequently had: "The Hickman Novel."

In his foreword, Callahan recalled his first day coming into Ellison's office, accompanied by Ellison's wife. "Beginning, middle, and end," he recalls her wondering aloud, staring at the piles. "Does it have a beginning, middle, and end?"

Callahan set out to determine the answer to that forty-year-old question. According to him, Ellison "dreamed of a fiction whose theme was the indivisibility of American experience and the American language as tested by two protagonists." These are, in *Juneteenth*, an African American jazz musician turned con man named Reverend Alonzo Hickman and an orphaned boy of "indeterminate race who looks white," Adam Bliss, being raised by Hickman. Bliss becomes part of Hickman's ministry, following him around as he preaches and occasionally scams his fellow men (in the name of God). Bliss finally leaves Hickman, during an evening celebration of Juneteenth, the holiday commemorating the end of slavery. He then "reinvents himself in the guise of a movie-maker and flimflam man" and finally becomes a "race-baiting" senator known as Adam Sunraider.

Juneteenth follows this fraught father-son relationship through the first half of the twentieth century in the segregated American South, up and down the Mississippi River, and from "Washington, D.C., south to Georgia and Alabama, southwest to Oklahoma, back again to the nation's capital" over the course of fifty years, exploring the "intellectual depths" of both two men, their "values and purposes."

Through Hickman and Sunraider, Ellison sought to characterize both American and African American culture, music, religion, politics, values, and desires. Ellison described the novel as a dialogue between himself, Mark Twain, and William Faulkner—with some Ernest Hemingway and F. Scott Fitzgerald in there as well. "In conception and execution," Callahan writes, "*Juneteenth* is multifarious, multifaceted, multifocused, multivoiced, multi-toned."

Excerpts of it were published, over the years, to eagerly awaiting fans. Saul Bellow, with whom Ralph Ellison briefly lived in Tivoli, New York, recalled that he had read "a considerable portion of it" and that "all of it was marvelous stuff, easily on a level with *Invisible Man*." And James Alan McPherson, after hearing an excerpt of the book in 1969, concluded that "in his novel Ellison was trying to solve the central problem of American literature . . . I think he was trying to *Negro-Americanize* the novel form, at the same time he was attempting to move beyond it." At one point Ellison and McPherson discussed the possibility that truly this was a novel in three volumes, which would each have to be published separately.

The finished novel was originally contracted to be delivered to Random House in 1965, which was then extended to the fall of 1967. Ellison told people that year that he was feeling good about finishing it, working hard on revisions at a summer house that he had bought in the Berkshires. Allegedly the novel was almost finished in November of that year, when a great tragedy occurred.

Ellison and his wife, Fanny, returned from shopping to find their house on fire. It would be completely destroyed, with all the furniture and personal possessions inside lost—including the manuscript of Ellison's novel. Fanny would later lament that she had not been able to break into the burning house to save the book, and sometimes this story involved firemen restraining her from entering the house to do so. "I knew right where it was," she would tell Callahan, years later.

But a few weeks later, Ellison wrote that while he had lost most of the revision work from the summer, he had it all very fresh in his mind and thought it could be redone by early the following year. "Fortunately," he wrote to critic Nathan Scott Jr., he "had a full copy of all that he had done prior to that summer."

But he would not turn in the manuscript the following year, or the year after that. His story about the damage done by the fire began to change, possibly as a justification for his delays. A year later he would tell one reporter that sadly he had lost 365 pages in the fire, and this tally would grow later to be more than 500. If on some level this was true, the larger problem was that, as he wrote privately to critic Richard Kostelanetz, the book had "become inordinately long—perhaps over one thousand pages—and complicated."

And there may have been deeper layers to the tragedy. Ellison's biographer, Arnold Rampersad, speculated in 2007 that while the fire might not have physically consumed his manuscript in progress, the experience had created a trauma that then became a deep wound for Ellison in the years that followed.

By the time of the fire Ellison had won the National Book Award (he was the first Black author to win the prize) and two presidential medals. He had joined the American Academy of Arts and Letters and worked at the American Academy in Rome. He'd helped to found the National Endowment for the Humanities, and dined at the White House with President and First Lady Johnson. *Invisible Man* had already become a crucial book in the American twentieth century canon.

The destruction of his Tivoli home by that mysterious fire would afterward loom symbolically in his mind. Officially, the cause of the fire had been faulty electrical wiring, but years after Ellison's death, Fanny wrote that he "knew, I'm sure, that it was arson, but he made no complaint to the town."

Their neighbors sent letters to the Ellisons, expressing their deep sympathy, and a hat was passed around to help collect funds for them to start over. But this wasn't enough. Ellison would drive up to inspect the ruined house, and then leave in melancholy. It would take more than six years to rebuild their home.

Meanwhile, the deadline for the second novel was moved to 1975. Then 1980. And then fourteen more years would pass with Ellison still hard at work, until his death in 1994, just after his eightieth birthday.

Juneteenth climaxes in the shooting of the racist Senator Sunraider by a young Black man. Over the course of several days in a hospital bed, Sunraider tries to reconcile with Hickman and his memories of his childhood as Adam Bliss, a member of the Black Baptist community. Sunraider thinks back to the Juneteenth night that he left. He dismisses the holiday initially as "the celebration of a gaudy illusion." Ninety years later, were the Black men and women of America really free?

In his introduction to *Juneteenth*, Callahan reminds us why the holiday is celebrated on the anniversary of June 19, 1865, and not on September 22, 1863, the day the Emancipation Proclamation was delivered by President Lincoln. The reason is that it would take two and a half more years for Union troops to march through the defeated South and reach the thousand men, women, and children enslaved in Galveston, Texas, to relay the news that they were now free. Callahan notes that the delay "is a symbolic acknowledgment that liberation is the never-ending task of self, group, and nation, and that, to endure, liberation must be self-achieved and self-achieving."

In the end, the dying Senator Sunraider reconsiders. He sees that leaving the Black community to pass as white was an "evasion" of his identity. That night he believed that he had escaped, but ultimately feels that he was cast out from "his true American self," and that his true kinship is to the people he has betrayed, both in his words and with his political power—he is kin, even, to the young man that shot him. Hickman and the community celebrating Juneteenth had been his family, and whatever his own unknown racial makeup might be, Sunraider ultimately realizes that he is also "somehow black."

According to Callahan, Ralph Ellison saw a meaningful parallel between his never-ending work in progress and the "'crazy country' he loved and contended with." If, at the start of "the Hickman novel," in the America of 1951, Ellison saw his chance to argue for "the indivisibility of American experience and the American language" and to contend with "race and identity, language and kinship in the American experience," then how must that story itself have evolved over the course of the next forty years?

Two days after the Supreme Court's decision in *Brown v. Board of Education*, Ellison wrote that he had "the whole road [of post-segregationist America] stretched out and it got all mixed up with this book I'm trying to write and it left me twisted with joy and a sense of inadequacy." He was working on it when Emmett Till was murdered. Working on it during the boycott of the Montgomery bus service and the arrest of Rosa Parks. Working on it when Martin Luther King Jr. led the march to Selma, and when he was assassinated. Working on it during the summer of 1967, when *Loving v. Virginia* was decided—working on it at the proud New England home that would soon be destroyed. Twenty-five years later, as the Los Angeles riots raged in 1992, Ellison was still working on it, by then with his IBM computer and his laser printer—trying to finish a novel that might encompass, and answer, the ongoing struggle of Black Americans in the twentieth century. Two thousand pages begins to feel like it could hardly scratch the surface.

Ambition is crucial to the spirit of great writing. We are driven to try and write the book that we've always wished to find on the shelf but no one's written yet. Each time we sit down to work, we're casting our lines a little farther than we've cast them before, out of the familiar and away from the safe. If we don't risk that much, then how can we expect anyone to risk their time inside our fantasies? But by doing this we have to be careful. We may spin a little too far, too fast, and become stalled. It's good that we want our work to be important, to be all-encompassing; if we're going to try to write at all, then why not at least try to write the definitive thing? Yes, most of the time we will eventually find we need to pull back, to settle for something a little less than we imagined at first—a book, instead of *the* book. In fact, the greater your ambition, the more likely you may be to stall out and need to rethink your scope, since the pressure to write something comprehensive can be overwhelming, even for a Ralph Ellison. But even the smaller project, fueled by that drive to be definitive, is in and of itself a marvelous creation. And the remainder of all that ambition? Let it stay there, until you're ready for the next book.

Ralph Ellison

As we've seen in the cases of *Bouvard and Pécuchet* and *Juneteenth*, there is some danger in getting sucked into a never-ending story, but it is clearly also very appealing. We spend so much time in creative life thinking about what to withhold or to pare back—there's something exalting then about playing around with expansion instead.

A former professor of mine, the postmodern novelist Steven Dixon, once described a particular method of expansive novel-writing to me that I think would be right up Ellison's alley.

First, you write out the plot of your story in a tight summary, single-spaced, on one page. You'll end up with roughly 500 words, or 30 sentences. These sentences should be tight—this is the tip of your iceberg, so make it as clear and solid as possible.

Next, take each sentence and write an entire page. Add description, interiority, dialogue, detail, all that good stuff. Let the idea of that original sentence grow without moving into the territory of the next—not until you reach the end of the page. Do this for each of the original sentences and you end up with around 30 pages. Simple.

Now you have a long rough draft of a short story. From here, if you wish, you can begin revising and cutting things back to tighten it back up.

But, if you're in for some *real* fun . . . expand again.

Across 30 pages of draft, you now have about 900 sentences. If you take each of those sentences and write *another* page around it?

Well, buckle up. This will take months, even years.

But by the end you will have something resembling a gigantic novel—or a trilogy of novels.

Fair warning: what you'll have at that point will not actually *be* a novel. What you will have is an *enormous* mess, full of contradictions and tangents and overwriting.

But an enormous mess can be shaped, whittled, divided, and transformed into something, or many somethings.

However far you go, you'll get to see how much bursting potential lies inside of every single, simple sentence.

Geniuses Keep Secrets

Patricia Highsmith

What is the best way to begin telling a story? You've got "Once upon a time . . ." naturally, or Snoopy's classic, "It was a dark and stormy night," but I have one to beat those. Ready? The best opening line in fiction is just four words: "I know a secret."

We open a book. We begin the first page to find a young woman about to tell us about the "queer, sultry summer" she spent in New York when Ethel and Julius Rosenberg were electrocuted. Why can't she stop thinking about them? What's wrong with her? She sees a cadaver's head and it follows her around like a "black, noseless balloon stinking of vinegar."

We're reading *The Bell Jar*, by Sylvia Plath, and before we even know who is speaking to us (Esther Greenwood) we know one of her deepest, darkest secrets. A thing that is on her mind that she cannot tell anyone else—only us. (We're very special, you see.)

We flip open *Beloved*, by Toni Morrison. Boom: we're in a house that is "spiteful" and "full of a baby's venom," where mirrors shatter suddenly, and ghostly infant handprints appear in cakes. What is going on here? Something bad, that's all we know. Something has been buried in this house. This house knows a secret. It's been hidden from everyone except, soon, from *us*.

Or there's a group of delightfully pretentious college students who've, well, recently murdered their friend, Bunny (we're now reading *The Secret History*, by Donna Tartt). And over there is a fellow standing at a window in a nice house somewhere, alone on the evening his clandestine lover is to be executed (*Giovanni's Room*, by James Baldwin). We could go on and on.

In all these books, and many, many more, we are hooked by the suggestion that we are about to be filled in on forbidding and powerful secrets.

And due to this, we're taught that to write well we need to dig down deep inside of ourselves and unlock the most hidden, scary truths we have. What are our biggest, worst secrets? What do we know that no one else does—or that no one else can face?

"The novel lies in saying something happened that did not," Elizabeth Bowen writes in "Notes on Writing a Novel." "It must, therefore, contain uncontradictable truth, to warrant the original lie."

This can be a *poetic* truth, Bowen says; it does not necessarily need to be a personal confession on the part of the writer, although fiction writers can and do often tap into this same source and direct it into new channels. But the novel must contain truth, and where else is a writer supposed to find new truths to share? In *Letters to a Young Poet*, Rainer Maria Rilke agrees with Bowen: "There is only one way. Go into yourself."

We champion writers specifically because of their willingness to mine their own inner life for use in fiction. Modern practitioners of autofiction like Rachel Cusk, Karl Ove Knausgård, Annie Ernaux, and Ben Lerner join in the age-old tradition that brought us Marguerite Duras, Jack Kerouac, Marcel Proust, and many others. They promise the beautiful structuring and ordering and poetry of a novel, but anchored in what's allegedly "true" instead of what's possibly not.

"To write is to sell a ticket to escape, not from the truth, but into it," writes Alexander Chee in his essay "How to Write an Autobiographical Novel."

But does this mean that exposure is the only way? That each novel must also be a confession? That the mark of a real genius is their willingness to reveal all about themselves, along with burning every bridge to others around them?

What then for those of us who are not willing to expose our real lives to the reader without a few layers of disguise?

I stand in awe of writers with the nerve to stand before strangers, nakedly and honestly—but I don't quite have that nerve. I'm protective of the real people I love in my life. I don't necessarily believe I have the blanket authority to take their stories as my own. I'm conflicted, eternally, over what right I have to represent them, over how ethical it is to sell something labeled "fiction" but marketed largely on its basis in real events.

To me, this question of "How much of this is based on your real life?" often becomes a way of restating that basic question—how can a great writer also be an ordinary person living an ordinary life? Do you need to have had an extraordinary life to write an extraordinary novel? And if you don't, then why can't any ordinary person living an ordinary life be a great writer?

Because, we believe, most of us would never be able to look so honestly at ourselves, or be perceptive enough to see inside those around us—and even if we could, we wouldn't be brave enough, or cutthroat enough, to share it with the world. We think a genius writer is, by nature, a fearless one.

But in my digging around into unpublished works by some of our greatest writers, one variety that I have come across is the manuscript abandoned out of fear. Books begun with the intention of exposing—the authors, the people around the authors—but then ultimately kept back, held from view. Are these failures of bravery, then, on the part of the authors?

Or is it that the mark of a truly great writer is knowing which secrets are to be shared, and which are not?

Suspense and Suppression:
Patricia Highsmith's *First Person Novel*

In a craft book called *Plotting and Writing Suspense Fiction*, the author Patricia Highsmith outlined her thoughts on various techniques that she'd learned from a lifetime of writing hugely successful psychological thrillers like *Strangers on a Train* and *The Two Faces of January*. In a chapter called "The Snags," she addresses common mistakes and problems would-be suspense writers might face. Among other things, she urges her readers to remain in the third-person perspective while writing, calling the first-person mode "the most difficult" and admitting to having twice been "bogged down . . . so emphatically that I abandoned any idea of writing the books."

What was it that Patricia Highsmith found so challenging about writing in the first person? You might think that the confessional mode would be a natural fit for a writer telling twisted psychological tales. When I first picked up *The Talented Mr. Ripley*, inspired by seeing the incredible 1999 film by Anthony Minghella, it immediately struck me as odd that the novel was written in the third person. The film had been so deeply personal, so close to the psychology of its sociopathic, lying lead character, Tom Ripley. But in the book, Tom is always at arm's length. All of Highsmith's novels are like this—except, as she says in her craft book, for two novels, both abandoned.

In Bern, Switzerland, at the Swiss Literary Archives, there are boxes and boxes containing Highsmith's personal letters and papers. In one of these boxes, marked "unfinished novels," there are fifty-nine pages marked with the oddly perfunctory title, *First Person Novel.*

What at first appears to be a series of letters turns out to be the opening of a strange book, in which a woman named Juliette Talifer Dorn sits in a German cottage, recounting to her husband her lifelong history of her love for other women. She decides that she will spend two hours every day that summer writing down these accounts, "for the benefit of her husband," as Highsmith put it in her own description of the novel to a friend.

Eric, the husband, is an electrical engineer, and they have a seventeen-year-old son named Philip John. She expresses love for Eric but cannot, she tells him with no small amount of regret, seem to stop herself from "practicing homosexuality, even if . . . she should wish to." At the time of her letter-writing, Juliette is having an affair with a ballet dancer, and her husband is understandably "bewildered" by this.

At some points called *Girls' Book*, and others *First Person Novel,* the book would in Highsmith's vision take shape as a mixture of letters and diary entries belonging to Juliette, forming a confession and history all at once. Juliette writes to Eric that she intends to go all the way back to the very beginning, to when she first realized that she felt this way, and trace her lesbianism through "the trail, the chain of crushes and loves" to the present day.

Highsmith's plan was to write seven stories, each "told from older and younger point of view" that would, through Juliette, explore and catalog her past relationships. Highsmith's notes make it clear that she intended to base many of these stories on real encounters from her own life, and actual women that she'd known and loved since she first began to realize that she was attracted to other women.

In the existing pages we learn about the earliest of these episodes. At age six, Juliette has an infatuation with a ten-year-old named Marjorie. Four years later, Juliette falls for a classmate, Helen, experiencing a for the first time a "tabu, unnatural" pleasure that she realizes she must keep in check. She resigns her feelings to the realm of "imagination," and it won't be until the next year that she discovers the word *lesbian* in a dictionary and puts a name to those feelings.

At fourteen, she lusts after another girl, whom she then pines after for three more years. As this is all going on, Juliette makes love to a man for the first time, "an indifferent experience she didn't particularly want to repeat." Her first real romantic relationship begins soon after, at a boarding school in Switzerland, with a girl named Veronica, whom she calls Verie. The girls end up separated from their classmates during a lightning storm and, in their fear and excitement, grip one another's hands and begin to kiss.

Juliette and Verie become lovers and are "gloriously happy" together. Traveling with Verie's family as her "old school friend," Juliette finds herself taken in and adored and accepted. Together she and Verie tour the grand capitals of Europe by train, and their love blooms. They fantasize about buying a house in California, or Italy. Verie seems unworried about them being caught and does not try to hide their love in public. But Juliette can't live so openly, and fears what will happen if people see them. In the end her fears are justified. The relationship ends when friends of Verie's family see them together in Rome and are just as unaccepting as Juliette feared they would be.

As a consequence of this, Verie's parents threaten to cut them off if she does not come home. The once-unconcerned Verie now begins to drink more heavily and the girls realize there is no way for them to create the life they want together. They separate, but as Juliette explains to her husband, she recognizes that Verie has, by then, formed a mold for all future lovers: "I grew conditioned to a physical type like Verie—not too tall, slim, but rounded and much softer to touch than she appeared to be, her short, wavy hair, her firm, round breasts that needed no brassiere, her slender feet braced against my insteps in bed, the slight depressions—favored by Rubens and odd in anyone as slim as Verie—on either side of her spine above the buttocks, little sinks that I could feel in the dark with my fingertips. All this has never left me."

And then—the book ends abruptly.

Just fifty-nine pages into the draft, Highsmith abandoned the *First Person Novel* project and did not return to it throughout the remaining thirty years of her life.

Patricia Highsmith was born in Fort Worth, Texas and moved between there and New York City as a young woman, living sometimes with her stepfather and mother—who had told Highsmith she'd tried to abort her by drinking turpentine when she got pregnant—and her grandmother in Astoria, who taught Highsmith to read and later helped bring her up in an apartment filled with books. Highsmith went to Barnard, studied playwriting and short fiction, and graduated in 1942 hoping to soon become a writer.

Highsmith spent the next six years working for comic book publishers, freelancing as a writer on pulp comics with titles like *Black Terror* and *Fighting Yank* and *Captain Midnight*. In her spare time, she worked on her short stories and began longer works. Finally, in 1950, she published her debut novel, *Strangers on a Train*, about two men, Bruno and Guy, who meet by chance, and Bruno's proposal that the two of them exchange murders, each killing the other's enemy so as to throw off the investigators afterward. The novel was a modest success at first, and then became even more popular after being adapted into a film by Alfred Hitchcock the following year. Just thirty years old, Highsmith was already becoming established as a promising author of psychological thrillers.

But in 1952, when Highsmith published her second novel, *The Price of Salt*, she did so under a pseudonym: "Claire Morgan." This would be her first book about women loving other women, and because *First Person Novel* would never get past page fifty-nine, it remains the only book she ever wrote about a same-sex relationship.

The Price of Salt revolves around a romance between young Therese Belivet and an older married woman named Carol Aird. The two meet in a department store, where Therese is working during the holidays and Carol is shopping for a toy. She gives Therese her address for the order's delivery, and Therese decides to use the address to send Carol a Christmas card. The two women begin to correspond and eventually begin a love affair. Though their relationship will ultimately cause Carol to lose custody of her daughter in her divorce from her husband, the novel ends on a surprisingly optimistic note—one of the very few in all of Highsmith's career, with Therese returning to Carol's embrace at last.

The Price of Salt had originally been referenced in Highsmith's notebooks as *The Bloomingdale Story* and later *The Argument of Tantalus: or THE LIE*. With it she was able to write in a voice that felt truer to her than usual, noting in her journals that she was eager to get back to work on this book that was far more personal than in her previous one, which had revolved around two men and their criminal intertwining. While readers of *Strangers on a Train* will find that a considerable homosexual tension exists between Guy and Bruno, any attraction they feel toward one another is neither verbalized nor acted upon—aside from their murderous pact. But in *The Price of Salt*, there is no subtext, and tellingly it is the only novel of Highsmith's in which no murder occurs.

"Oh, I shall be myself then!" she wrote at one point, while working on *The Price of Salt*, exalting in her ability to express herself so freely.

But in the end, Highsmith was not willing to publish *The Price of Salt* under her own name, which was not uncommon at the time for writers of fiction that involved homosexual love. Though Highsmith was now known in New York literary circles, and able to have open relationships with women while in the bubble of Greenwich Village (where many of her novels would ultimately be set), she knew she'd face scandal and even possible criminal action by publishing a novel about two lesbians in 1952. Moreover, Highsmith's own feelings about her sexuality were complicated and, in her diaries and letters, she still held out some hope that she might yet find a way to cure herself of her homosexuality.

It was this same desire that had led Highsmith, back in December 1948, to take the holiday job working at Bloomingdale's, where she met the real-life woman, Kathleen Senn, who inspired the character of Carol Aird. With *Strangers on a Train* still not published, Highsmith needed money, in part to help pay for twice-weekly psychoanalysis sessions. In her diary, she wrote that she "wanted to get myself in a condition to be married." Highsmith knew already that she did not enjoy sex with men, which she likened to "steel wool in the face, a sensation of being raped in the wrong place." She believed this was due to Freudian issues of her own and that they might be fixed through therapy— an idea that, in 1948, was entirely within the mainstream. Just a few years later, in 1952, when the American Psychiatric Association put out its first *Diagnostic and Statistical Manual of Mental Disorders* (DSM), homosexuality was placed within the category of "sociopathic personality disturbance" and classified as a "sexual deviation" akin to pedophilia. It would not be completely removed from the DSM until its fifth printing in 2013, almost twenty years after Highsmith's death.

But whatever Highsmith's intentions were as she'd worked at the desk in the toy department at Bloomingdale's, she became utterly entranced by a customer named Kathleen Senn. The tall, blond, beautiful woman entered wearing a mink coat and bought a doll. Highsmith saved a copy of the receipt for the doll, which had the woman's home address on it. Immediately after work that day, Highsmith went home and wrote an eight-page outline for *The Price of Salt*, where Highsmith's fantasies of reaching out to Senn and beginning a love affair became, instead, the basis for her second novel.

Biographer Andrew Wilson, in his book *Beautiful Shadow: A Life of Patricia Highsmith*, explains that writing *The Price of Salt* initially had been a liberating thing for Highsmith, and it "allowed Pat to release herself from what was to become her most reliable artistic forgery: the male 'voice' of narration and an apparently heterosexual orientation." Highsmith's own diaries confirm this, writing in December 1949: "How grateful I am at last not . . . to spoil my best thematic material by transposing it to false male-female relationship."

But the day after finishing writing *The Price of Salt*, Highsmith's journals recount a troubling episode. After having a few drinks she'd boarded a bus that would take her close to Senn's home in Ridgewood, New Jersey—she had the address still saved from the Christmas purchase, years earlier. Highsmith hid outside the house until she saw a woman in an aqua dress drive by, with blond hair and dark sunglasses. Unsure if it was even Senn, Highsmith left in a hurry, feeling ashamed and unsatisfied.

Highsmith's diary entry from the next day gives her dark reaction: "yesterday I felt quite close to murder, as I went to see the house of the woman who almost made me love her when I saw her a moment in December, 1948. Murder is a kind of making love, a kind of possessing. (Is it not, attention, for a moment, from the object of one's affections?) To arrest her suddenly, my hands upon her throat (which I should really like to kiss) as if I took a photograph, to make her in an instant cool and rigid as a statue."

Ironically, as Wilson points out, the truth was that Senn, totally unbeknownst to Highsmith (who had never spoken to her after that day in 1948), was also deeply troubled. She was an alcoholic and had been institutionalized for mental illness twice. Senn would, coincidentally, kill herself in the garage of her home in Bergen County shortly before *The Price of Salt* was published, totally unaware of her role in the novel's inspiration.

Meanwhile, Wilson notes, as *The Price of Salt* got closer and closer to release, Highsmith unraveled quickly. Consumed with shame and guilt, she drank until she blacked out, losing sometimes days at a time from memory. At one point she confessed to her agent Margot Johnson that she had been seeing Johnson's girl-friend, Kay Guinness, behind her back—a self-destructive act both in the doing and the telling. Johnson did not drop Highsmith (though she did break up with Guinness), and instead introduced her author to a new lover, Sonya Cache, a Parisian woman—going so far as to provide them with her own apartment, as she had done previously, so that the two of them could sleep together. It briefly seemed to help Highsmith's stability.

"I had almost forgotten that pleasure beyond all pleasures, that joy beyond all treasures," Highsmith wrote. "The pleasure of pleasing a woman . . . beyond creative satisfaction."

But it didn't last. Cache had another lover already, whom

Highsmith called up on the phone to confront. It did not end well. "And anyway," Wilson notes, "she was still secretly seeing Kay"— now her agent's ex. Around this time Highsmith began abusing "dental gas," which provided the "total anesthesia" that could "relieve her, if only for an hour, from being Patricia Highsmith."

If writing *The Price of Salt* had been so liberating for Highsmith, then why did she never write another book like it? Why did she abandon *First Person Novel* so early in the going? In her anxiety over the publication of the earlier novel we can see how difficult it was for Highsmith to face exposure, and how it strained against her insecurities and repression.

But *The Price of Salt* made Highsmith famous in new ways as "Claire Morgan." Marijane Meaker, whose own lesbian novel, *Spring Fire*, also came out in 1952 (under her own pseudonym, "Vin Packer"), recalled in a memoir that every lesbian in the bohemian enclaves of lower Manhattan had a copy of *The Price of Salt* on their shelves, and word got around quickly that Highsmith was the real author. It was remarkable at the time because it had a happy ending, of sorts. Meanwhile other lesbian authors like Meaker had to end their novels with their characters being punished or reformed as "straight" in order to get a publisher to accept the books. It was illegal to send "proselytizing" materials for a "vice like lesbianism" through the mail.

Spring Fire, which sold 1.5 million copies, ends with its main character having a "heterosexual awakening," thanks to the help of her doctors. Another book of Meaker's came with cover copy that described the story as "frightening picture of how the blight of sexual distortion spreads, corrupts and finally destroys those around it." So to Meaker and other literary lesbians at that time, Highsmith was not just an incredible writer, but a groundbreaking force—a legend in her own time.

Meaker recalled first seeing Highsmith in a "dark, cozy" Greenwich Village lesbian bar called L's, a few years later: "A handsome, dark-haired woman in a trench coat, drinking gin."

In an interview with Terry Gross on NPR's *Fresh Air*, she explained that their admiration for one another began in literary appreciation: "I loved her writing. I think we shared a common theme, which was folie à deux, a sort of simultaneous insanity, two people involved with each other very closely, often in a crime. I think that was—and her writing, of course—was what drew me to her before I even knew her."

Meaker was more out than Highsmith at the time, and politically active in the New York gay rights movement. She and Highsmith eventually began a two-year romance, during which Highsmith wrote several more books and regained a happiness and stability she had not had since before publishing *The Price of Salt*.

And it was during this period that Highsmith started to write *First Person Novel*.

When, in May 1960, Highsmith began writing the new book by "Claire Morgan," she initially thought she might return to the perspective of Therese, making this book a kind of sequel to *The Price of Salt*. Ultimately, however, because Highsmith "couldn't figure out how to introduce Therese into the narrative," she moved off this plan and introduced the character of Juliette instead. The fifty-nine pages of *First Person Novel* are written in a confessional mode, with Juliette opening up to her husband about her attraction to women, but they do not express shame or beg for forgiveness. Juliette presents her homosexuality to her husband as long-standing, as genuine, as real and loving—if often ending in tragedy.

First Person Novel seems, like *The Price of Salt*, to show Juliette embracing her sexuality and, if anything, asking her husband to understand and accept it as something natural, if misunderstood. This would have been groundbreaking for Highsmith, and for lesbian fiction generally at that time, but we'll never know for sure, because Highsmith abandoned the book a few months after she began writing it.

It happened around the time that she and Meaker ended their two-year relationship. Meaker talks about these sad months in her memoir. She and Highsmith moved into a house together near Doylestown, Pennsylvania, and even made plans to adopt an orphaned child from Korea together, but they soon found that they could not make it work. Highsmith could not settle into a calm, domestic life. She drank too much; she had affairs. They fought and eventually decided to split up, so quickly after first moving in together that Meaker recalls her embarrassment in needing to call the same moving company—the only one in the area—that had brought their stuff into the house, to now bring it all out again. A local newspaper article about their planned adoption ended up running within days of Highsmith deciding to leave for good.

Many years later, when *The Price of Salt* was republished in the 1990s by Bloomsbury as *Carol,* at last with Highsmith's own name attached, she explained her decision not to publish under her own name in a new afterword. Highsmith said it was a matter of its content being so different from that of *Strangers on a Train*, or her later novels of psychological suspense: "If I were to write a novel about a lesbian relationship, would I then be labelled a lesbian-book writer? That was a possibility, even though I might never be inspired to write another such book in my life. So I decided to offer the book under another name."

We now know that she was, at least for a time, inspired to write another such book. She had once felt she had more to say on the subject of lesbian relationships. But after walking away from *First Person Novel*, and from Meaker, she'd never again write directly about those topics in her fiction.

Instead, early in 1961, Highsmith became absorbed in writing *The Cry of the Owl*, a suspense novel about a stalker named Robert Forester and his victim, a woman named Jenny Thierof. But while this may seem like a return to safe ground, it may have been more complicated than that. Wilson points out that Highsmith's new novel merely resumed her previous strategy of transposing her own homosexual desires onto a male character's perspective—one that was now twisted into stalking. Wilson notes that the descriptions of Jenny's house, as related through Robert's enthralled perspective, bear similarities to the home of Kathleen Senn, the real-life Carol. Rather than engaging directly and positively as she'd begun trying to do only a few months earlier, Highsmith was instead, with *The Cry of the Owl*, transposing her romantic feelings for Senn into the mind of a criminal man, taking her own real-life stalking and building a novel around it.

She wrote *The Cry of the Owl* quickly, finishing the entire first draft by July, and finalizing it six months later. The novel was published in 1962. Though several critics wrote that it might be her best achievement yet, Highsmith privately confessed her disappointment with the book, "one of her weakest," finding the protagonist Robert to be "square . . . a passive bore."

She had, after all, abandoned the far more honest character of Juliette and her many real-life-inspired loves for the relative safety of Robert the stalker—but his story, no matter how criminal and twisted, could at least be published under her own name.

Following this, Highsmith wrote in her diaries again, reflecting back on her past relationships. Whereas a year earlier she'd seen these loves with different women as inspiring material, she now looked back on her diaries and saw "a chronicle of unbelievable mistakes."

Throughout the rest of her long career, Highsmith would stick with the *Strangers on a Train* mode. Her books became definitive in the psychological thriller genre. Where themes of homosexuality are present in her work, they're most often about male characters, and their desires are generally subsumed beneath layers of criminality and murderousness. Take, for example, *The Talented Mr. Ripley*, where the young con man Tom Ripley develops an infatuation with the wealthy Dickie Greenleaf as the two travel across Europe together. The premise sounds a lot like the adventures of Juliette and Verie in *First Person Novel*—but as discussed before, the perspective has been changed, to third person, and so have the genders of the characters. And in this case when Tom's true feelings are exposed, they are repulsive to Dickie, and Tom ends up murdering the man he loves with an oar, before assuming his identity and trying to live large off Dickie's money. The strong homosexual attraction between Tom and Dickie is never directly addressed or acted on—Tom wants Dickie, but the novel allows a reader to believe that he wants Dickie's money, Dickie's life, and most of all *to be Dickie*—and this conflation is what propels the story forward.

It calls to mind that line Highsmith wrote in her diary the day after she went to Senn's house in Ridgewood: "Murder is a kind of making love, a kind of possessing." This would be the engine that powered most of her novels.

By 1963, Highsmith had left the United States and made her home permanently in Europe, where she'd remain for the next thirty years before her death from cancer in Switzerland. Meaker's memoir ends with a few chapters about seeing Highsmith again, twenty-seven years after their split, in what would be the final years of Highsmith's life.

One day, Highsmith appeared on her doorstep, drunk and ranting. The transformation of her old lover, from the "handsome, dark-haired woman" in the trench coat at L's bar to the miserable and angry woman there before her, left Meaker shocked and deeply saddened.

"I knew Pat when she was young and not yet so jaded and bigoted," she wrote in a 2007 article for *Mystery Scene*. "The internet is filled with stories of her meanness, and prejudice, and also of her introversion, of her being a loner. I met that Pat many years after we broke up."

Meaker took Highsmith in and the two caught up. She was shocked, she wrote, to find how much more bitter Highsmith had become, and how much more bigoted. As Meaker recounts, in their discussion Highsmith repeatedly, casually made racist and antisemitic statements. Highsmith's diaries and journals from the period show more of the same, and while living in Switzerland she made something of a pastime out of writing antisemitic letters to the editors of newspapers there, using a variety of pseudonyms.

The two met for lunch the next day and talked more soberly about Highsmith's career and reminisced about the gay bars in Europe they'd once gone to.

Highsmith recalled how the ones for men would always have a large "G" in the guidebook, and the ones for women would have a small "g" instead.

"That's a good title," she said, "*Small g.*"

Meaker agreed that it was, and Highsmith continued. "And everyone's waiting for me to do a lesbian book since I was so successful with Claire Morgan. So I think I'll do it."

They spent the day together in Montauk, drinking beer and

catching up. In the end, Highsmith did write *Small g*, and it was published in the months after her death. Only it was not the Claire Morgan "lesbian book" she'd envisioned with Meaker, but another lurid murder story, written in the third person.

If she had finished *First Person Novel*, or other books like *The Price of Salt*—if she had been able to live her life openly and free of secrets, as "Claire Morgan" or even as herself—it's hard not to wonder if Highsmith might have had a happier life.

But it is also hard to deny that her methods of transference and suppression, in their own way, led to some pretty remarkable art. By the time she died at age seventy-four, she had written twenty-two novels, and become lauded worldwide for her work. She won the O. Henry Award, the Silver Dagger, an Edgar Allan Poe Award, and the Grand Prix de Littérature Policière, and was named a knight of the Order of Arts and Letters by the French Ministry of Culture.

The *Times of London*, in 2008, put Highsmith at the top of their list of the fifty greatest crime writers, saying: "She broke most of the rules that govern the writing of crime fiction. She followed none of the usual formulae. There are no heroic cops, tough private eyes or amateur sleuths; often there is no mystery and therefore no solution; good does not necessarily triumph over evil." They cite her novels about Tom Ripley as her greatest literary accomplishment: "the charming, good-looking, bisexual, conscience-free con man who goes on to become a killer. He is amoral and a psychopath. Yet, far from being repulsive, he emerges as a sympathetic, even attractive, character."

Highsmith found a way to write honestly, if not about who and how she loved, then mainly about the power and the pain of our darkest lies and secrets. About the delicious pleasures of the evilest behaviors, and of our deep desires to shed our own skins and instead become someone else. Tragically, her methods of sublimation did not lead Highsmith into a happy life, but they did push her into a strange kind of genius. In our own lives we may find there are numerous things that we must, or even just prefer to, leave off the page. It isn't necessary to bare your whole soul, to expose every moment of your private life. Even the most fervent autofictioneers wouldn't claim to have done that. Writing a novel can be therapeutic, but that doesn't mean it must also be a confessional in order to succeed. There's always something compelling about a novel you know is based on true events, and in my experience at least, readers will never stop asking how much of what you wrote is "real." Tell them it is all real, but also that none of it is. You don't have to let your own life be the only thing your work is about. We're all just as interested in your imagination, in your empathies for the stories of others, and in all the lives you lead that aren't your own.

FAIL LIKE A GENIUS

Patricia Highsmith

Shame is a powerful emotion, something that guides our anxieties and fears and guilt and all our least fathomable behaviors. In other words, it can be the source of a lot of great storytelling.

Take a piece of paper and write out a list of things you keep secret or feel some shame over. What are the embarrassments of the past that you lie awake at night reliving, or wish you could undo? Keep the list to yourself (or, better yet, bring it to your next therapy session) but take one of the secrets on the list and give it to a fictional character. Write a page where someone, not you, confesses the story in their own words. If it helps, start with the words, "I have to tell you this before I go," or "It's time you knew the truth," or "I've never told anyone this before but . . ."

The aim here is to take something secret and difficult and let yourself *play* with it. Give that secret to someone else. Transform it into a similar but different secret. Maybe it turns out differently this time. Maybe it leads to something better.

This can be healing, but it can also make for great writing, and more than anything else—it can simply be fun.

Geniuses Burn Bridges

J ust as we might believe that a genius author is one willing to reveal all their deepest secrets on the page, we similarly are convinced that greatness in art requires a willingness to tell sometimes brutal truths about those around us. Ernest Hemingway's classic novel *The Sun Also Rises* revolves in part around an affair between the main character's love interest, Lady Bret Ashley, and his other friend, Robert Cohn. Hemingway's actual friends, Harold Loeb and Lady Duff Twysden, who were having a real-life affair, were horrified to discover that Cohn and Ashley were barely disguised versions of themselves. Hemingway's weak defense was that he had, one drunken night, told a roomful of people, including Loeb and Twysden, "I'm writing a novel. Everybody's in it."

When Sylvia Plath wrote *The Bell Jar*, she published it under the pseudonym "Victoria Lucas" mainly to protect her mother, and initially she didn't want it to be released in the United States where more people knew her family. Despite this caution, several women who worked with Plath at magazines in real life were upset that she used "secrets" they told her to flesh out the secondary characters in the novel's scenes where Esther Greenwood works at a women's magazine. Allegedly, the book ruined two marriages.

Terrible mothers, abusive fathers, unfaithful spouses, the betrayals of friends and lovers: these are fruitful topics for a great novel, but transmuting real-world examples to fiction will likely cause some real-world trouble. As much as it troubles me that would-be writers may think they need to flay themselves on the page in order to write something great, I also fear they may believe that the next best path to excellence is by skewering everyone who has ever trusted them. It's true that this might lead to great material, but as the case of Truman Capote's unfinished novel *Answered Prayers* shows, when writing about real people they know any great writer needs to tread carefully.

"A Severe Insult to the Brain": Truman Capote's *Answered Prayers*

After Truman Capote published his novella *Breakfast at Tiffany's* in 1958, society women across New York City scrambled to stake their claims that the heroine, Holly Golightly, had been based on them. Everyone wanted to see themselves in the brassy, sweet, freewheeling, innocent, and wild character who threw lavish parties and rubbed elbows with the elite, despite her true origins as a runway child bride from the countryside. According to biographer Gerald Clarke, "half the women [Capote] knew and a few he did not claimed to be the model for his wacky heroine." This list included Babe Paley, Gloria Guinness, Oona O'Neill Chaplin, and Gloria Vanderbilt. Capote himself claimed to have based the character on an unnamed German refugee he knew who had successfully infiltrated Manhattan's high society. Others speculated that Holly was actually based on Marilyn Monroe. When activist Marguerite Littman passed away in 2020, the headline of her *New York Times* obituary declared her to be "the Inspiration for Holly Golightly," prompting a fresh wave of articles, sixty-two years later, over who *really* held that title.

In all likelihood, the character of Holly was probably based initially on Truman's mother, Lillie Mae, who had fled to New York after divorcing four-year-old Truman's father, and who spent her time introducing herself at parties as "Nina" while hoping to fall in love with a rich man. She'd return in defeat and heartbreak to Monroeville, Alabama, where she'd left Truman with relatives At the time he was Truman Streckfus Persons, crushed by his mother's abandonment and aiming, himself, to rise above his rural surroundings to the penthouses of Manhattan someday. (And so perhaps the true model for Golightly was, at least on some level, Capote himself.)

As a literary star, Capote would indeed rise into café society, and even more so after publishing *In Cold Blood*, a journalistic deep dive into the brutal and senseless murder of a family in Holcomb, Kansas. Moving beyond literary celebrity, Capote became a celebrity, period, traveling with heiresses and movie stars. In 1966 he took his profits and threw the famed Black and White Ball at the Plaza Hotel, attended by the likes of Lady Bird Johnson, the Duke and Duchess of Windsor, Gloria Vanderbilt, Andy Warhol, Harry Belafonte, Frank Sinatra, Brooke Astor, Mia Farrow, an Italian princess, and the maharani of Jaipur. Everyone wore masks, though everyone knew who was who. Publisher Jason Epstein described the masked ball as nothing short of a revolution: "Until that night . . . New York society observed the rigid caste-based system it had followed since the Knickerbocker days, one dominated by a handful of families." But after the Black and White Ball, everything changed. Capote had upended the entire social order.

It was a high point in the life and career of an outsider—a queer, Southern fiction writer from an unknown family—who had forced his way not just inside, but to the very top.

But a few years later, Truman Capote would fall from grace, shunned by these same celebrities and the members of the New York glitterati. Many of the same women who had tried to claim themselves as the original Holly Golightly, enchanted by the idea of inspiring a literary character, suddenly found themselves appalled by the characters that he'd actually based on them in his novel in progress *Answered Prayers*, which dished the most private dirt and shared the most salacious gossip he knew about the wealthy people who had made him so famous.

Answered Prayers is an example of how catastrophically things can go for a writer who reveals too many secrets—especially the secrets of others. Writing it would ruin Capote's life and leave him exiled from almost everyone he'd grown to love—even though he never even published most of it.

Quite possibly he never even *wrote* most of it. The version published posthumously is incomplete—the surviving bits are those he published as excerpts in magazines and that sparked the backlash against him. Many would later claim to have read more, or to have heard Capote read more, while others would claim it was all a farce. No one knows how much more existed and, if it did, what happened to it. Capote's own explanation was that he left the only copy in a locker at the Los Angeles Greyhound bus depot and never looked back.

By all accounts Capote began writing his last novel decades before his death from liver disease in 1984, long before *In Cold Blood*, even before *Breakfast at Tiffany's*. For more than thirty years, Truman Capote described the book to anyone who would listen, as a Proustian novel, based on real stories straight out of New York's 1950s café society. "It is the only true thing I know," he said. "I was born to write the book . . . it means *everything*."

The title is taken from the wisdom of Saint Teresa of Ávila: "More tears are shed over answered prayers than unanswered ones."

According to his biographer Gerald Clarke, Capote envisioned the novel as a "large, sprawling story that spanned thirty years, moved between two continents, and included a vast and influential company of players."

All we have of it today are three chapters, plus "Mojave," a fourth chapter, which he later cut out.

The first chapter, "Unspoiled Monsters" is almost a novella by itself, introducing the narrator, P. B. Jones, a bisexual hustler living in a room at the YMCA and trying to write a novel called *Answered Prayers*. He is "an opportunist, a heel, a rat," according to Clarke—clearly a stand-in for Capote. "P.B. isn't me, but on the other hand he isn't *not* me," Capote said. "I'm not P.B., but I know him very well."

Jones recounts his life story, from the time of his orphaning in a St. Louis movie theater to being raised by nuns and spending time as a sex worker before eventually landing in New York City's literary world. It is here that he gets to peer inside of high society and assumes the companionship of the novel's heroine, Kate McCloud, for whom the second chapter is named.

Kate McCloud is like Holly Golightly on steroids. Glamorous and cultured, she is, according to P. B., his "very own *Death in Venice*: inevitable, perilous as the asp at Cleopatra's breast." Supposedly she was modeled on as many as half a dozen different society women Capote knew well from that world.

Indeed, most of the other characters in the three extant chapters are drawn more directly from famous and powerful people of the time. Hotel magnates. Wives and ex-wives of steel tycoons. Celebrities and countesses. George Davis of *Harper's Bazaar* and Katherine Ann Porter. And in his darkly funny stories, Capote hung out all the dirtiest laundry that he had been noting in decades of running in their circle.

Indeed, at first, he relished this tell-all quality. When "Unspoiled Monsters" was published in *Esquire* magazine in 1976, Capote posed for the cover as an assassin, holding a stiletto. *Women's Wear Daily* dubbed him "The Tiny Terror." Capote allegedly teased friends that if they were not careful he would put them in the book. He described the book in *People* as being like a gun: "There's the handle, the trigger, the barrel, and, finally, the bullet. And when that bullet is fired from the gun, it's going to come out with a speed and power like you've never seen—*wham!*"

The most damaging of all was the third chapter, "La Côte Basque, 1965," named for a real restaurant on East Fifty-Fifth street in Manhattan where high society often dined. In this story, P. B. lunches with an old friend named Lady Coolbirth, who spends the meal gazing around the celebrity-packed room, scathingly dressing everyone down. Some of the guests, like Gloria Vanderbilt and Princess Margaret, both real acquaintances of Truman's, are included with their names unchanged. Others are thinly disguised and involved in highly libelous stories. One, "Ann Hopkins," is known to have shot her own husband in the face with a shotgun and gotten away with it by claiming she thought he was a burglar—just coming out of the shower. This is, almost exactly, the true life story of socialite Ann Woodward, who remained part of the in crowd even after.

In another such story, Coolbirth spots a powerful political figure and relays a tale of a steamy one-night stand he once had with the wife of a former governor, who failed to mention that she was having her period. The next morning, the man finds his sheets covered in bloodstains "the size of Brazil" and ends up desperately scrubbing them in the tub with a bar of soap before his wife gets home. People in the know—meaning many of Truman's friends—

recognized instantly that this was based on a rumor about the real-life former New York governor, W. Averell Harriman.

Tennessee Williams, who appears in "Unspoiled Monsters" as Mr. Wallace, one of P. B.'s johns, captured the fury provoked in those who had entrusted Truman with their secrets: "This thing Capote has written is shockingly repugnant and thoroughly libelous. Capote's a monster of the first order, a cold-blooded murderer at heart. He's a liar and everybody knows he is."

The turn against Capote was swift and cruel. He was threatened and snubbed constantly by people he thought were his dearest friends. Even as copies of *Esquire* flew off the stands, Truman was banned from the high society events where he'd long been a fixture.

Sometimes "I know a secret" has more power than we're really ready for.

Many have questioned why Capote published the excerpts, instead of keeping it all under wraps until the novel was completely finished. He likely did not need the money. More likely, Capote was too proud of them to hide what was looking like the best work of his life. Clarke argues that they are his "most mature piece of fiction" and "contain some of the best writing he ever produced."

Still, Capote could have guessed that some, if not most, of his friends would despise him for what he was writing.

William Todd Schultz, in his book *Tiny Terror: Why Truman Capote (Almost) Wrote* Answered Prayers, views the whole affair as something akin to a suicide attempt. He argues that Capote never expected, and did not know how to handle, the immense success that followed *In Cold Blood*, and that *Answered Prayers* was, on some level, his way of stopping the ride. Releasing it before it was finished may have been an act of desperation, not of over-confidence.

The standard thinking is that after the fury that followed the *Esquire* chapters in 1976, Truman Capote never wrote any more of *Answered Prayers*, falling into a deep despair, abusing alcohol and drugs until his death eight years later. This is what Jack Dunphy, Capote's longtime companion, believed: that while Capote pretended publicly to be working hard on the book in the intervening years, he was never able to progress in his work on it.

In an enormous oral biography of Capote assembled by George Plimpton, many of those around Capote speculated about what happened to *Answered Prayers*.

Norman Mailer, one of Capote's greatest literary enemies, recognized the bind that Truman was in. New York society, in Mailer's mind, had "swallowed his talent." *Answered Prayers* stemmed from a desire to exact revenge on the beautiful people who had seduced and distracted him from his work. Mailer imagined that Capote, a "little Napoleon," believed that writing those chapters would increase his power among the jet set, but "he didn't understand the true social force of New York—that even he could be eighty-sixed. The book . . . probably died in him ten years earlier."

Capote's editor at Random House, Joseph Fox, writes a note at the opening of the published version of *Answered Prayers*. He believes that there is another possibility—that Capote did write as many as four more chapters, including "A Severe Insult to the Brain," "Yachts and Things," "Father Flanagan's All-Night N-----r-Queen Kosher Café," and "Audrey Wilder Sang," but that they did not live up to his hopes for them, and he then deliberately destroyed them during the final years of his life, when he was "almost incoherent because of drugs or alcohol or both."

This would explain one mystery, which is that so many of Capote's friends later recounted times when he shared some of the missing chapters with them. Joe Petrocik recalled an evening in Sag Harbor when Capote got up in front of them and read sections from "A Severe Insult to the Brain" (the phrase is listed as the official cause of death on Dylan Thomas's certificate—Capote used it often to refer to the city of Los Angeles). But Petrocik admitted he was "never sure whether or not he was just telling me the story. He had pages in front of him which he was apparently reading. He would look up. He was quite the actor . . . I never did actually see the words on paper."

Author John Knowles claimed to have seen physical pages from the rest of *Answered Prayers*, but that years later Capote told him in Southampton that he'd come to believe none of it was any good. "I don't know," Knowles said, "I think he burned hundreds and hundreds of pages."

But director Frank Perry told another story. "I asked him how everything was going and he said, 'It's wonderful. . . . Look at that, finished pages, two and a half inches. It's wonderful.' Later on, being a cynic, I drifted over to riffle through the manuscript. It turned out to be a Missouri bankroll, which is to say, the top three pages had typewriting on them and the rest were blank."

Alan Schwartz, Capote's literary executor, claims to have been "absolutely astounded" to find no trace of the missing chapters after Capote's death. He recalled that Capote had tried many times to get Random House to fork over the rest of his advance, claiming that the novel was basically done.

Clay Felker, the founder of *New York* magazine, remembered that he offered Capote $35,000 for the next excerpt from the book. Capote spent an entire morning at his house recounting one chapter in lurid detail. He said he'd give it to him that weekend, but Capote later backed out. He met Felker again and began to describe a whole different part of the book, a suicide that Kate Mc-Cloud witnesses. "I just have to tighten a few screws," he said. Felker claims he would have paid $100,000 for the chapter. But Capote never delivered it.

Capote was known to exaggerate and to lie. He was also, reportedly, often disastrous during these years. John Knowles recounted how Capote once lost $4,000 worth of cocaine in his front yard, and later got so inebriated that he fell out of bed fifteen times in one night. Knowles witnessed Truman having hallucinations and drug-related seizures. Once he walked into traffic and nearly was run over by a bus. "I think he just decided . . . I'm going to be stoned all the time. And die."

Alan Schwartz recalls that, at one point, Capote claimed to him that the novel was finished and that a former lover, John O'Shea, had stolen it and gone to Florida with the manuscript in the trunk of his car. Capote asked Schwartz to file a lawsuit, demanding the return of the pages. Later, Capote claimed to have gone down to Florida and personally blown up O'Shea's car. "One day little Johnny went downstairs and his car wasn't there. Instead there was a big puddle where a car used to be." Nobody believed him.

Producer Lester Persky claimed for a long time to have the manuscript locked in a drawer in his house that he couldn't get into. When he finally did pry it open there was nothing there.

Joanne Carson, wife of Johnny Carson, whose affairs were discussed openly in one excerpted chapter, recalled that Capote gave her a key to a safe-deposit box on the morning of his death. But there was no number on the key and furthermore, she had no idea to what box, in what bank, or even in what city it belonged. She claimed to have read, firsthand, "Father Flanagan's . . . ," "Yachts and Things," and "Audrey Wilder Sang." She described them in some detail to George Plimpton—who says that he then personally went to Alan Schwartz to ask about the safe-deposit key after that.

Schwartz replied, "Yes, I think there was a key. There was no clue as to what it did unlock, or if it did, what was inside. We could never find the safe-deposit box. There was a key, and we tried to track it everywhere. We couldn't. So we're left with that."

Capote's favorite story about *Answered Prayers* was that he had locked it up at the Greyhound station in Los Angeles—hidden it deep inside the "severe insult to the brain" itself.

Could it be true? In 1991, Greyhound moved their station from Seventh and Maple, where it had been since the 1930s, though the old building itself still stands. As much as I'd like to believe that the lockers are still in there somewhere, I suspect that they were hauled away long ago.

Most scholars have long since abandoned hope of ever finding *Answered Prayers* squirreled away somewhere, though in 2012 researchers from *Vanity Fair* did stumble across an unfinished manuscript of "Yachts and Things" among Capote's papers at the New York Public Library, where they had been available for more than two decades. The six typewritten and hand-edited pages are still up on their website.

Nevertheless, it seems most likely that Capote either never finished or destroyed the rest of *Answered Prayers*, and that he spent the eight years between the publication of the *Esquire* chapters and his death in a slow deterioration, dreaming about how wonderful the chapters would be if he could only manage to write them well.

By either not writing them or not publishing them, he spared himself any further social damage, and the possible loss of the friends who did stick by him. Many of these people are the same ones who later reported to Plimpton on the spectacular excerpts they saw, or read, or heard, reinforcing the speculations that Capote himself may have desired.

And there's something fitting in that we are left with only rumors about a novel born of and killed by gossip. Perhaps on some level, this was Capote's intention. Years before he released the excerpts, in 1971, Capote joked on the *Dick Cavett Show* that the book would be his "posthumous novel"—"either I'm going to kill it, or it is going to kill me."

If more tears are shed over answered prayers, then what about finished novels?

If he could not write, or could not publish, the novel itself, then perhaps he decided to leave behind the next best thing—an enduring literary mystery.

The tragic story of Truman Capote's final novel highlights a subtle but important distinction when it comes to writing about other people. Just because his swans eagerly claimed to be the muse behind Holly Golightly, that didn't mean they *actually* wanted Capote to base a character on them. It's one thing to see elements of yourself reflected in a fictional creation, and another to see yourself exposed publicly on the page. I'm sure it helped that Holly was a lovable and sympathetic character and hurt that Truman's socialites in *Answered Prayers* were held up for mockery. But the shift in tone may not have mattered as much as the degree of resemblance. With Holly, Capote had taken bits and pieces of many of the women he admired and sprinkled them over elements of his mother's life and his own. The result that no one person was quite all of Holly, or fully revealed in her. With *Answered Prayers* Capote forgot, or intentionally neglected, to take those precautions, and it cost him everything.

Fail Like a Genius

Truman Capote

Capote's situation illuminates the dangers of writing about real people in our lives, but in general my advice to students is that you probably can get away with a lot more than you think.

To fight our fears over this, I prescribe some exposure therapy: "steal" a story from someone else and write it out yourself. It doesn't necessarily need to be a secret—just some other person's story that you've always enjoyed or admired or even coveted. It could be the tale of how your parents met, or the day your brother set the garage on fire, or the story of how your ex once vomited on the Easter Bunny at the mall. Whatever jumps to mind—write it. Get all the details in there that you can.

Remember, nobody else ever has to see this but you. Burn it when you're done if you want!

But before you do—try making it harder to recognize. Change names. Set it a hundred years in the past. Move the action to the other side of the country. Make it science fiction. A bit of disguising can go a long way, and far from watering down your story, this can open new dimensions.

Always ask permission if you're worried. They may say no, and you'll need to deal with that if they do. But in my experience they're much more likely to be excited that you've chosen them as your muse.

Geniuses Get Rejected

Richard Wright

One of the hardest truths about creative life is that sometimes you can do everything right and still fall short in the end. We want to think that publishing and art are a purely artistic meritocracy, where genius-level work always finds its audience eventually. But most writers I know have had the experience of working for years on a truly incredible novel, only to spend months getting kindly worded rejections from every editor and publisher out there. I have gone through this on multiple occasions, and it is agonizing. There are often a few kind sentences in the email about the book being "brilliant" and "compelling" and "powerful" before the axe falls—"In the end I can't think of how to market this" or "I'm just not convinced that readers will love it like I do" or "I'm not sure that this is the time for this book."

It is tempting to read between the lines of these rejections, to think that the editors are just being nice and that they can't say they out-and-out hated the book, or that I'm an awful writer, or that the novel is a total mess. This would (for me) be easier to understand than what they're really saying, which is that the book itself is great, that my writing is doing everything it should be doing and more, but that, strictly from a business perspective, they don't think readers will want to *buy* it.

When I speak with editors and agents they tell the same stories from the other end of the process. Every one of them has a book they believed in with all their hearts but couldn't make a convincing case for as a product. An agent has to persuade an editor that a book is not only incredible, but sure to sell well. An editor then has to persuade their whole team, including their bosses, of the same, and not just other editors but also representatives in marketing and sales, who eventually will need to convince booksellers to stock it, and readers to buy it. There's a whole chain of faith that must proceed unbroken between your pen and the reader's eyes in order for a book to succeed. In the end, lots of perfectly great books don't make it through to the end of these discussions, to the heartbreak of most involved.

As much as a writer may believe that any publisher can *make* anything into a best seller through sheer force of will and expenditure of marketing dollars, this simply isn't how it works.

We can tear our hair out over the cursed intersections of capitalism and art, and we can yearn for some imaginary bygone days when things worked differently (although they really didn't)—or we can accept that sometimes our best work just did not meet its moment and we've got to get on with our creative lives anyway.

Well-meaning friends of mine are always quick to make marketing suggestions, like "dystopias are so hot now—why not set your new book in the middle of an apocalypse?" But even if I was inclined to chase trends like this, because it can take years to finish a novel it is typically a fool's errand to write to the market's current desires unless you can do so very fast. The craze for vampire romances that is dominant when you sit down to write chapter one will have become a frenzy for novels about Parisian librarians during World War II by the time you get to chapter thirty.

Even once a book is finished being written, and even if that book gets sold, it is usually well over a year before it gets to the shelves. There's no predicting what will be going on in the world by then—just ask any author whose books came out in 2020. There's also no controlling what else will be coming out around the same time as your book. A professor of mine once lamented the "failure" of one of his novels because it happened to be published the same week as Dan Brown's *The Da Vinci Code* and all the usual media oxygen had been sucked up, leaving his book to quietly asphyxiate.

Terrifying. But it happens all the time.

Now, let's say that on top of all that, you're also someone writing about topics that some in the reading public find challenging or uncomfortable. The calculations over what's going to sell will inevitably collide with questions about what's controversial. Great novels often pierce assumptions and humanize stories that might be otherwise relegated in our society. While one editor may see a book on a contentious topic as a potential boon that will attract lots of attention to itself, another may see it as too risky and take a pass. Because the acquisitions process is inherently a cautious one, it can be difficult to push a more contentious book through.

Over the past few years I've been heartened by the number of books I see on shelves that challenge systemic racism, misogyny, and the patriarchy. Following the Black Lives Matter and #MeToo movements, there was a renewed push for the publishing industry to be more equitable in its acquisitions, to hire more editors of color, and to highlight voices that might have gone overlooked even a few years earlier. But today many of those big steps forward have been reversed. It remains important work, half done and barely begun.

In the end, whether you are a marginalized writer or, like me, about as unmarginalized as can be—when a book gets rejected, we don't usually know exactly why. Does the fault lie with our writing? With us, personally? Is it the tastes of the editors? The contours of politics? Or the particular fascinations of the reading world in that particular moment? As writers facing rejection we're often lost, unsure of where the issue lies.

It is important to be open to feedback and to criticism, and to find ways of learning from even the stingiest bad review. (Believe me, I've gotten some doozies and as much as I've hated it, I've still found ways to improve from them.)

But it is also important to understand that we may have succeeded at ninety-nine things along the way, even if the hundredth didn't quite work. And that sometimes there may be a hundred and first thing that has nothing to do with us or our writing at all.

After all, some of the greatest writers of the twentieth century have found themselves shelving manuscripts that were deemed by their publishers at the time to be too controversial for readers.

Descending into the Dark:
Richard Wright's *The Man Who Lived Underground*

Richard Wright changed the course of literary history with his novel *Native Son*, and while it is a classic today it was plenty controversial with readers at the time it was published. But even this genius, even after that early success, found himself walking a fine line with his second novel, which was to focus on the brutality of police violence against Black bodies. Indeed, it was not until more than fifty years after the death of Richard Wright that a publisher would put out his novel *The Man Who Lived Underground*.

In 1944, Wright published a short story in *Cross Section: A Collection of New American Writing*, edited by Edwin Seaver. The story, "The Man Who Lived Underground," was about a Black man named Fred Daniels who lives in the sewers of a major city. He is hiding out after being tortured by police into confessing to a double murder that he did not commit. As time goes on, Daniels grapples with that trauma and discovers a profound and surprising freedom. Alone in the dark underground world, he is at last living apart from society and racism. It's a remarkable and complex story, one of those pieces of short fiction with so many layers that it has the feel of being an entire novel, condensed.

Few reading the story in 1944 knew that, actually, this was precisely the case. *The Man Who Lived Underground* had been an entire novel, written by Wright two years earlier, but had been ultimately turned down by his publisher. The book remained unpublished for nearly eighty years, until in 2021 it was put forth at long last by the Library of America at the behest of Wright's grandson, Malcolm, himself a prominent film director, who had discovered the lost novel among his grandfather's papers and finally brought it to the public.

But why did it take eighty years? In 1942, when Richard Wright was writing *The Man Who Lived Underground*, he was at an early height in his career. Wright had recently won a Guggenheim fellowship, and was the widely acclaimed author of the novel *Native Son*, published in 1940. That book is about a young Black man named Bigger Thomas growing up on Chicago's South Side in the 1930s, who accidentally murders a white woman named Mary and is eventually caught and executed. *Native Son* won widespread attention and success for the way it subtly and powerfully examined the systems of societal racism that lead to Bigger's crime and continue to hang over his eventual capture and execution. With the book, Wright became the first African American author to have a book selected by the Book of the Month Club (though the organization insisted on editing out some of the book's sexual content, which has only recently been restored in a new edition). The novel was adapted into a Broadway play, with Wright's help, and directed by none other than Orson Welles. In one year, with one novel, Richard Wright had become one of the the country's most prominent Black authors.

With all this success, why would Wright's publishers reject his next book?

Wright got the idea for *The Man Who Lived Underground* from a real-world story. In the 1941 issue of *True Detective* magazine, Wright came across an article called "The Crime Hollywood Couldn't Believe" by writer Hal Fletcher. It was about a man who "lived in the sewers beneath Los Angeles for more than a year, staging a series of burglaries from an underground bunker." Inspired by this kernel, Wright launched into the project with a "written at white heat," in the words of Wright's wife Ellen.

The Man Who Lived Underground, Wright believed, "'stemmed more from sheer inspiration' than anything he had written," or so he wrote in his letter to his agent Paul Reynolds as they prepared to submit it to Edward Aswell at Harper & Brothers on December 12, 1941. He felt that, among other things, it marked "the first time I've really tried to step beyond the straight black-white stuff."

Unfortunately, "neither Reynolds nor Aswell shared the author's enthusiasm," according to a note included with the 2021 publication. Aswell ultimately turned it down.

One possibility here is that the book just wasn't ready—Wright had, after all, written it in nine months. But then again, Wright had written the much longer *Native Son* in *five*. For his first novel he wrote longhand, getting up at six a.m. to sneak out to a park bench in Fort Greene Park with pen and paper to work every morning, rain or shine, for four hours straight. After reading the morning's work to Ellen over a late breakfast, he'd type it up all afternoon. He was logging fifteen-hour working days, and in the end said that he never wanted to work like that again. With *The Man Who Lived Underground*, Wright changed his methods—using a new Dictaphone to record his voice as he composed the book verbally, and then typing it later. This new technology may have made the writing easier, but the change it brought to his style may have backfired. Even after sending it to Aswell, Wright found himself working on the text, trying to "sharpen language, tighten episodes, and trim the narrator's overt psychologizing of his protagonist, Fred Daniels."

Still, even if the novel still needed work, it would have been possible for Aswell to accept it in partial condition and then to work with Wright on making revisions. But Aswell didn't send it back with notes. He simply said no.

Wright's biographer Hazel Rowley suggests that the novel was rejected not because of its lack of quality, but because of its content. She writes that it "portrayed all too clearly the arbitrary 'justice' of the world at a time when publishers were looking for more rousing stories." Though no one expected a new novel by Richard Wright to shy away from a frank depiction of racism in America, something about *The Man Who Lived Underground* was so unsettling that his publisher balked.

The Beinecke Rare Book and Manuscript Library at Yale University holds one of the two existing manuscript copies of Wright's novel, along with 118 slips containing written comments by two reviewers. The first set appear to belong to Paul Reynolds, and the other to Kerker Quinn of the University of Illinois, the editor of *Accent* literary magazine.

One thing that both reviewers noted about the novel is its "uneasy mixture of realism and allegory," which made the book feel like an extreme departure in style from the literary naturalism of *Native Son*. During Daniels's time living in the sewer, he has numerous fantasias and hallucinations, and there is something deeply fabulist about the tone. Malcolm Wright, in his foreword to the new publication, speculates that the book was meant to feel allegorical, being an attempt at a reversal on Plato's allegory of the cave. In the classic philosophic text, Plato describes the way the real world would appear to someone who had lived all their life inside of a dark cave, only to emerge into the light. Having departed the cave, a person would have great difficulty returning, knowing what they know now about the larger world.

In Wright's novel, the situation is reversed. It is by descending into the dark sewers that Daniels becomes free *of* the real world. Living down there, he is not only safe from the threats of the police but liberated from racism and race. Just as the former cave dweller in Plato's allegory cannot return to the darkness, Daniels, now free underground, cannot bring himself to return to the light of the aboveground "real" world.

"The stubborn constraints of societal patterning are not in the darkness of the cave," Malcolm Wright notes. "They permeate the bright world aboveground."

Perhaps, Rowley suggests, Wright's vision of liberation by escape and separation from the world of white power was not the "rousing" story that Aswell was looking for. This is supported by Aswell's next move: he instead asked Wright to refocus his energies on another book Wright had proposed, titled *Black Hope*—a book that would have followed the lives of Black domestic workers in the familiar literary naturalistic style and, given the title, would have had the "rousing" overriding message Aswell was seeking.

But Wright never completed *Black Hope*.

Some of the 118 slips written by Reynolds and Quinn cite another related reason that the book was turned down in 1942. The "extended depiction of police brutality," Quinn wrote, was "unbearable."

The book opens with Daniels being picked up for the murder of Mr. and Mrs. Peabody, and being repeatedly abused by the police officers interrogating him for dozens of pages. He is slapped, kicked, punched, and beaten with a blackjack as they show him photographs from the scene of the crime and insist that he sign the confession, ramping up their attacks until he finally agrees. Wright describes the scene in vivid detail, with all the powerful literary naturalism that Aswell and Reynolds said they wanted.

The passages are upsetting, to be sure, but it is hard to find them shocking now, in a time when the violence of police brutality is shown in body camera footage on the news and social media on a regular basis, when the descriptions of assaults like this one fill the pages of newspapers and magazines without end. In other words, in 2021 the novel's violence might have come off as being toned *down*—but in 1942 it would have landed quite differently, even with the many readers who had applauded *Native Son*. Malcolm Wright remarks that the novel depicts a world where "race is supremely deterministic; eclipsing notions of Truth and Justice." This is a depiction of the world that, even today, many are deeply uncomfortable with, and highly invested in suppressing.

Malcolm notes that it was Wright's decision to set the book aside in 1942, around the time of the birth of Wright's daughter Julia (Malcolm's mother). Wright was then highly preoccupied by the question of what world he was bringing a child into, and Malcolm wonders if he had a change of heart about the novel after becoming a father.

Kerker Quinn went on to publish two short excerpts from *The Man Who Lived Underground* later in 1942. Eventually, a consolidated story version would be printed in the posthumous collection of Wright's work *Eight Men*.

Though Richard Wright gave up on publishing the novel, he later gave the carbon copy of the manuscript as a gift to Sylvia Beach of Shakespeare and Company in Paris. He did not ask or expect her to publish it, but she decided to bind the copy lovingly, underscoring its importance. Now held in Princeton's Firestone Library, Beach's was one of the two copies used to create the 199-page version published in 2021, taking into account all of Wright's own edits on the pages themselves.

But in his lifetime, Wright never returned to the idea of it becoming a novel.

Malcolm Wright describes how the novel "captures [the] environment of fear" in Jim Crow America and highlights how its sinister suppression reached far beyond the South: "In these pages, he had poetically distilled the rewarding and dangerous condition of Otherness . . . represented here with unparalleled raw and flowing creativity." Malcolm Wright goes on to explore this term of Otherness: "All members of oppressed minorities hold an innate understanding about it. The pain and violence of being othered can engender insights and freedoms of a kind not easily shared with those who have never left the bosom of comfortable belonging. Standing outside, looking in, the Other sees our relationship with the world in ways those not estranged from society simply cannot." This understanding indeed throbs like a bruise throughout the text of *The Man Who Lived Underground*, only relieved by Daniels's total separation. Wright's novel was written more than a decade before the declaration by Supreme Court Justice Thurgood Marshall, in *Brown v. Board of Education,* that "separate is not equal," but Wright's novel makes the compelling case that Othered is also not equal—and that some self-imposed separation may indeed be a solution to a life of perpetual Otherness.

It's a concept that many today still struggle mightily with, but which has begun to get the discussion it deserved back in 1941. Wright's dark vision was of a man forced to live alone in the sewers in order to find happiness and freedom and finding that exchange to be worthwhile. Reading the novel today begs the question of whether a Black person like Daniels, after all this time, is any closer to feeling a security of freedom and happiness while remaining aboveground like anybody else. However we answer it, we can be glad that Wright's question has at last been asked of us.

Incidentally, if *The Man Who Lived Underground* all sounds familiar, then you're not wrong. The basic premise does indeed seem a bit like that of *Invisible Man*, which Ralph Ellison would publish a decade after Wright's book failed to be published. Critics, including none other than Shirley Jackson's husband, Stanley Hyman, went so far as to suggest that *Invisible Man* had been inspired by the story version of Wright's novel. Ellison dismissed this, writing in one letter, "As for my narrator, he comes out of Dostoevsky's *Notes from Underground*, not Wright's 'Man Who Lived Underground.'" Though it would seem from that statement that Ellison was aware of Wright's story, it could also be true that he was familiar with the same article that had inspired Wright, who no doubt was also drawing some inspiration from Dostoevsky himself, as even the title might suggest.

In any case, Richard Wright's novel sat in a time capsule for decades. Today, with Wright's place in American letters secured, we may look back critically at the editorial judgment of Aswell and

Quinn. We may even see their decisions as a suppression, a way of forcing Wright to produce something more hopeful about racial equality, though he didn't feel much hope for it at the time. I don't think that's a wrong way to see it at all, and from Malcolm Wright's foreword to the new publication, it seems clear that this is how he sees it too.

Still, in the mind of Aswell and Quinn, the decision may have been more nuanced. It was their job to evaluate what the readership that Wright had earned with *Native Son* was going to do with his new work. If it was a letdown, a flop, for whatever reason, then his career might have taken a big step backward. We know that Quinn liked the work enough to publish it in a shorter form, but perhaps he sensed that Wright could do better—as much as I enjoyed *The Man Who Lived Underground*, it doesn't hold a candle to the masterpiece of *Black Boy*, which he'd go on to finish next. I think it may be telling that Wright did not return to his lost novel later in his career. He may have come to see it as less than he was capable of, in the end.

As writers we don't often consider the publication process from the perspective of the editors. Sometimes they make bad decisions, for bad reasons, no doubt about that. But far more often, I think, their hearts are in the right place, and they are striving to get the best possible book out of the writers they love, and then to make sure that book does as well as it can. At the very least it should be a good reminder to all writers that rejection doesn't mean that we're deficient, or awful, or talentless. It may mean that we are ahead of our time. Or it may simply mean that our best idea is still around the corner, waiting for us to keep looking for it.

Fail like a Genius

Richard Wright

One surprising twist in the story of Wright's lost novel is a technological one, the possibility that his sudden shift to using a Dictaphone affected his writing style and confused his editors. I find it incredibly relatable as someone who eagerly tries out every new gadget and gizmo that promises to make the writing process easier, despite the fact they don't tend to stick for me. What if a transcription app could turn my voice memos into text, and I could write the next *On the Road* while literally driving across the country? What if I bought a laptop that runs on AA batteries and uses an e-ink display that does nothing but word processing so I can avoid distractions? Or a digital scanner to import my hand-scrawled drafts? In the end these things never seem to work out for me, but I'm always eager to try the next. Who knows when I might need to do something in a new way?

What didn't quite work for Richard Wright in 1940 was essential for Richard Powers in 2007, who explained in an op-ed for the *New York Times* that he'd gotten so used to writing through computer dictation that he no longer had a keyboard attached to his computer. There are times when I feel some relief that if I ever broke my fingers or got carpal tunnel, I might still adapt to some new process.

Until then, I do think it is a good thing to experiment with new ways of writing, as an artist needs to dabble with new techniques in painting or a chef should try new methods of cooking to keep things fresh and make discoveries—writers should always be on the lookout for breakthroughs.

So, see what happens if you experiment with new techniques! I've played with voice transcription services like Otter.ai, used special electronic notebooks with Bluetooth pens, and composed in different software. So far I've found that going old-school tends to win the day, and I prefer to break out my old manual typewriter, or just write longhand in a plain $2 spiral-bound notebook. You may not find a permanent change in your ways of writing, but you might find an interesting new voice emerging for a character, or a fresh style that can be incorporated into something you're working on: a transcript, an interview, an email, or a letter. Surprise yourself, and feel the process become new again.

Geniuses Cave Under Pressure

James Baldwin

In Mark Twain's classic American novel *The Adventures of Tom Sawyer*, the young rapscallion Tom starts out by getting into various kinds of fun trouble: stealing jam from his Aunt Polly, playing hooky from school, sneaking out of his room, and getting in a fight with another kid. As punishment, Tom's Aunt Polly makes him spend his Saturday whitewashing their fence. For the crime of having fun when he was supposed to be working (at school or at home), Tom will now have to work while everyone else is off having fun.

Famously, Tom soon begins to act as if the whitewashing itself is so fun and enjoyable that he dupes his friends into coming to help him paint the fence. He even cons them into paying him for the pleasure of doing his chores for him.

Twain sums up the moral of this little episode for us this way: "If [Tom] had been a great and wise philosopher, like the writer of this book, he would now have comprehended that Work consists of whatever a body is obliged to do, and that Play consists of whatever a body is not obliged to do." He suggests that this explains why grown-ups so often pay good money to do things that might be considered work if they were getting paid for it, like driving stagecoaches around, or climbing mountains. I've always wondered where Twain felt that writing books fell on that scale. Is it Work or Play?

I wonder this often when I am working hard on a novel or a story, feeling overwhelmed and overloaded, watching the world pass by my window and trying to remember what my friends' faces look like. It's hard to explain to others how exhausting and isolating it can become, because most of them would love to have time to sit around making up stories all day.

Most of us start off writing because it is a fun diversion from our actual work. We begin to scribble things down, enjoying the use of our vivid imaginations, for no particular purpose and without any specific ambition. Because we're not in any way obliged to do it, it is pure Play.

But at some point, as we've gotten older and started thinking of ourselves as writers, this changes. We take our creative life more seriously, think about publishing, and even begin to refer to our writing as our "work"—as in, "this is my work in progress," or "I'm working on a novel." Inevitably, we begin to feel obligated to do it. *Octavia Butler wrote every day*, we tell ourselves. *She got up at four and wrote before her awful day job.* Cultivating a steady writing practice becomes an important part of getting better, and of making progress. But as Tom Sawyer and Mark Twain would remind us, this can also suck all the fun out of it.

This may well be the root of some unfinished novels I've written about already, where blocks emerged or progress stalled because a project steadily became unenjoyable. But in the case of author James Baldwin and what would have been his final book, *Remember This House*, the obligation that paralyzed him wasn't to himself, or to his editor, or even to the book itself. He'd promised to write a book about the great heroes of the civil rights movement, to share with readers all the things he'd witnessed in his lifetime as an activist and a journalist. He felt a deep obligation to write it, but by the end of his life, Baldwin had written almost nothing at all.

"There Are New Metaphors": James Baldwin's *Remember This House*

The idea for *Remember This House* first came to Baldwin in 1979, while he was living abroad in France. He decided he'd travel back to the American South and write about the lives of three leaders of the civil rights movement: Medgar Evers, Malcolm X, and Martin Luther King Jr. He'd share it all: how he had known them, and how they had crossed paths and purposes with one another in their fight for racial equality. Baldwin would ruminate on the terrible tragedy that, within five years, each of those men had been assassinated in that fight.

Baldwin had touched on these topics in 1963's *The Fire Next Time* and then in 1972 with *No Name in the Street*, but he had a lot more to say. He wanted to travel to Atlanta, Selma, and Birmingham to talk with the widows, brothers, and sisters of his subjects. Most of all, he would speak with their growing sons and daughters. A decade after the deaths of these men, he wondered how they and their cause appeared to their children's generation.

Baldwin approached the *New Yorker* to write an article on the subject, but soon realized the project would be far too big. He ultimately proposed *Remember This House* as a new book to his literary agent, Jay Acton. He wrote to Acton that he did so "in a somewhat divided frame of mind . . . this is a journey, to tell you the truth, which I always knew that I would have to make, but had hoped, perhaps (certainly, I had hoped) not to have to make so soon."

Baldwin was about to turn fifty-five, he remarked with some

astonishment. Time was passing, and the civil rights movement had become the civil rights era. Baldwin felt an obligation to look back on it, but also a reticence. "It means exposing myself as one of the witnesses to the lives and deaths of their famous fathers. And it means much, much more than that—a cloud of witnesses, as old St. Paul once put it."

To write this book would mean bearing witness. It would mean facing those children and the memories he held of their fathers. It also meant facing the question of whether the equality they had fought and died for was any closer at the dawn of 1980.

Publisher McGraw-Hill soon paid a $200,000 advance for the book—the largest in Baldwin's career.

But when Baldwin died of liver cancer, eight years later, at his home in the south of France, he had only written about thirty pages of notes for *Remember This House*. Over the final years of his life, Baldwin made several attempts to write the book but found it to be "impossible." Indeed, he could not bring himself to even begin the necessary research—to go back to the South and speak to the descendants of those civil rights heroes.

"I can't be a pessimist," James Baldwin said in one interview, "because I'm alive. To be a pessimist means that you have agreed that human life is an academic matter. So, I'm forced to be an optimist. I'm forced to believe that we can survive whatever we must survive."

It was a stirring and powerful public claim, but according to his assistant David Leeming, as the 1980s had progressed Baldwin's former optimism had given way to a deep cynicism when it came to the "unlikelihood of the white world's changing its ways." In the essay "The Evidence of Things Not Seen," Baldwin had written about a string of unsolved murders of Black children in Atlanta, and the failures of both the white police force and the city's Black leaders to act in the crisis. The "New South" was a myth, Baldwin understood. Whites were eager to believe that America had already become more equal, that if there were Black politicians and policemen and television and movie stars, progress had been achieved. But Baldwin saw the reality of suburban white flight, of the rise of Black imprisonment, of racists no longer aware of their racism. The American Dream for Black Americans could never be achieved if whites did not genuinely desire to share it. Looking back, Baldwin felt that the moment had been missed, that the old language of equality and civil rights had become meaningless and that if there was real progress to be made in the future, a "new language" would be needed. If Baldwin had once hoped that *Remember This House* might find this "new language," as time went on he realized more and more how distant that future was.

Still, he never totally gave up on the idea of writing it. Even when he was finally so ill that he could not travel, Baldwin asked Leeming if *he* might go to speak with the widows and the children in Baldwin's place. He could not shake his feeling of obligation to write the book—now not only his obligation to the families of the assassinated civil rights leaders, but also to the publishers.

Not long before his death he asked Leeming to help him sort some papers at his desk, including *Remember This House*, which he hoped to return to "in a day or so." In the days before Baldwin passed away, he had Leeming read aloud bits of *Pride and Prejudice*, and they watched a favorite Charlie Chaplin film. His life's work, and his unfinished business, would go on to inspire generations of activists to come—those who still believed in forging that new language he needed.

Baldwin knew that the work for *Remember This House* was going to be draining and difficult and depressing, and so he stalled. In many ways we might be glad that we did. Instead of tracking down grandchildren in the New South, writing once more about the failures of America to keep its promises and live up to its supposed ideals, Baldwin was able to spend those final years of his life engaged with other work that brought him joy.

He wrote poems and essays, collected two volumes of his nonfiction, and translated some of his plays into French. He lived happily in a beautiful villa in a medieval town called Saint-Paul-de-Vence, surrounded by beauty, and was visited often by the many lights of his generation: Sidney Poitier, Harry Belafonte, Nina Simone, Josephine Baker, Stevie Wonder, Maya Angelou, Toni Morrison, and many, many others. Instead of spending his final years with the ghosts of the civil rights era, Baldwin spent them creating a bohemian paradise for Black luminaries. (One of the projects that Baldwin worked on instead of *Remember This House* was a play about this remarkable space. He called it *The Welcome Table*, and it centered on a range of vibrant discussions and ideas between the luminaries who came to visit him.) The house remains today a writer's retreat, "La Maison Baldwin," welcoming fellows from around the world to come and work there in the rooms that became his happiest home. At the new National Museum of African American History and Culture in Washington, DC, a wide-ranging exhibit now collects various artifacts and photographs from "Chez Baldwin" and celebrates his creation of a unique and "vibrant abode" that inspired dozens of artists and thinkers of a coming generation, a "place for healing, gathering, and writing."

And Baldwin's death was not the end for *Remember This House*, which took on a strange afterlife. In 1987, McGraw-Hill sued his estate to recoup the $200,000 advance he'd been paid—plus interest. Their chairman, Joseph L. Dionne, took the view that "Mr. Baldwin effectively received an interest-free loan of $200,000 to write a book as to which we await evidence that he ever wrote more than a very rough 11-page draft. As a publicly owned company, McGraw-Hill is not in a position to waive repayment of that sum."

It's still relatively uncommon for a publisher to sue a writer for the return of an advance when they've failed to deliver a book. In 2012, when Penguin sued *Prozac Nation* author Elizabeth Wurtzel and eleven other writers over books they'd never finished, it was an odd enough occurrence that it made international news, with articles in the *Guardian* and the *Telegraph* quoting shocked editors and literary agents.

Even less common is a publisher suing the estate of a deceased author to get their money back on an unfinished book—but that is what happened in Baldwin's case.

Back in 1987, in response to McGraw-Hill's lawsuit, the *New York Times* interviewed a variety of other prominent publishing executives, none of whom could think of any prior situation in which a deceased author's estate had been sued for repayment of an advance. One industry lawyer said that doing such a thing had always been "considered simply not cricket." Still, it took an outcry from the Authors Guild to convince the publisher to retract the lawsuit, which, according to Baldwin's family, would have ended in the eviction of his eighty-nine-year-old mother from her home.

Once the suit was finally dropped in 1990, the rights to *Remember This House* reverted back to the Baldwin estate, where they remained for almost two decades, and might have been forgotten forever, if not for Baldwin's sister, Gloria Karefa-Smart, who one day handed them over to a filmmaker named Raoul Peck.

Peck had been studying the estate's archives for several years, trying to make a documentary about Baldwin. She told him that he could have the notes, and that she believed he'd know what to do with them.

Imagine being handed the pages of an incomplete—really, a *barely begun* project—that one of the greatest literary giants of the twentieth century had found "impossible," and being asked to steer it home after almost forty years.

But that's just what Raoul Peck did.

"A book that was never written!" Peck wrote, in the print companion to his documentary *I Am Not Your Negro*. "That's the story. . . . My job was to find that unwritten book." Using a new, visual language, and Baldwin's own words, he finally took the journey that Baldwin had once found so impossible.

I Am Not Your Negro organizes excerpts from the thirty extant pages of *Remember This House* with other bits and pieces of Baldwin's letters and notes and interviews, to tremendous effect. Peck described his role in its creation as similar to a "librettist crafting the script for an opera from the scattered works of a revered author."

Baldwin had written in a tiny note that he hoped *Remember This House* would be "a funky dish of chitterlings." Peck took this concept to heart, combining Baldwin's words with all manner of other media: still images, film clips, speech excerpts, news footage, song lyrics, a Chiquita banana advertisement—even excerpts from Baldwin's own FBI file. Just as Baldwin wanted, Peck illuminates the three civil rights heroes through Baldwin's own memories, but he also bears Baldwin's witnessing to a new generation, a new millennium, where so many of those same old struggles persist. The film ran internationally, made millions at the box office, won the BAFTA Award for Best Documentary in 2018, and was nominated for Best Documentary Feature at the Academy Awards.

On the title page of that thirty-page manuscript for *Remember This House*—dismissed as worthless by McGraw-Hill, but of such immense value to Peck—Baldwin wrote the first word as "Re/ member," which, according to Leeming, suggested his desire to "put a broken 'house' together again." To not just recall, but to reassemble the "'house' of the fallen heroes."

In the companion book to *I Am Not Your Negro*, Raoul Peck shares a 1973 quote of Baldwin's, which was sent to him by Baldwin's sister Gloria in 2009. It describes, in greater detail than before, what that "new language" he'd been looking for would consist of. Even as he was himself unable to find it, Baldwin sensed what it would someday turn out to be:

```
There are new metaphors. There are new sounds. Men
and Women will be different. Children will be differ-
ent. They will have to make money obsolete. Make a
man's life worth more than that. Restore the idea of
work as joy, not drudgery.
```

It's a powerful idea, and I love especially that this last line so pleasantly echoes Twain's parable of Tom and the whitewashed fence, and the importance of making Work into Play again. Usually as I read about these unfinished works, I'm left in a glum wistfulness, trying to imagine what could have been *if only* things had ended differently. But in the case of *Remember This House*, I'm glad he didn't force himself to write it, as I'm glad that a future genius found a way to make it, joyfully, anyway.

Although I don't recommend failing to deliver on a six-figure advance unless you *are* James Baldwin, I think it's helpful to remember that we don't *have* to write anything unless we want to write it. We especially don't have to write anything because we feel obligated to write it. Life's too short, for one thing. For another, signed contracts aside, we must remember that we never owe our art to anyone but ourselves. And that sense of obligation, whether financial, existential, or otherwise, can be the death of creativity—which means that sometimes the only way to move forward is to rid yourself of the idea that you must make progress. Make your work a joy, not drudgery, and see what begins to grow out of the space you've cleared away.

FAIL LIKE A GENIUS

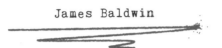

James Baldwin

How do you break up with a book? By now we've seen projects left unfinished by their authors for all kinds of reasons: crumbling confidence, a growing lack of interest, some heartbreak, or a crippling block. As integral as persistence is to the writing process, so is resilience, or an ability to dust oneself off from a failure and start fresh.

So often I encounter a truly brilliant student who is partway through a novel they're *sure* is going to be their debut triumph—only when I read the book I see it is nowhere near the level of their present abilities. Often this will be something they've been working on for years, and ironically the problem is that in the meantime they've learned so much and become so much better than when they started out. That's good news—there's great promise on the road ahead, but it may mean that the book can't come with them.

It really is like a breakup, the end of a long-term relationship that has opened your eyes to the world, taught you about yourself—and, yes, it has flaws, but you've even come to love those flaws too, so why won't everyone else?

How can it be all these things and still now need to be let go?

What I'm about to propose might sound crazy, but I promise I've tried it myself and found it shockingly helpful. If and when the time comes to set aside your own *Remember This House*, sit down and actually break up with it. Write it a literal Dear John letter—*Hey, book, this is Kris, I think we both know that this hasn't been good now for a while* . . . You're going to feel ridiculous at first, but you're giving yourself a chance to think through what you've loved about the work and what you think you want to do better next time. Be specific, spell it all out—the book can't storm off in tears. If your book isn't capable of appreciating your honesty, then at least you will. And on the other side of that is the closure you both need.

Geniuses Ask for Help

Clarice Lispector

As a young reader, I fell into the habit of scanning the acknowledgments sections in my favorite books, hunting for literary Easter eggs. I was always looking out for interesting little hints about the author's personal world. Who did they thank, and how did they thank them? Did they credit influences and creative allies? Did they think themselves too cool for acknowledgments at all, or give pages of gushing gratitude for all who ever helped them in even the tiniest way? These things reveal something genuine about the author, and how they considered (or didn't) the vast web of people who contributed to their book's existence.

Watching a movie or a television show, we're used to seeing a stretch of end credits. At the theater or the opera, you'll be handed a program filled with names—all organized in a precise manner. But with a novel, anything seems to go. Aside from citing direct quotes from other works, there is no formal requirement to recognize anyone who may have had a hand in creating the work. The impression is left that, by default, our genius author has done it entirely on their own, even if they graciously (but optionally) choose to thank those who smoothed the way.

This is surely never the case. There is always some crew of publishing professionals involved, and friends, early readers, writing retreats, organizations that provided grants, etc. These are involved in almost every book, whether they are properly acknowledged or not.

Acknowledgments sections can be as brief as a paragraph or as long as several pages. Very short ones are sometimes tucked onto the copyright page in very tiny print. Most are perfunctory lists of names provided without any context whatsoever in an understandable effort to credit people for their contributions while respecting their privacy. Sometimes these are delightfully cryptic in-jokes; Andrew Sean Greer thanks, in *Less*, "the Evens and Odds" and "the Dolphin Swimming and Boating Club." At the back of *Our Country Friends*, Gary Shteyngart thanks (among others) a friend who taught him to prepare the Piedmontese dish vitello tonnato, which he "highly recommends." These sections can tell you a lot about what writers see as necessary support, what they think deserves special mention, and how private they are about their process. Naomi Jackson, in *The Star Side of Bird Hill*, thanks more than a hundred people over nearly four pages; by contrast, the entire acknowledgments section of Bryan Washington's *Memorial* is a spare list of twenty-nine first names (a few are grouped together) and "The Riverhead crew" and that's that. For my own part, in my first acknowledgments sections I make a point to thank the owners of the coffee shops where I do all my writing.

A writer often uses the space to thank their readers, as Aleksandar Hemon does in his latest novel *The World and All That It Holds*: "First, I want to tell all of my readers that without them this book is a paper brick and I am nothing." (Within the four-page mini-essay that follows, he goes on to credit everyone that he can think of, including the "singing voice" of Damir Imamović who recorded an album to accompany the novel, and then his own electronic dance music project Cielo Hemon, the tracks of which he says are "neither visible nor audible to anyone other than me, but were crucial in creating both works of art." At the end of the section, Hemon implores everyone to get up and go out dancing.)

The tradition of the acknowledgments section began 500 years ago, according to an article by Sam Roberts, among authors in Europe and England. Roberts spoke with a reference librarian at the Library of Congress about the practice and learned that back in the sixteenth century, writers would include an *impensis* (Latin for "at the expense of") to credit those who had financially backed their project, and sometimes also to woo potential future patrons. Authors would also commonly include an *imprimatur* (more Latin for "let it be printed") in respect for the church or another "official body" that had permitted the work to be licensed. These two impulses remain today, intertwined in the contemporary acknowledgments section—there are those who supported the writing effort financially, emotionally, through research, etc., and those publishing professionals essential in creating the book itself.

We've seen already the hidden figures surrounding the geniuses discussed here—never quite so solitary or monolithic as the myth would have us believe. F. Scott Fitzgerald's published letters show he wrote constantly for advice, encouragement, and financial support from just about everyone he knew: Maxwell Perkins, Edmund Wilson (who he calls "Bunny"), his wife Zelda (even when they were separated), his daughter Scottie, his longtime friends Gerald and Sara Murphy, Ernest Hemingway, on and on. Who would Franz Kafka have been without Max Brod, or Vladimir Nabokov without Véra? Harper Lee, discussed in a later chapter, and Truman Capote each supported the work of the other throughout their lifetimes. Flannery O'Connor based characters (and whole ideologies) on her friend Maryat Lee. And, as complicated as their contributions surely were, Ted Hughes and Stanley Hyman each played significant roles in the working lives of Sylvia Plath and Shirley Jackson—both for better and for worse.

All of which is to say that while writing can oftentimes be presented as a deeply solitary act, it is rare to find any genius of literature who did what they did without a good deal of help.

We better understand the nature of genius by looking at it as a network of connected energies, instead of as a lone pulse of electric greatness.

"The fact of the matter is that there are many hands tapping the writer's keyboard," says Colum McCann in his acknowledgments for *Let the Great World Spin*. No man is an island; it takes a village. "This isn't a game of *Survivor*," my MFA director, Alan Ziegler, said to my incoming class in 2003. "You don't win by being the last one voted off the island." Instead, we succeed by helping one another become better. If you give strong feedback to a classmate, in theory they'll do the same for you. "If you leave this program with one thing," Ziegler said to us, "I hope it is a few classmates whose work you love, and who love your work too, and who will continue to critique and support you in the future." I took his meaning to be that we'd need this network of readers and friends more than we'd need all the knowledge and advice of our professors—and after twenty years I have concluded that he was 100 percent correct.

"Breathing Together":
Clarice Lispector's *Água Viva* and *A Breath of Life*

The world nearly lost Clarice Lispector in 1966. After taking a sleeping pill on a September evening, she got into bed to smoke a cigarette and soon woke to find her apartment engulfed in fire. "In a panicked attempt to save her papers," Benjamin Moser writes in his biography *Why This World*, "she attempted to put out the fire with her own hands."

Lispector's son eventually walked her over to a neighbor's, but not before she had been badly burned from head to toe, her clothes melted onto her skin. Footprints of blood marked the carpet where she had stepped.

Had she died that night, Clarice Lispector would still have been remembered as one of Brazil's most famous writers. At forty-six, she was the author of eight books, including *Near to the Wild Heart* and *The Passion According to G. H.* Her masterful, mystical stories and novels were like nobody else's, and beyond this she was a fashionable and public figure, mesmerizing both on the page and in real life. One critic wrote that her work had "shifted the center of gravity around which the Brazilian novel had been revolving for about twenty years."

Thankfully, Clarice Lispector did not die that night. She was, however, hospitalized for three months with third-degree burns, experiencing immense and lasting pain. Her right hand, which she had used to write, was blackened and horribly bent. She kept family, friends, and neighbors nearby, and in time she pulled through—if to a life irrevocably altered.

Along with facing a grueling physical recovery, Lispector had lost all her unfinished work in the fire. She had been struggling for some time to follow the success of *The Passion According to G. H.* Now, after this serious trauma, Lispector began to despair, feeling increasingly isolated from society.

Through this, she published two novels for children and wrote, in 1968, a novel called *An Apprenticeship*, which critics enjoyed, though she expressed dissatisfaction. Soon after, she announced that she would not write another book. When asked why in an interview she replied, "What a question! Because it hurts too much."

But Lispector did keep fighting—not to get back to her old self, but forward into something else: what would eventually amount to a second life of letters. She reinvented everything: her style, her methods, and even the very questions at the heart of her writing. In the years following, she would write dozens of new stories and several beautiful novels, including the masterpieces *Água Viva* and *The Hour of the Star*, which would carry her reputation beyond Brazil and into the waiting world.

To face these huge new challenges, Lispector enlisted help.

She began to see a psychiatrist, Jacob Azulay, five days a week, an hour a day—for the next six years. Sometimes, he recalled, she would write sentences and fragments in his office. She told him that she felt like an insect who had shed the skin of the being formerly known as Clarice Lispector.

She also hired an assistant named Olga Borelli, who, according to Moser, "would become a key figure in the last years of Clarice's life and whose tireless dedication and intellectual affinity facilitated the creation of Clarice's great final works."

A former nun, Borelli had been an ardent fan of Lispector's writing and, after seeing her on a television program one night, decided to call her under the auspices of fundraising for a charity. They spoke on the phone and two weeks later, the women met and became close friends.

Borelli thenceforth dedicated her life to the remainder of Lispector's. Borelli became a part of Lispector's day-to-day routines. She cared for her, talked with her, comforted her, and played a singular hand in the construction of her late works, editing and arranging them from disparate fragments, including her very last—*A Breath of Life*, published in 1978, a year after Lispector's death from cancer.

A Breath of Life (*Sopro de vida*), which was translated into English for New Directions in 2012 by Johnny Lorenz, is primarily a conversation between two characters: an unnamed male Author, and Angela, the character that the Author is creating. "The title," according to Moser, "refers to the creation, mystical or 'Franken-steinian,' of one being by another."

Over the book's one hundred sixty pages, Angela and her Author discuss the connections between creator and creation and what it means to breathe life into another being, even a character. There is a strong preoccupation with knowing that creation means, inevitably, death. Some critics have noticed that the voices of the two characters often switch and merge together. The Author has a tendency to override Angela's voice, who in turn sometimes influences her creator's mannerisms in spooky ways.

Publishers Weekly called it a "schizoid duet" (in a nice way) when the book was translated into English—the Author and Angela being two sides of Clarice Lispector. But in some sense, the novel as we read it is truly a "schizoid trio," for between the arguments of Angela and the Author, who together may make up Lispector, there is also Borelli—the woman who transcribed, edited, typed, retyped, and reedited hundreds of fragments during Lispector's lifetime, and, after Lispector's death from ovarian cancer, ultimately organized those fragments into their final form.

In a half-page introduction to the book, Borelli briefly notes her role in finishing Lispector's unfinished "definitive book," which was, "in the words of Clarice, 'written in agony,' for it was born from a painful impulse she was unable to contain." Reflecting on her eight years of working closely with Lispector, Borelli remarked, "I wrote down her thoughts, typed her manuscripts and most of all shared in her moments of inspiration."

According to Benjamin Moser, Lispector had never before permitted her literary work to be edited by anyone. Now Olga Borelli would be more than just an editor, but a silent collaborator. A "sensitive, well-educated reader with a refined sense of lan-guage," Borelli would later write her own memoir of her time with Lispector. Organizing and editing was exhausting for Lispector at this stage, and she was prepared to fully abandon a several-hundred-page mess she was calling *Loud Object*. Instead, with Olga's help, they shed its skin and exposed a ninety-six-page masterpiece, *Água Viva*.

When I've spoken to friends about this, they're often shocked and even quite uncomfortable with the idea of collaborating on a book with someone else. Writing can be so personal, so intimate, that we are often nervous to share it with others at all, let alone ask them for help in arranging and editing it. I know writers who are phobic about even *discussing*, in the broadest of strokes, what they're working on with anyone, until it is completely finished. This may be a strategy for protecting our ideas, or of protecting ourselves in case the project falls apart, but it contributes to an already very isolating process. For many writers, stalwart introverts that we tend to be, this may be no issue at all. But I hope that the case of Lispector and Borelli will show that there are other options available. We've seen already that writing is often assisted by many others behind the scenes, only mentioned in acknowledgments and dedications.

If you have a Max Brod or a Véra Nabokov in your life, should they have to remain behind the curtains? Collaboration is common, if not assumed, in the lives of most screenwriters, playwrights, dancers, musicians, and, frequently, visual artists.

If two heads are better than one in other art forms, why not in literature?

Borelli described her method of working with Lispector as "breathing together" and likened the experience to building a puzzle, in this case out of sometimes scavenged fragments of writing, "on the back of a check, a piece of paper, a napkin . . .

some even smell of her lipstick. She would wipe her lips and then stick it in her purse."

A Breath of Life began to emerge not long after *Água Viva* was published, in similar small unordered fragments. In her introduction, Lispector wrote, "This I suppose will be a book made apparently out of shards of a book. . . . My life is made of fragments and that's how it is for Angela."

Throughout the book, the Author, and Lispector, struggles with having to come to an end, meaning that Angela will come to an end. "Do I kill her? Does she kill herself?" he asks. Angela remarks later, "At the hour of my death—what do I do? Teach me how to die. I don't know."

Four years later, upon Lispector's death, all that existed of the novel was a "mountain of fragments."

Moser notes that it was "not only published but also, to some extent, *written* after Clarice's death" by Borelli, "breathing together" with the memory of Lispector. Thus the book, Moser argues, achieves its perfection "precisely by its incompletion and imperfection."

Some of her changes, Borelli admitted after the book's publication, were more about her concern for Lispector and her family than about what would best serve the book. For instance, Lispector had the Author confess, "I asked God to give Angela a cancer that she can't get rid of." She had told several people throughout her life, including Azulay, her psychiatrist, that she knew she would someday die of "a nasty cancer"—and indeed, when Lispector was hospitalized in 1977, a few days after publishing *The Hour of the Star*, doctors soon diagnosed her with terminal ovarian cancer, although she was never told that this was what she was dying of. Thinking of the impact on Lispector's loved ones, Borelli left out the cancer line.

After her diagnosis, Lispector spent three months in the hospital, but this time she did not leave. Olga Borelli passed the time with her, taking dictation right up to the day of the hemorrhage that would end Lispector's life.

We may have this idea of a genius as being "peerless"—a solo act, with the brilliance of the artist so beyond the level of those around them that they are forced to go it alone. But even a cursory look at the lives and practices of most writers will show this is hardly ever the case. We need a lot of people to make the process work—partners and spouses, friends and editors, managers and representatives, colleagues and sounding boards. Why draw the line there? Why not share the words themselves with others? Aren't we, essentially, doing this already? If your work is something that is meant to be shared with others, then others can and should be able to assist and advise you in the making of that work.

Many writers I know are happy to finally escape the workshop process, but soon enough the question comes: who will read us now? Yes, it can be annoying to listen to others complain about your work, week after week, but we may soon discover we were relying on it more than we knew. Just as my MFA director had predicted, within weeks I found myself being ever more grateful to have met a few other wonderful readers that I could stay in touch with afterward, some of whom are still on my panic call sheet now, twenty years later.

Often, I feel uncomfortable reaching out to friends for test reads, or even just general editorial advice. I convince myself that they're far too busy, or that they will feel pressured, even burdened, by my asking them to read what I'm working on. But when I get in my own head too badly, it helps to think about Lispector and Borelli. Their unique kind of collaboration remains uncommon, brought about only because of an extreme medical need. But there's no reason it has to be a last resort. Flip through a few acknowledgments sections and you'll be reminded how ordinary it really is to ask others for help, and to depend on partners and friends in the creative process.

Don't be afraid to let others in to your process. You might be surprised what it brings.

Fail like a Genius

Clarice Lispector

Clarice Lispector's process of generating thousands of fragments, to be later assembled with Olga Borelli's help, is certainly already a method we could try on our own (or with a friend). We've talked already about how shorter "low stakes" writing can be useful, and seen how physically rearranging index cards can be helpful in building a larger whole from smaller pieces. It could be interesting to do something like Lispector and Borelli did, where you generate dozens of fragments and then turn them over to someone else to place in their own order.

But another fun approach to collaboration is to create a *Nest of Ninnies*—a 1969 experimental novel, cowritten by poets John Ashbury and James Schuyler. They wrote the entire 191-page book one line at a time, beginning with Ashbury's opener: "Alice was tired." From there, Schuyler wrote: "Languid, fretful, she turned to stare into her own eyes in the mirror above the mantelpiece before she spoke." Schuyler passed it back to Ashbury, who wrote the third line . . . and you get the idea. They did this for years, without consulting each other as to where the story was going, letting it always be a surprise for the other. In the end the book is, truly, unique in being a completely equal collaboration of their two imaginations.

This could be done more easily today—imagine a novel or story composed via tweets or text messages—a fun activity taking up only a few minutes a day, slowly evolving. However you do it, you'll get to witness the moves another writer might make and learn to adapt to those moves as they adapt to yours. You'll learn to be flexible and accommodating, while booting loneliness directly out of the process. Will it produce a beloved experimental novel in the end, or simply be a way of keeping your skills fresh? There's no way to know until you dive in. All you need to start is a friend and a first sentence.

Geniuses Try Another Way

Zora Neale Hurston

When students of mine are first beginning to workshop their writing, I tell them there are three objectives to the process. The first is to share their work with others to get critical feedback that guides them in taking the next steps. Their peers will weigh in on what's working well and what's not, and the author can see how the piece can be improved in revision. Easy.

On the other side of the equation, the second objective to workshop is to train to become better readers and critics—which also helps them be better writers. By analyzing other people's work, they'll fine-tune their own tastes and clarify their ideas. Seems straightforward as well.

But what's the third goal? You take feedback, you give feedback. What else is there?

The last piece of the puzzle is actually learning how to *ignore* feedback. When do you listen to advice, and when it is OK to disregard it?

In my MFA thesis workshop, our small group was dominated by several vocal classmates whose work veered toward the most violent, pornographic, and nihilistic direction possible. It was the early 2000s; Chuck Palahniuk was in vogue at the time, and this cadre was very interested in following that style. Each story they wrote, every chapter they turned in tried to top the shock value of whatever the last writer had turned in.

Unfortunately, I was trying, at the time, to write a wholesome YA novel about two boys in a boarding school who start a secret society. Week after week, the Palahniuk fan club insisted that my characters should do more drugs, have more sex—never mind that they were thirteen years old—and their beloved English teacher ought to have multiple degenerate vices I won't get into here.

I'm not saying that the novel they wanted me to write wouldn't have been a good one—in fact, maybe it would have even sold to a publisher, which I can't say about the book I did end up writing. But at the end of the day, I just did not *want* to write that other novel. And no amount of pressure from my peers could change my mind. Week after week, I disappointed them more and more as I continued to ignore their advice.

You could certainly argue that this was all just a huge waste of my time. If I had been in a different group, with more like-minded writers, maybe I would have gotten useful advice and made my book even better. But instead, I got something else that was still very valuable. I learned to stay true to my own taste, and to stand up to criticism seeking to urge my writing in some other direction. In that one semester I came to understand more about what made my voice *mine* than I did in all my other years of workshop.

That's been incredibly useful since then, now that being a professional writer means putting my work in front of opinionated bloggers, career literary critics, and even just regular readers who enjoy posting blunt comments. If someone tells me I'm being "too clever" or "too sentimental" it helps to be able to think back on that old workshop and remember that my work may just not be up their particular alley. I know now that literature is a bigger world than they think it is, and that it has a lot of different alleys to go down.

People sometimes talk about the need for a would-be writer to "have a thick skin"—another genetic-seeming trait, like the "eye for detail" or the "ear for dialogue"—but I don't care much for that metaphor, which makes it seem like authors come with a suit of armor because criticism is a battlefield.

What we actually need is a compass: a sense of what direction we're moving in and why it is the right one for us. To get better, we *must* listen to others and honestly consider their feedback, but that doesn't mean we give every piece of advice equal credence. What are the things that are not up for compromise in your work? If you say "everything" then there's a problem . . . but if you say "nothing" that's potentially worse.

Ultimately, every writer must know what is vital to their work and what isn't.

It's one thing to ignore a loud classmate in workshop, or to shut out a critique from a newspaper columnist or some blogger with an axe to grind. But what happens when the pressure is coming from within the system? What happens when it comes from an editor, even, who says they really love your work except that there are just a few major things you'll need to change completely if they are going to put it out into the world? This is where it gets very, very hard indeed.

I was reminded of all this as I delved into the story behind Zora Neale Hurston's first book, *Barracoon*, which was not published for almost eighty years after she finished it—in large part because she refused to compromise on certain key elements of the book in order to please publishers at the time it was written. Her refusal meant that a book she'd spent years researching, at great personal cost, would be scuttled—and even more difficult, it would mean Hurston having to entirely abandon the kind of scholarly life she thought she'd live.

"Not One Word from the Sold": Zora Neale Hurston's *Barracoon*

In her considerable career, Zora Neale Hurston wrote four novels, three books of poetry, at least two plays, and several books of nonfiction. But before this she was training to be an anthropologist, and her first book-length work, later lost for decades, was going to be a work of documentary, even academic, nonfiction. *Barracoon* aimed to tell the story of the last surviving African slave in America, a man named Cudjo Lewis, who relayed his firsthand account of enslavement to Hurston for what was going to be her doctoral thesis in anthropology. The twisting story of what became of this book, and of Hurston's plans to go into the social sciences, reveals much about the ways that writers can benefit greatly from exploring different forms of writing.

The journey to *Barracoon* began on December 14, 1927, at 3:40 p.m., when thirty-six-year-old Zora Neale Hurston boarded a train at Penn Station in New York City, bound for Mobile, Alabama. She had already published a few short stories and some poetry, and sometimes collaborated with friends in the theater world like Langston Hughes. But her main focus was anthropology, and the research she wanted to do to complete her dissertation and pursue a life in academia.

Her mission that day in 1927 was to interview a man formerly named Oluale Kossola, who now went by Cudjo Lewis, the last surviving African brought to the United States on the last known slave ship, the schooner *Clotilda*. In July 1860, the *Clotilda* had illegally brought 110 enslaved African men, women, and children to Mobile Bay. The US Congress had banned the importation of slaves in 1807, but slavers continued to flout the law throughout the US Civil War—some, like Timothy Meaher, the owner of the

Clotilda, were said to take it as a challenge. The *Clotilda* had picked up its unlawful human cargo in Whydah, in the Kingdom of Dahomey, today part of the nation of Benin. After making its crossing of the Atlantic, the ship was snuck into Mobile Bay and the 110 surviving Africans, including Oluale Kossola, were sold. To avoid legal consequence, Meaher decided to scuttle the *Clotilda* up a nearby river and then burned it to cover his tracks.

Kossola and the others worked in enslavement for five and a half years, most in an area called Plateau-Magazine Point, not far to the north of Mobile. Once freed, the surviving men and women appealed to the Meaher family to provide them with land and help them establish a town. But the Meahers refused, and said they took no responsibility. They even continued to deny the existence of the *Clotilda*, and claimed that the stories of the men, women, and children brought to the United States onboard it were nothing but lies. The descendants of the Meahers continued to assert those lies until 2019, a year after *Barracoon* was finally published, when the remains of the ship, burned all the way back in 1860, were positively identified by researchers at the bottom of a river off the bay, where Timothy Meaher had attempted to destroy it 160 years earlier.

Back in 1865, the freed Kossola, now Cudjo Lewis, settled in the area of Plateau with the others freed by the Civil War, and together they started the community of Africatown that persists today.

And it was there that, beginning in 1927, Zora Neale Hurston spent three months interviewing Lewis as part of her anthropological research.

Hurston had attended Howard University, but later accepted a scholarship to finish her studies at Barnard College in New York City, becoming that school's first (and, at the time, only) Black student. While at Barnard, Hurston began working with Franz Boas, a professor at neighboring Columbia University now considered to be the "Father of American Anthropology." Boas opposed the then-mainstream ideologies of "scientific racism" that contended that there were biological differences between members of different races that determined their capacities for intelligence and so on, frequently based on examinations of cranial shape. Boas helped to overturn previous studies that were thought to have proved that descendants of African and Indigenous races were deficient based on skull shape and size. The research conducted by Boas revealed that these were not stable racial traits, but the result of differences in environmental factors including health and nutrition. He championed the idea of cultural relativism, rejecting the then-common hierarchies of human races and civilizations that prized Western European culture over all others.

Hurston finished her bachelor of arts in anthropology in 1928 and became a graduate student under Boas, intent on building further on her interviews with Cujdo Lewis and exploring the cultural narratives of formerly enslaved Africans. Hurston was working on a broader collection of African American folklore, which she had begun gathering in her hometown of Eatonville, Florida, and which would eventually be published as *Mules and Men*.

Her anthropological work was funded by a woman named Charlotte Osgood Mason, a "patron of Harlem Renaissance luminaries," who cared so deeply about Hurston's project in Africatown that Mason went so far as to donate money directly to Lewis when he fell into need. Hurston dedicated *Barracoon* to her this way: "To Charlotte Mason, My Godmother, and the one Mother of all the primitives, who with the Gods in Space is concerned about the hearts of the untaught."

On March 25, 1931, Hurston reported to Mason that she was

nearly done with her book, *Barracoon*, documenting Lewis's incredible life, beginning with his time in Africa as a member of the Kingdom of Dahomey and his capture and sale by members of a warring tribe, leading to the brutal Middle Passage. Lewis spoke about his life in slavery during the Civil War, and then the experience of living as a free man during Reconstruction and the Jim Crow era, and on through World War I and entering finally into the Great Depression. It was an unprecedented collection of the knowledge of one of the few formerly enslaved people to recount such a life in firsthand terms.

"All these words from the sellers, but not one word from the sold," Zora Neale Hurston remarked in her original introduction to *Barracoon*. It is clear Hurston wanted to remedy this with her work with Lewis and saw his voice as a vital and important piece of history, which she was in a unique position to preserve and to put forth to the world with great craft and accuracy.

Hurston submitted her book to publishers in September 1931. There was some interest right away, but they soon became stuck on the way Hurston had written the book to capture Lewis's voice. Viking Press asked if it could be rewritten "in language" instead of "dialect," meaning that they wanted Hurston to take Lewis's words and reshape them into "proper" English.

Hurston refused, arguing that capturing Lewis's speech accurately was a "vital and authenticating feature of the narrative." She insisted on maintaining "the orality of the spoken word" and ultimately refused the revision, even knowing that it likely doomed the project's prospects for wide publication.

How is it, then, that fifty years after Mark Twain was able to publish *The Adventures of Huckleberry Finn*, in which Jim and many other Black characters speak in the same types of "dialect" that Viking complained about, Hurston would run into such resistance? Harriet Beecher Stowe's own attempts in *Uncle Tom's*

Cabin, written even thirty years earlier than Huck Finn, didn't seem to be an issue for readers. Could it be that Twain and Stowe were white authors writing Black voices, and Hurston was not?

You may begin to sense similarities between Hurston's situation and that of Richard Wright in a previous chapter. Though her case happened years earlier, both books would ultimately meet the same fate, only finally being published three years apart, in 2018 and 2020 respectively.

Back in 1931, Langston Hughes, Hurston's friend and a fellow Harlem Renaissance luminary, told Hurston that her difficulties with Viking were a sign of the times. Things had changed, according to Hughes. During the 1920s big publishers had been excited to buy books by Black authors, then very much in vogue. They could afford to take risks on what might be challenging texts for their white readers. But after the Great Depression, they were no longer willing to gamble the same way on what they called "Negro material."

Even as a scholarly text, *Barracoon* struggled. Following the approach used by Boas, Hurston had rejected the traditional objective-observer stance for a "participant-observer" stance, making it clear in the text that she maintains a personal involvement with her subject and using the book to reflect on her own thoughts and reactions as well as Lewis's. For one example, at one point, Hurston describes how Lewis would sometimes refuse to speak with her and did yard work while she sat there waiting for him to return to the interview. She wrote about how sometimes she would drive him into town in order to get him to agree to continue the interview. And she, through Mason, had even paid Lewis to keep providing material for the book, which was considered unethical by her fellow anthropologists.

These colleagues wanted to be able to independently authenticate Lewis's story and separate it from Hurston's storytelling—worried that she was tilting too heavily into her own fictionalized accounting in her efforts to bring Lewis and his story fully to life.

Today we might say that Hurston's techniques simply presaged the New Journalism of the 1960s and 1970s, where writers (most often white and male) like Tom Wolfe, Gay Talese, Truman Capote, and Norman Mailer saw great success in blending fact and fabrication—going "gonzo," in the words of Hunter S. Thompson. Even in Hurston's time, similar techniques were used to great effect by writers like George Orwell, whose *Down and Out in Paris and London*, published in 1933, employed those same strategies to bring lower-class life to readers, all funneled through the perspective of Orwell as he lived and worked among them. Orwell owned up to numerous omissions and, later, fabrications in that work without much consequence. But in Hurston's case, her perspective choices left her stuck between academia and commercial publishing without any good options.

Lucky for all of us, Hurston took this rejection as a reason to get out of scholarship and into literature. The same roadblocks to her scholarly and journalistic work would become trailblazing achievements in her fiction.

Those supposedly problematic African American dialects that Viking complained about would, in 1937, become a defining feature in her first novel, *Their Eyes Were Watching God*. With that novel and her later work, Hurston created room for generations of twentieth-century Black writers to follow their own explorations of what today we'd call African American Vernacular English.

In the end Hurston's ability to move fluidly from nonfiction to fiction would steer her career in a better direction. It is telling that even as she worked to train as an anthropologist, she was writing and publishing poetry, and working on plays with Langston Hughes. Ironically, what may have seemed like a "safer" path into academia would turn out to be something she was glad to have left behind.

Barracoon might have faced other challenges as an academic work, even if editors had been ready to accept Hurston's narrative style and use of dialect. Following Hurston's death in 1960, a scholar named Robert Hemenway accused her, in 1972, of improperly appropriating language from another book, Emma Langdon Roche's *Historic Sketches of the South,* published in 1914. In her foreword to *Barracoon,* Hurston did not credit Roche or the book, but only more broadly the "Mobile Historical Society" that had provided Hurston with background materials—likely including Roche's book. But why not credit Roche directly, particularly in what was at the time an academic work, where issues of plagiarism could have ruined Hurston's fledgling career?

Hemenway offers a number of speculative possibilities—perhaps Hurston consciously or subconsciously wanted to leave academia, due to a tense relationship with her advisor and other academic mentors, or a growing desire to leave scholarship behind for fiction. Or maybe Hurston intended to later include footnotes or some other credit to Roche but, because the project was never picked up for publication, simply never added these into the manuscript before it was abandoned.

It's certainly possible that Hurston knew she would be in for greater scrutiny if *Barracoon* was published, and that this contributed to her choice to keep it in her drawer, instead of going back to Cudjo Lewis's story later on. All we know is that at the time she was interested in publishing it, she was faced with stiff enough resistance that she moved on. Richard Wright would do much the same thing with his novel, ten years later.

But we also know that, possible plagiarism aside, the very

factors that were criticized in 1931 make *Barracoon* as it was finally published in 2018 a valuable document for modern readers. Thanks to Hurston's powerful writing, and because we are so brought *in* to the story through her participation and Lewis's voice, a reader today will see Lewis as much more than a historical recording. He is a full character. A living, breathing man, doing his best to survive in the South during the Great Depression, still struggling to reconcile his kidnapping some seventy years earlier.

Hurston took her "dialects" from one arena where they were a roadblock, and moved into another form of storytelling where she could make new kinds of magic with them. She took the rejection of her nonfiction work in stride and tried another mode that ultimately fit better for her. Crucially, she didn't give up on nonfiction work either—she'd publish more in her lifetime, as times and tastes and attitudes changed. In Hurston we see the same determination and perseverance in the face of rejection that we've seen be so crucial for other writers, but here paired with a flexibility and open-mindedness when it came to how she expressed herself, which would become key to her success.

FAIL LIKE A GENIUS

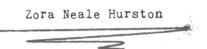

Zora Neale Hurston

After our workshop is over, I typically recommend that student writers take a few days and then send me a brief, typed revision plan. The purpose of this little extra step is to consolidate all the opinions and ideas that came flying at them over the course of our class discussion, and to give them a chance to turn it all into something actionable.

But with Hurston in mind, we might flip this around and create a non-revision plan instead. What advice are we rejecting, and why? In your plan, respond to feedback you won't be pursuing, and explain your reasoning.

There's a long tradition in literature of being contrary, of being opposed to specific things on principle. Susan Sontag is "Against Interpretation," as Philip Lopate is "Against *Joie de Vivre*," as Ben Metcalf is *Against the Country*, and Michel de Montaigne was "Against Idleness." It is good to be stubborn sometimes. Illuminating what we are *against* helps us better sort out what it is that we are for. For Zora Neale Hurston it might have been "Against Whitewashing Language," which just as easily could be "In Support of Vernacular Speech" or something along those lines.

The next time you get a piece of criticism you disagree with, take a few minutes to articulate why you think it *isn't* valid. It might even turn into an essay of your own. At the least it will help you pinpoint what's important to you as a writer, and that is valuable indeed.

Geniuses Bounce Back

Harper Lee

There may be nothing more difficult in the creative life than dealing with rejection. It can feel at times like nothing will ever work out. You begin to doubt your abilities, your choices, your sacrifices. As a teenager I remember reading an early chapter in Stephen King's *On Writing* where he described his difficult start as an author of short stories. He took a long nail and drove it through a piece of wood and set it on his desk. Each time a rejection came in the mail he'd jam it onto the spike and watch as the pile grew and grew. I am glad I read this anecdote when I did, because I had already begun to amass my own little pile—in my case thumbtacked to a corkboard near my desk, a collection of colorful preprinted slips that fluttered at me whenever my fan blew on them. Back then I had to mail physical copies of each short story to literary magazines, including a self-addressed stamped envelope (or SASE, as the magazines abbreviated it) that they'd use to send me the bad news, six to twelve weeks later—if they ever sent it. These days it will happen through email or Submittable, and I miss the satisfaction of tacking those paper slips to the corkboard, though I don't dread going to the mailbox and seeing envelopes with my own handwriting on them anymore.

At least I knew, back then, thanks to Stephen King's candor, that it was normal to face steady rejection at the start of your career. What I didn't realize then was that this doesn't necessarily go away later on—even after publishing two novels I still find myself getting a stream of rejections for short stories, and there's been lots of rejection to face while writing longer things too. At one point, I had a story get rejected fourteen times in eleven months. Then, in one afternoon, it was accepted by two different magazines within the span of a single hour.

When rejections happen, and they always happen, it helps me to think of Stephen King's stack of slips, and to think about the many other writers that I'd consider to be great geniuses who found themselves getting the equivalent of their own SASE back in the mail. Already we've seen cases where writers have needed to persevere through years and years, through draft after draft, before finally finding success in the end. But in my experience, it isn't just perseverance that a creative life requires, but resilience. That is to say, it isn't only about continuing to slog along much longer than we'd expect, but also about bouncing back up again after each setback.

The best illustration of this that I've come across in my search of unfinished novels is an odd one—a circuitous mystery involving one of the most classic novels of the twentieth century, Harper Lee's *To Kill a Mockingbird* and its strange "sequel," *Go Set a Watchman*, which arrived decades later, under dubious circumstances, and which finally turned out to be something else entirely.

Harper Lee's First Draft: *Go Set a Watchman*

On July 14, 2015, the literary world received a treat—or at least what seemed to be a treat—fifty-five years in the making. Harper Lee's novel *Go Set a Watchman* was published by

HarperCollins to intense fanfare, with bookstores staying open overnight and millions of preorders on Amazon. It was only the second novel ever published by the eighty-eight-year-old author.

Her first, *To Kill a Mockingbird*, published in 1960, had become a near-instant American classic, winning a Pulitzer Prize and then becoming a Best Picture–nominated film starring Gregory Peck. To this day it remains a staple of middle and high school English courses and sells hundreds of thousands of copies each year. A Broadway stage version of the novel, adapted by Aaron Sorkin, won nine Tony awards in 2019 and became the highest-grossing American play in history.

I was assigned to read the novel three years in a row in school—I can't think of any other book I was even told to read twice. I wasn't complaining. Its appeal for me then was mainly that I badly wanted to be friends with the narrator, a young girl named Jean Louise Finch, known to all as "Scout." I wanted to run around with her and her friend Dill, getting up to all kinds of trouble in Maycomb, Alabama. Their fascination with their reclusive neighbor "Boo" Radley was how I felt about most grown-ups at that age—mysterious figures whose lives I was adjacent to but did not understand. Scout was sensitive and tough at the same time, never giving in to the swirling cruelties around her. ("Want to play Boo Radley?" the other boys in my eighth grade class began yelling that year, right before they'd pretend to stab you with a pair of scissors . . . give me Scout and Dill any day.) Gradually, the novel moves into what it is best known for: the ballad of Atticus Finch, Scout's father, who is defending a Black man named Tom Robinson who has been accused of raping a white woman named Mayella Ewell. Scout observes the trial, along with the explicit racism of her town and country when her neighbors attempt to lynch Robinson. Atticus goes on to boldly defend Tom Robinson, despite the community's pressuring, and eventually proves that Mayella had

seduced him willingly. Nevertheless, the all-white jury finds
Robinson guilty. He is ultimately killed trying to escape prison
before his appeal. It's a heartbreaking exposure of American
racism and the corruption of the processes of justice that, until
then, I'd been taught would always come out on the side of truth
and law and goodness.

After intense and widespread acclaim following *To Kill a
Mockingbird*, Harper Lee moved back to Alabama to care for her
dying father in 1962. In 1964, in what would become one of her
last public interviews, she spoke about her desire to become the
"Jane Austen of South Alabama," but after that she published only
a few essays, and never another novel—not for decades. And Lee
remained largely silent as a public figure, though she did speak out
occasionally against school boards and libraries seeking to ban *To
Kill a Mockingbird* as "immoral." Lee was appointed to serve on
the National Council on the Arts by Lyndon B. Johnson, and forty
years later she received the Presidential Medal of Freedom from
George W. Bush, and then the National Medal of Arts from
Barack Obama.

All because of one single, incredible book.

But why did she not follow through on her goal of writing more
about South Alabama? In 2011, her friend the Reverend Thomas
Lane Butts of the Monroeville Methodist Church gave an interview claiming that Lee had told him why she never intended to
publish again: "Two reasons: one, I wouldn't go through the
pressure and publicity I went through with *To Kill a Mockingbird*
for any amount of money. Second, I have said what I wanted to
say, and I will not say it again."

By this time, Lee, at age eighty-five, was living in an assisted
living facility following a stroke some years earlier. In depositions

for a lawsuit in 2013, Lee revealed that she had declining hearing and eyesight, and had, in her ill health, been taken advantage of by the son-in-law of her literary agent as he sought to "dupe" her out of the copyright to *To Kill a Mockingbird*.

That she would stand up to someone trying to trick her was not shocking. But then, in a separate lawsuit soon afterward, Lee also sued the Monroeville County Heritage Museum for selling *Mockingbird*-themed merchandise in its small gift shop. Onlookers in Monroeville and elsewhere were baffled by the long-reclusive author's sudden lawsuit against the small, not-for-profit museum, whose gift shop sales tallied around $28,000 a year. The museum owners and other residents were skeptical of her true involvement in the suit. News reports noted that Lee herself was "profoundly deaf and almost totally blind." How could she be behind this?

Many speculated that the lawsuit was instead coming at the behest of Lee's older sister Alice, then 102, who had once been a lawyer with a powerful local firm, Barnett, Bugg, Lee, and Carter. Monroeville residents believed that the suits were being brought by a real estate lawyer at the firm, Tonja Carter, who had been given power of attorney by Harper Lee in order to represent her in the earlier lawsuit against the literary agent's son-in-law. In those court filings, Carter had asserted that Lee's "mental capabilities" had not been affected by her 2007 stroke, even as others disputed this. Suspicions grew that Carter, not Lee, was the one behind the suit against the museum. Meanwhile, Carter restricted visitors to Lee and even threatened to sue Lee's former neighbor, Marja Mills, over her memoir *Mockingbird Next Door*.

That same year, it was Carter who revealed the existence of a long-lost second novel by Lee, called *Go Set a Watchman*.

People both inside and outside the Lee family knew that Lee had worked for over a decade on a "true-life murder mystery" based on a serial killer in Alexander City, which she had titled *The*

Reverend. In a 2015 *New Yorker* article, Casey Cep described the forty-year speculation around that book, which was supposed to be "perhaps something like *In Cold Blood*"—the genre-smashing true crime book written by Lee's longtime friend Truman Capote (and the model for Dill in *Mockingbird*). Cep met with Tom Radney, the white lawyer for the Black preacher Reverend Maxwell, who had been investigated for those murders. On the condition that it not be quoted directly, Cep was able to read a chapter of the manuscript that Lee had sent to the Radney family. Though Lee felt certain that the accused Reverend Maxwell had been guilty, the book would have described how the white Radney helped to defend and ultimately acquit the Black (alleged) murderer—a tidy reversal of Atticus's eventual position in *Mockingbird*. Lee abandoned the project, though Radney and his family remain eager to see the book published, and Cep notes that "when Harper-Collins announced that Lee would finally publish another book, the Radneys thought it might well be this one. It wasn't, but they haven't given up."

In a press release on February 3, 2015, the publisher at Harper-Collins announced the acquisition of the "recently discovered" novel by Lee, titled *Go Set a Watchman*, to be published in North America and the United Kingdom on July 14. The press release describes how Tonja Carter found the manuscript "affixed" to an original typescript of *To Kill a Mockingbird*. The release declares it to be a "masterpiece" that "will be revered for generations to come."

The release contained a statement from Harper Lee, provided through Tonja Carter.

In the mid-1950s, I completed a novel called *Go Set a Watchman*. It features the character known as Scout as an adult woman and I thought it a pretty decent

effort. My editor, who was taken by the flashbacks to
Scout's childhood, persuaded me to write a novel from
the point of view of the young Scout. I was a first-
time writer, so I did as I was told. I hadn't realized it had survived, so was surprised and delighted
when my dear friend and lawyer Tonja Carter discovered it. After much thought and hesitation I shared
it with a handful of people I trust and was pleased
to hear that they considered it worthy of publication. I am humbled and amazed that this will now be
published after all these years.

The release described *Go Set a Watchman* as being "in many
ways like a sequel to Harper Lee's classic novel." But Lee's own
description of the book said it was completed "in the mid-1950s"
and therefore *before* she'd written *To Kill a Mockingbird*.

How could it be a sequel, written first?

Go Set a Watchman is narrated by a twenty-six-year-old Jean
Louise, who has returned to Maycomb to visit with her father,
Atticus. The novel is set in the 1950s, twenty years after the period
in which *To Kill a Mockingbird* would eventually be set. And so it
seemed reasonable to read it as a sequel to that novel.

In this light, millions began to read, at long last, and many came
away shocked.

The heroic Atticus Finch, who had so powerfully defended Tom
Robinson in *To Kill a Mockingbird*—and for many readers had
been an icon for fifty years, sticking up for the law and standing
up to bigotry—was presented now in *Go Set a Watchman* as a
racist.

After Jean Louise finds a pamphlet in her father's papers called "The Black Plague," she tails him to a white supremacist meeting. She watches in disgust as her father introduces a man at an event who delivers a deeply racist speech. Later, Atticus tells Jean Louise that he does not think Black people should be granted civil rights because they're "not ready." He says that he disagrees with the Supreme Court's decision in *Brown v. Board of Education* and thinks it is unconstitutional. The novel ends with Jean Louise losing her illusions of her father as the hero she believed him to be.

If *Go Set a Watchman* is read as a sequel to *Mockingbird*, then Atticus's transformation is both dark and painful. It is, sadly, completely possible that someone who once upheld the ideals of racial equality might later become corrupted by racist propaganda. Still, at first, readers and reviewers alike were highly confused. Maureen Corrigan at NPR described the book as a "mess" and compared Atticus's transformation as being akin to Captain Ahab rewritten as a "whale lover."

Some suspected that the book, coming so suddenly at a moment when publishers were desperate to find books to speak to the conversations about racial inequality inspired by the Black Lives Matter movement, was cynically assembled from bits and pieces of other earlier drafts of *To Kill a Mockingbird* in order to capitalize on the emerging discourse. Others noted it was strange that there seemed to be no mention whatsoever of the trial of Tom Robinson or many of the other memorable events of *To Kill a Mockingbird*. The novel reads as if these events never occurred.

Close readers soon began to pick up on another clue: passages that were nearly identical to ones found in *To Kill a Mockingbird*.

In the first chapter of *Go Set a Watchman*, for one example, the town of Maycomb is said to be named for "Colonel Mason Maycomb, a man whose misplaced self-confidence and overweening willfulness brought confusion and confoundment to all who rode with him in the Creek Indian Wars." The language is very close to another description found in *To Kill a Mockingbird*: "Colonel Maycomb's misplaced self-confidence and slender sense of direction brought disaster to all who rode with him in the Creek Indian Wars." A description of Scout's Aunt Alexandra's corset is identical in both books: "drew up her bosom to giddy heights, pinched in her waist, flared out her rear, and managed to suggest that Aunt Alexandra's was once an hour-glass figure." One article found several longer passages involving entire duplicated paragraphs, word for word, or nearly so.

What was going on?

Finally it became clear that *Watchman* was actually Lee's *first* attempt at *To Kill a Mockingbird*, never envisioned as a follow-up. The characters of Jean Louise and Atticus were created there, as was Maycomb—in the 1950s, in a story about a young woman coming home to see her father and discovering his racist inclinations in a South that was being transformed by the civil rights movement.

Lee's editor liked the characters and the world of the story, but was most compelled by the scenes where Jean Louise recalls her youth during the Great Depression era. She urged her to rewrite the novel focused on that time in these characters lives, and owing to that revision, *To Kill a Mockingbird* was born.

Perhaps as Lee wrote about Atticus and Scout in the 1930s, she continued to bear in mind her expectations of where they'd each end up in another twenty years. If she did consent with full knowledge to the publication of *Watchman*, then she intended for readers to grapple with Atticus's turn, and to chip away at the façade of the "white savior" narrative in that way. We don't know, unfortunately, how much of this Lee considered, if any at all.

Imagine Harper Lee as a child, the youngest of four, born in Monroeville, Alabama. Her father, an editor and lawyer who served in the Alabama legislature for over a decade. She is, through him, a distant relative of Robert E. Lee, the famed Confederate general. Her father wants her to become a lawyer, but she drops out of college a semester early and moves to New York City to work at a bookstore and manage airline reservations so she can write in her spare time.

She's twenty-three years old. She writes a series of stories about Monroeville and gets an old friend (who happens to be Truman Capote) to show it to his agent, who sells her pages to an editor at J. B. Lippincott. Only the editor says they won't publish her disjointed collection of reminiscences—they want her to quit her job and turn it into a novel instead.

She does. She takes all those fragments and forges them into *Go Set a Watchman*, a real novel—her very first. She sends it back and the editor at Lippincott, a woman named Tay Hohoff, turns it down.

Once again, Lee is told to go back and start over. Write an entirely new book based around a handful of scenes Hohoff liked most—all flashbacks to the character's childhood, minor moments in the scope of all she'd been writing. Instead of a novel about a young woman going home to Maycomb in the present day, dealing with the struggle for civil rights, Lippincott wanted a totally different one, about Maycomb in the Great Depression, when Jean Louise is a young girl.

How many writers would simply give up in that moment, having been sent back, if not to square one, then pretty close to it?

Lee remained resilient. She revised. For two and a half years she took the book apart at the seams and salvaged its scant remains. Lee recalled later that during those years she very nearly threw the entire thing out of the window on several occasions.

Even when she came back with *To Kill a Mockingbird* and the new novel was accepted, Lee was told in no uncertain terms that the book would probably sell poorly—Lippincott expected to print only a few thousand copies in total. Lee said in a 1964 interview that she was simply "hoping for a quick and merciful death at the hands of the reviewers." At best, she said, she could glean some "encouragement" that might propel her on to the next thing. In the end she got more encouragement than she knew what to do with.

There's a reasonable debate to be had over whether *Go Set a Watchman* should have been published differently, or even at all. But I am grateful in the end for something even rarer than a lost masterpiece—the opportunity to trace the unlikely evolution of an American classic, to see the radical ways that a novel can be changed in the revision process, to a point where fifty years later it isn't even immediately obvious to anyone how the drafts relate to one another. In the face of setback after setback, Lee pushed ahead, still believing herself to be capable of more even when encouragement was nowhere to be found.

If we can borrow an ounce of her strength in starting over, who knows what we might end up creating next?

FAIL LIKE A GENIUS

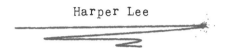

Harper Lee

Too often we think of revision as a refining procedure, where we take the work we've done and "polish" or "tighten" it—making mostly minor, surface-level changes that don't deeply affect the underlying structure. Lee's example shows us the power of *big revision*—one where the attitudes of characters are totally turned upside down, where huge leaps are taken in the timeline, where only a small handful of language remains from the original by the end.

What happens if you rewrite your third-person novel into the first person, with interiority and perspective and language belonging fully to that character? What if you set it twenty or thirty years in the past, like Lee did? What if you relocate it to another city, or state, or country? What if you take the whole thing and tell it from the perspective of a different character entirely?

Whatever the tack you might take here, the key is to swing *big*. Do something that will force you to do away with the bulk of what you have already. It's OK! It's not wasted. You may end up going back to some of it, or most of it. All you're doing in the meantime is coming at the story from a new direction, and seeing what that can teach you about the deficits of the previous direction. Ultimately the right answer may be some new balance between the two, or three, or more versions. But you won't ever find out if you're not first willing to overhaul.

Geniuses Are Mere Mortals

Virginia Woolf

(20)

On the afternoon I finished writing my first novel—which had taken me the better part of two years—I took a walk from my apartment to the grocery store a few blocks away on Manhattan's Lower East Side. I'm sure I was picking up milk or something—my mind was not at all on the task at hand. I wasn't wearing headphones or talking on my cell phone, just walking and thinking about the book and feeling an incredible relief about being "done." In this strange haze, my mind elsewhere, I stepped off the curb without looking and nearly got run over by a city bus.

I felt the wind of it passing, about an inch from my nose. Instinct kicked in and I leaped back onto the sidewalk—people around me were shouting, rushing over to see if I was OK and thank God, I was. And I suppose I was still not quite ready to absorb the fact that I could have died, so the first thought I had was, "At least the book would have been finished!"

This isn't to say I didn't care about anything else—it was just the first thought to come to me in a long line of them. But it stayed with me. It was a whole new relief. If the worst had happened, this thing I'd been making wouldn't be left behind in a heap of disconnected pieces, full of plot holes and character inconsistencies and typos, like Fitzgerald's or any of the others I'd been studying.

Until that moment, I had not realized how anxious I'd been, over the previous twenty months or so, about this exact outcome. A primal fear of incompleteness had been weighing on me, but that fear was also driving me the whole time.

Each time I am working on a new writing project, this feeling returns. It's like I can hear the clock ticking. When I get to sit down to work each morning, I try to feel some gratitude for being there, able to inch it closer to the end.

It's a powerful feeling—and one that I like to think has been felt in some way, shape, or form by everyone else who has ever written anything they've hoped might outlast them.

A Novel for the End of History: Virginia Woolf's *Between the Acts*

Virginia Woolf's final novel is not her best remembered, or her most loved, and she herself did not think much of it at the time that she committed suicide, on March 28, 1941. *Between the Acts* was published after her death by her husband, Leonard, who included this brief note: "The MS. of this book had been completed, but had not been finally revised for the printer, at the time of Virginia Woolf's death. She would not, I believe, have made any large or material alterations in it, though she would probably have made a good many small corrections or revisions before passing the final proofs."

Between the Acts is not incomplete like *The Pale King* or *The Love of the Last Tycoon*. Woolf's last novel reads fluidly from beginning to end; there are no obvious missing sections. We know that she revised it thoroughly. But we also know that she died while still unhappy with the book. In her final message to Leonard, she asked him to burn her notes and papers—which thankfully he didn't do. But would that wish have included *Between the Acts*?

Is this Kafka all over again? Or something else?

Between the Acts is set in a small village in rural England, likely based on the real town of Rodmell, in Sussex, where Virginia Woolf and her husband, Leonard, had spent time outside of London for nearly thirty years. The Woolfs had bought a property in Rodmell known as Monk's House, which Leonard Woolf remarked had been unchanged since the time of Chaucer. While taking in some peace and solitude in the countryside, Virginia Woolf became captivated by the town's position within English history.

Rodmell had been, in many ways, untouched by modern times. According to Woolf's biographer, Hermione Lee, there was "no bus, water, drains or electricity," and to reach the town from the closest major road, Virginia and Leonard had to either walk, ride a bike, or hire a horse-drawn carriage. The town itself was little more than "a pub, a mill, and a forge . . . the church and the school, a village shop, a post office, a bakery, a Club Room (rebuilt as the village hall), a cricket pitch, and several farms."

There, the Woolfs met people who, in fifty years, had never gone past the hill in the distance, and had no intention to ever do so.

Walking through the fields around the town, Woolf felt surrounded by the "relics of passing civilizations." She could see chalk carvings from pre-Christian England, barrows from the Iron Age, fortifications from the Roman conquest, and so on.

The community there had continued, largely untouched by modernity, for generations. Their plainspoken neighbors had names that reached back to the great survey of England performed for William the First, a kind of census known as the Domesday Book, conducted in 1086. Being faced with nearly a thousand years of history had a profound impact on Virginia Woolf, but she was moved as well by something else: its impending end.

Because she also felt that all this history and continuity was presently under threat, a preserved world now decaying around her. Of the 160 families who had lived there 35 years earlier, only 80 remained. None of the boys, according to the local reverend, were being taught to plow. Most would leave to live in other towns, rather than stay and continue the farmwork their fathers had done. Wealthy gentrifiers (like her and Leonard) were taking over the country homes that went up for sale, seeking respite from the hustle and bustle of the city, and the chance to adopt a simpler life, if only transiently.

This world and these themes were what Woolf wanted to present to her readers in *Between the Acts*. She began writing the novel, then called *Pointz Hall*, in the autumn of 1938. She wrote in her diaries that it was a welcome escape from some more serious work that she was doing on a biography of painter Roger Fry, a Bloomsbury Group member who had died a few years earlier, in 1934.

Woolf often took pleasure in working on "illicit" books, according to Lee, particularly her novels, at times when she was supposed to be deep in a "task" book that she'd agreed to write.

Woolf's previous novel, *The Years*, had attempted to explore English history by tracing the changes in urban society through the fifty-year saga of a single family, the Pargiters, between the 1880s and 1930s. Each chapter in the book focuses on a single year in their lives, and many scenes take place in London or Oxford.

Lee argues there is a similarity between this penultimate novel and the final one. Both deal "with the disappointed and ineffectual lives of a family, a class, a country, 'between the acts' of the two World Wars, and re-enact the traumas of the First."

With *Between the Acts*, Woolf focused on an English country house in a town resembling Rodmell, and the events take place over the course of a single day. The townspeople are putting on a pageant about English history, written by one of the locals, Miss La Trobe. As the performance is being prepared and staged, various domestic dramas unfold among the residents of the house—there's a failing marriage, some generational strife, and a plot involving a visiting friend presumed by the others to be a homosexual. Each of these episodes rise and fall in between the rehearsals and preparations, each ultimately interrupted and unresolved as the pageant itself is put together and, that evening, performed for a local audience.

The pageant itself is written in verse and aims to map a variety of English styles throughout its literary history—beginning with a Shakespearean romance before moving into a Restoration comedy and then at last into a triumphant Victorian "panorama." Passing through these styles, La Trobe presents her audience with a summary history of English literary progress. A reader might imagine that this would build to the contemporary moment, in which Woolf and other celebrated intellectuals in the Bloomsbury Group had created their international modernist literary moment. Woolf and others had pioneered new ways of writing, in streams of consciousness, using perspective and fragmented narratives to capture new uncertainties and shift the possibilities of art in a world that had, during the First World War, come totally undone and now found itself hanging only delicately together again.

Miss La Trobe, in the final scene, called "Ourselves," has the actors come out holding large mirrors, which they turn toward the audience, thus bringing them onto the stage, in a sense, and thus the pageant. The experimental gesture suggests that they've quite literally arrived at a moment for reflection on their own place in an ongoing history.

It's a powerful image, but after the pageant ends, the novel concludes with a scene where Miss La Trobe drinks alone at the pub afterward, mostly disappointed with how the play came together. She considers it a failure. But she steadily forms plans for something new to come next. The other characters, their dramas still unresolved, disappear as the night falls over the countryside, and the novel ends.

And what comes next? Presumably, a second act—if they are all currently "between" two—with history and the past behind them and the future up ahead.

Sadly, in that moment, this looming next act was looking grim.

While Woolf finished the first draft of *Pointz Hall* in the fall of 1940, England was speeding headlong into the Second World War. Britain was officially at war with Germany. Gas and food were being rationed; children were evacuating from the cities. Identity cards were required for all citizens and had to be presented upon demand by the authorities. Refugees were pouring into England, residents in coastal areas were relocated. Cardiff and Plymouth had been bombed. As Woolf finished her draft, the Blitz had begun in London and other cities, resulting in enormous destruction and mounting deaths. Any day could easily be the last one, for anyone in England, including the Woolfs.

Their home in London had already been destroyed by bombing, and Leonard and Virginia had gone to live in Sussex year-round to be farther from the destruction. But even way out in Rodmell, among the "relics of civilization," there was no hiding from the war. She and Leonard heard, each day, of more devastation and destruction, of the deaths of more of their friends and countrymen.

They worked and waited, waited and worked.

Initially Woolf had been "very pleased" with how *Pointz Hall* had come together. When she shared it with Leonard, however, he gave it a heavy critique. She was frustrated, and on top of this, her "task" book, the biography of Roger Fry, had met a poor reception that summer as well. It's hard not to imagine how hopeless it all must have seemed—how little it would seem anyone needed a book about the life and times of an art theorist and his postimpressionist aesthetic theories. And did they need a novel about country life in Rodmell, now, at the height of the Blitz?

Initially Woolf was determined to get back to work right away on a new draft. But by January 1941 she was experiencing the return of a hard despair that she had been visited by several times before in her life. Woolf found herself depressed, and largely unable to read or work on *Pointz Hall*.

Instead of going into revisions of the novel, Woolf got through her block by doing some work instead on short stories. In one, "The Symbol," a woman witnesses the death of an Alpine climbing party and becomes obsessed with the mountain where they'd died.

Lee points to a passage from the story that seems to reflect Woolf's own feelings of extreme detachment at that time:

```
To tell you the truth, I have practically no emotion
left. I am sitting on a balcony and at one o'clock
the gong will sound. I have not cut my nails. I have
not done my hair. . . . Vanity of vanities, all is
vanity. When the doctor came I assumed a grave
expression. Yet he guessed that I had only one wish—I
can't even now write that down.
```

Woolf likely suffered from what we'd today call bipolar disorder. It had manifested early in her childhood, following the death of her mother when she was thirteen. Her family soon began noticing her "madness": wild mood swings taking her from deep depressions back up to extended manias. Their family doctor thought it might be cured if Virginia took up regular exercise and rest. He also prescribed that she cease her tutoring and her hobby of creative writing, which he believed were straining her mentally.

At this time, it was commonly held by doctors (all male) that the minds of girls and women were inherently incapable of education or creative work, and that attempts to move beyond the domestic sphere were the root of "hysteria" and other kinds of mental illness like Woolf's. Fortunately, she did not take this misogynistic guidance seriously, but when she collapsed again after her father's death a few years later, and then tried to throw herself out of a window, she was institutionalized. Again, her doctor seemed to believe her mental state stemmed from her ambitions as a writer, and from her education—rather than from grief or from a chemical imbalance, as we'd likely understand her situation today. But in a time when such understanding was still decades away, Woolf's depressive episodes would recur periodically throughout the rest of her life.

Lee notes that Woolf faced these recurrences each time with "exceptional courage, intelligence, and stoicism," and also emphasizes that Woolf was not "mad." She had an illness that could not be treated, only poorly managed, during this particular historical moment. Especially in the hands of doctors inclined to believe that it was being brought on by Woolf reading too many books and straining her feeble female mind, she had reason to be skeptical of their allegedly expert advice. From Woolf's own perspective it was those very books—great literature and great art—that had proven they reliably held the power to pull her out of her despair.

Lee reminds us as well that Woolf thrived throughout most of her life. In spite of her illness and a society without any way to help her with her "glooms," she was one of the century's most innovative writers, a founder of a defining artistic movement, who in her fifty-nine years of life wrote incredible novels, dozens of short stories, book-length essays, works of criticism, plays, and more—works that changed the world, in their way, and continue to do so today. Lee urges us to consider her incredible lifelong strength, rather than dwell heavily on the way her life ended, and I could not agree more.

But what about *Between the Acts*? Did she want it to be her ninth and final novel? As Woolf's depression increased in the winter of 1941, her initial enthusiasm over *Pointz Hall* subsided. Still, she pushed herself and completed a revision late in February 1941, which is when she finally retitled it *Between the Acts*. However, Woolf wrote in her notes that she found it to be "a completely worthless book."

Woolf lived her last months in a time of extreme upheaval, when any future for England as a nation or its literature as a potent cultural force must have seemed in enormous doubt. It may have seemed to Woolf, in the depths of a depression, to be a history-ending moment—there was no reason to think it wouldn't be cataclysmic. Given everything Woolf was struggling with at the time, it makes sense that her outlook on her last book was dim.

In the depths of a depression, it could have been hard to see its value. With all the grand ambitions she had for the book initially, begun years earlier in better times, Woolf may have felt that it came up short, just as Miss La Trobe feels about her pageant at the end of the novel.

Writing a novel is an act of faith only made meaningful by the ever-present possibility of failure. By that same logic, then, an outcome of failure is, in and of itself, also meaningful. This is what

I see in the final scene of *Between the Acts*, and it is a message worth hearing loudly still.

⌒

Both La Trobe's pageant and Woolf's domestic dramas are heavy-handedly symbolic. Still, there are moments where the novel does reveal those "continuities" that Lee wrote about, which struck Woolf so powerfully when first coming to Rodmell thirty years earlier. And there are moments where the novel presents powerfully that decaying fabric as well—the absence of the older families, the boys who'll never learn to plow, the gentrification of the upper classes coming into the villages. Still, if Woolf's dream had been to take a big sweep at all of English history, to show how a country house like that one straddled a whole millennium— *Between the Acts* does not quite get there. But if it fails, it fails meaningfully.

Reading the final pages of *Between the Acts*, feeling a dissatisfaction with it, knowing Woolf felt it too, we are left with two options. A scholar might simply file it away as a "lesser" work to disregard and unrecommend. But a writer might, instead, see something: a residual potential. World events and brain chemistry were not on Woolf's side in 1941, but what about us? What about now? Is quaint, frozen-in-time Rodmell so unlike a thousand other villages and towns right now, surrounded by history, threatened by a loss of their young generation, old families being replaced by urbanites heading to the country? Today it is a Maine fishing village, or a Rust Belt town in Ohio, or a medieval mountainside in Sicily, or a settlement off the coast of New Zealand somewhere. How would a Miss La Trobe from our own little world create a pageant from our own culture's grander history? Will it go over any better with the crowd in the end? Can we pick up where one of the greatest geniuses in the last century left off? Maybe that's hubris, or a disaster waiting to happen. But then again . . .

This, truly, is the greatest thrill of so much unfinished business. It invites us to pick up where someone else left off. To accept a passed parcel, no matter how messily wrapped, from long ago. *Here*, they seem to say, *I couldn't get this to work, but could you?* Once we see that these geniuses aren't so different from us, it feels less sacrilegious to pick up where they left off.

The curtain is rising. The next act begins now, and it begins with you.

FAIL LIKE A GENIUS

Virginia Woolf

Virginia Woolf first began writing *Between the Acts* while she was hard at work already on the biography of Roger Fry. Woolf's own biographer, Hermione Lee, observed that she often worked on two books at once in this way. First, she had the "task" book that she felt under some obligation to write, and second she had the "illicit" book that she stole time away from the first one to write on the sly.

I've noticed that I do this too. There's nothing I enjoy more than "cheating" on one project with another. As soon as I chart out the first thing, inevitably I'll have some barely-thought-out side project where my attention wanders.

Writing requires careful planning, goal-setting, and strategizing, especially when one is trying to make time to do it in between actual paying jobs and family responsibilities and all the rest. But when we get too organized what starts out as a secret, daring, "illicit," joyful, even selfish thing that we were doing for the pure pleasure of it . . . turns into work. We may find that we've lost the fun completely.

Juggling two books at once may seem like a bad idea, but it may be a great way to keep the fires burning. Great writing should always feel a little "illicit," so go ahead and indulge—write what excites you, when it excites you—and if what happens next surprises you, all the better.

In any case, whatever your main focus is, don't hold yourself back from playing around with something else on the side, especially if it feels fun and lower-stakes than the first thing. Maybe it goes no-where. Maybe it reinvigorates your original project. Maybe it overtakes it, in the end. Maybe it becomes the start of your next great masterpiece. There's only one way to find out.

Geniuses Are Never Finished

Michelangelo, Kurt Cobain, Sanditon, and Drood!

O nce I began looking for unfinished works, I found them everywhere. The interest that was piqued all those years ago as I read *The Love of the Last Tycoon* for the first time has, by now, reverberated through my practices as a writer and as a teacher. My eye more and more drifts away from the perfect, the finished, and toward that which isn't and can never be.

Sightseeing in Florence at the Accademia Gallery, I was as eager as the thousand other tourists to see Michelangelo's exquisite sculpture of David, one of the icons of beauty and perfection and completion. Study it for ages and you won't find a contour that needs a bit more shaping or a line that isn't quite right. It is downright miraculous, and looking at it I can understand why people in Michelangelo's day called him Il Divino, or "the divine one," and believed that he was the literal tool of God. The David is one of those things that manages to not only live up to its own hype but exceed it. It is what we're all taught that great art *is*.

But then I wandered a few rooms down, trying to escape the crowds for a moment, and came across four more Michelangelo sculptures, not nearly as famous as the David, but to me just as striking in a different, even more powerful way.

"The Prisoners" (sometimes also called "The Slaves") are four human figures that seem to be emerging from individual blocks of marble. One character, a representation of Atlas, is nearly fully formed, but his legs remain bound up in the rock. Another has no head and seems to be almost trying push himself out of the raw marble. The next is barely more than a torso and one leg, folded up as if climbing out of the bed of rock. The last covers his face, his hand still attached in marble to the opposite shoulder, his other arm lost behind him. Unlike in the David, studying these Prisoners I can see the still-rough marks of Michelangelo's chiseling, the places where the marble goes from smooth to coarse and irregular.

These sculptures are called *non finito*, or "not finished," and one guidebook describes them as representing "the eternal struggle of the human spirit to free itself from the material world."

But this suggests that Michelangelo designed them this way. That he intended for these sculptures to remain in this state. Or perhaps he began them thinking he would complete them and then decided, along the way, not to. Are they, in other words, *finished* by remaining unfinished? Or were they abandoned along the way, discarded because they were not coming out right, or because something else interrupted the great sculptor—another block of marble, or some more pressing financial demand?

Scholars have noted that Michelangelo left works unfinished in this manner more and more often as his career developed, and some contend that it was an artistic choice, an attempt to represent the nature of art itself, or to exemplify a larger spiritual struggle. In the philosophy of art put forth by Plato, all works of art are "unfinished" in that they can never completely represent their counterparts in heaven where all things are entirely free of the constraints of physical materials. Michelangelo leaving his Prisoners trapped in that very unfinished material could then be seen as a reminder of our earthly distance from the divine.

Meanwhile, others argue that Michelangelo left an increasing number of works non finito because of more mundane, human reasons. In some of his letters he indicates that other works had to be abandoned in progress because the pope or one of his other demanding patrons were pushing Michelangelo move onto something else.

Whether a work of art is left incomplete by intention or by circumstance, it holds a value that is even more interesting because of that incompleteness.

In Book 35 of *Natural History* by Pliny the Elder, written in 77 AD, he says this about the appeal of the non finito:

```
It is a very unusual and memorable fact that the
last works of artists and their unfinished pictures
. . . are more admired than those which they fin-
ished, because in them are seen the preliminary
drawings left visible and the artists' actual
thoughts, and in the midst of approval's beguilement
we feel regret that the artist's hand while engaged
in the work was removed by death.
```

By this logic, the Prisoners have some added power today, centuries after Michelangelo's death, because they will never be finished. Their roughness reminds us that he was not divine, but a man, then alive and now dead. Seeing his non finito works, his unfinished business, we feel grief at the loss of him that we don't feel when we stare at the David, through which the sculptor has almost made himself immortal.

One random afternoon in the fall of 2002, as I was driving in my car and listening to the radio, I heard something so incredible that I had to pull over.

Kurt Cobain's voice was coming out of the speakers.

It was a Nirvana song, clearly, but it was not one that I'd ever heard before.

At this point, Cobain had been dead for eight years. And in truth, he'd been dead since I—a musical late bloomer—had first listened to Nirvana, in the late '90s. I'd thought before about how my older cousin, who had seen Nirvana perform in Buffalo in 1993, and who had mourned Cobain's suicide as the news had broken, would always fundamentally have a different experience of his music than me. He'd seen him *alive*, but to me, Cobain had always been dead.

But since I had become a late fan, I'd sought out everything Nirvana had ever recorded along with all the live albums I could find. By 2002 I thought that I'd long since come to the end of the catalog, but suddenly, there on the radio, was something new.

The song, "You Know You're Right," I'd later learn, had been one of the last recordings done by the band and had never been finished, but plans to work further on the track after an upcoming tour were ended by Cobain's suicide. Since then, it had been tied up in a legal battle between Cobain's wife, Courtney Love, and the surviving members of Nirvana. But someone leaked the MP3 on the internet. Fans had begun passing it along to each other, and now radio DJs were broadcasting it widely without permission.

All I knew at the time was that it felt like I was being visited by a ghost. What a gift! To get something more, long after I'd thought it was all gone. So what if it was still a little raw, still off-balance? Wasn't that, if anything, better? More interesting?

As Pliny observed, the unfinished work of art takes on a special dimension—it forces us to consider that the artist was a person, not a god. It reminds us that the work was *all* made in the first place. We have to ask ourselves practical questions in experiencing the work. Why had the artist stopped making it, or ceased revising it, or chosen to leave it off the B-side?

We don't think about these things in the same way when we listen to "Smells Like Teen Spirit" or stand in the presence of the David. Their apparent perfection can fool us into feeling like they sprang forth fully formed from the marble block, or the 1969 Fender Mustang electric guitar in Lake Placid Blue. The non finito reminds us that they didn't. Of course they didn't. This makes them more incredible, not less.

I used to worry about leaving behind work that is incomplete, but studying the many strange afterlives of these unfinished novels has altered my thinking. Rather than see the non finito as tragic, I've begun to see them as something else, something quite special: as little gifts from beyond.

Take Jane Austen, for one example. I spoke previously about her early finished but abandoned works like *Lady Susan* and her later unfinished book, *The Watsons*. But she left behind another unfinished novel, *Sanditon*, which was only about eleven chapters when she died in July 1817.

She had begun working on the book that January, but gave up after about ten weeks, too ill to continue. The book revolves around a fishing town on the British coast called Sanditon, which one of the characters, Mr. Parker, hopes to reinvent as a seaside resort. At the time these were popular destinations, particularly for those recovering from illnesses, and the idea surely came to Austen under the same circumstances. As she was suffering more and more from an unknown illness—today believed by some to have been either Addison's disease or Hodgkin's lymphoma—Austen thought back on the year she herself had spent living in the seaside town of Worthing in 1805, and her friendship with a man named Edward Ogle who was creating a similar modern resort. In the novel, the three children of Mr. Parker are all pronounced hypochondriacs, who use their "poor health" as an excuse to sit around in Sanditon doing nothing all day—a humorous poke at the society types who Austen saw making similar excuses to go on long holidays at the beach for medical reasons.

Sadly, Austen's own health really was in decline, and there's some evidence that she ignored many of the warning signs, though it isn't clear that the doctors of the time would have been able to do much to help her. The unfinished novel was still in its first draft form but was eventually published almost a hundred years later, in 1925, as "Fragment of a Novel." What exists of the book does a fine job of setting up the premise, introducing us to the characters and to the world of Sanditon, but gets almost nowhere beyond that.

But almost a hundred years after its delayed publication, the "fragment of a novel" inspired Welsh screenwriter Andrew Davies to adapt *Sanditon* into a TV series. Airing on iTV in the UK in 2019 and then in the US on PBS's *Masterpiece* anthology, the eight-part series takes the initial twelve chapters that Austen wrote as source material, but for the final episodes they needed to continue the story beyond where she'd stopped.

Davies's adaptation then became something else—a *continuation*, a "finishing" of the original unfinished work. That's a bold thing to do, on the one hand, and Davies acknowledged in interviews that there was a lot of pressure in taking up a project left behind by one of the language's greatest authors.

But at the same time, why not give it a try? Making a *Sanditon* for TV was already an adaptation, no different than in 1995 when Andrew Davies did it for the six-episode miniseries of *Pride and Prejudice*. It's always a collaboration with the deceased, going beyond the source material in many other subtler ways that we're more comfortable with when the novel itself was "finished."

And Davies isn't saying that he has now finished Austen's novel. Without knowing how Austen would have concluded *Sanditon*, all anyone can say is that it presents *a possible finishing*. Someone else might come along at any time and tie things up in some other way entirely.

Originally the *Sanditon* series was not meant to go beyond the eight episodes that were aired, but the show earned such an ardent following that fans began a campaign to pressure PBS to bring it back for a second season. They eventually did so, and at the time of this writing, the series has since had a full third season as well. We might think of these new seasons almost as *sequels* now, moving far beyond the original scope of Austen's unfinished novel, developing new stories and characters to live and love in the world that she created.

Similar TV adaptations have been made of other unfinished works. In 2016, Amazon created a TV series based on *The Last Tycoon*, starring Matt Bohmer as Monroe Stahr and Lily Collins as Cecelia Brady. It was canceled after one season, unable to get much further past where Fitzgerald had left the story himself.

At the time of my writing this, the TV writer and director Ryan Murphy is creating a new season of his *Feud* anthology, based on *Capote's Women* and the author's betrayal of his "swans" with the writing of *Answered Prayers*. Will that show renew some interest in solving the many mysteries around the unfinished book? I suppose there's always some chance that someone manages to find the Greyhound bus locker or the safe-deposit box where he claimed to have stashed it. But failing that, there's no resolution in reach. *Answered Prayers* will go on being a whole host of possible books: a success, a failure, a masterpiece, a middling effort, an utter farce. As long as it remains unfound, it is all of those things at once, and none of them, and so we can't let it go.

As I've worked on this book over the past several years, almost everyone I've mentioned it to has had some suggestion for something else I have to read. These unfinished books are obscure by nature and yet beloved by any true fan of any particular writer. Did I know that Longfellow left behind unfinished poems? What about Charlotte Brontë's *Emma Brown*? Or Willa Cather's *Hard Punishments*, set in medieval Avignon? There's Roberto Bolaño's *2666*, which he'd originally planned to publish as five individual books, but which after he died were instead released as one gigantic epic. What about Büchner's *Woyzeck*? Hunter S. Thompson's *Prince Jellyfish*? The three existing chapters of *The Decembrists*, a follow-up to *War and Peace* that Tolstoy never finished? (He'd even planned to write a third book, to make a full trilogy.) For my entire life, Robert Caro has been writing his Years of Lyndon Johnson series and, at age eighty-seven, is supposedly almost done with the fifth and final volume. And then there's the seemingly endless wait for George R. R. Martin to publish *The Winds of Winter*, which wouldn't even yet conclude his Song of Ice and Fire.

Shakespeare's *Timon of Athens* was drafted but never completed by the Bard, and another play, *Two Noble Kinsmen*, is known to have been written in collaboration with another playwright, John Fletcher, but it isn't clear if they worked on it together or if Fletcher finished it for him later. And in the opera world there are unfinished works as well, by Mozart and others. Some, like Alban Berg's *Lulu* or Puccini's *Turandot*, were left unfinished by the composers' deaths and were only "completed" by others afterward.

What are they? What might they have been?

The work is never finished.

At the Museum of Modern Art in New York City, there was a major exhibition in 2017 called "Unfinished," featuring 197 non finito works from the Renaissance to the present day, including by artists like Titian, Cézanne, Turner, Rembrandt, Pollock, and Rauschenberg. "Unfinished" invited visitors, à la Pliny the Elder, to consider the inherent beauty of these works. Each piece is both a glimpse into the creative process that wrought it and an invitation to the viewer to continue the project. How would you finish what they didn't?

This may seem unthinkably bold. In a literal sense, to walk up to an unfinished Cézanne with your own wet paintbrush would be a criminal act. But as you look at the canvas that wasn't painted, or the marble that wasn't chiseled, you must be privately considering how you would have proceeded, if you were them. So why not carry that impulse on, to your own canvas, or your own block of marble, and see what comes?

In truth, this happens all the time. Art communicates, passes ideas from one generation to the next, one century to the next. Even finished, it invites us to continue the thought. And when unfinished, it almost demands it.

In 1870, when Charles Dickens died of a stroke after writing six of the twelve expected installments of *The Mystery of Edwin Drood*, the author was scarcely buried when writers began scrambling to try and finish the novel in his absence. Because the book was being put out serially, at the time of his death the reading public had already voraciously consumed the first three sections. Everyone was aware that after these, the novel would still only be half done.

One writer, Robert Henry Newell, living in America, took a stab at completing the book, rushing to get his version out by the end of that same year. But audiences found his conclusion to be farcical and unappealing. A journalist, Henry Morford, tried again a year later. Morford's book was published as a "sequel" he and his publisher claimed was a collaboration between the deceased Dickens and the author Wilkie Collins, who denied having anything to do with it. A year after that, a Vermont painter named Thomas Power James wrote another version, and alleged that he had done so while psychically channeling the spirit of the dead Dickens, and that he was merely its "ghost writer." (Improbably, this version was the most successful, in part because Arthur Conan Doyle wrote that he found the style convincing and believed James's claims. This edition sold millions of copies across America and Europe.)

In 1985 the British American musician Rupert Holmes, best known at the time for writing the song "Escape (The Piña Colada Song)," decided to adapt the Dickens novel into a musical comedy. The play is officially called *The Mystery of Edwin Drood* but is often informally called *Drood*, or *Drood!* with a theatrical exclamation point.

Holmes's Dickens adaptation ended up winning five Tony awards that year, including Best Musical. One of the secrets to his notable success in a field where so many had failed before was that the musical cleverly presents the audience with a Choose Your Own Adventure where, each night, the theatergoers vote on what will happen in that night's performance.

The play, then, becomes a new experience each time, and so invites repeat attendance. In artistic terms, it succeeds by not claiming any single ending is the one Dickens would himself have chosen. Rather, Holmes allows for a full range of possibilities, making a metareference to the chaotic sequeling and finishing that had been going on for a century already. The musical becomes an embrace of unfinishedness and incompleteness. The story might go many different ways, and all of these options are essential parts of the whole, even the ones you didn't happen to see.

This, to me, speaks to one of the most real and powerful appeals of these unfinished works, and gives the best reason I've found as to why we're drawn back to them again and again.

Their incompleteness is a gift that will never stop giving. The blank pages at the end, the revisions still unmade to the beginnings—it not only presents us with a glimpse into the process, but it invites us to become a part of that process ourselves.

Geniuses: They're Just like Us!

The geniuses I've written about in this book *are* geniuses—my intention has never been to dethrone them, but only to dismantle our idea of what we mean when we call them that. Maybe they were indeed born with some gifts, some talents, that we weren't—maybe there are some people with an "ear for dialogue" or an "eye for detail." Savants and prodigies do exist, and I can't explain them away, nor would I want to. What's crucial is that the rest of us do not hold ourselves to those impossible standards. If you were blessed with musical gifts or a mathematical mind, then by all means, make the most of that. But if you, like me, were born without these things, as is overwhelmingly likely, I believe whatever we weren't given by nature, we can still develop in nurture.

"Talent is insignificant," James Baldwin remarked in an interview. "I know a lot of talented ruins. Beyond talent lie all the usual words: discipline, love, luck, but, most of all, endurance."

In school, and for two decades since then, I rubbed elbows with writers who I will happily admit were far more talented than I was. Not all, or even most, of those people are still writing today. Why? I ask myself—and I take no pleasure in seeing them move on, though mostly they seem quite happy doing other things. Talent alone isn't enough.

If the writers in this book have some amount of talent in common, then they have that in common also with thousands of others who never got very far at all. What matters far more are all those other things that Baldwin describes—and those traits can all be studied, learned, and practiced. (Aside from "luck," which is often crucial—but luck will change, too, on a long enough timeline.)

In one of his last major interviews, David Foster Wallace spoke to the French magazine *Le Nouvel Observateur* about the writers that he admired most. After rattling off a healthy-sized list, Wallace pointed out that these giants, to him, were not only giants of technical prowess or canonical importance, but giants in their willingness to embrace the world for all its complexities and harms and contradictions. Of these he said, "What are envied and coveted here seem to me to be qualities of human beings—capacities of spirit—rather than technical abilities or special talents."

This, I think, is the true common denominator of these geniuses. None of them were perfect, and some not by a long shot. But we look up to them nonetheless because they share in something like that capacity of spirit, and we can share in it too, especially when we remind ourselves that every genius is a failure, every genius is only mortal, every genius is only human—unfinished and incomplete.

In my copy of *The Love of the Last Tycoon,* there is a line in the first chapter that I underlined three times, there in the beautiful sky-blue room with huge windows. Cecelia/Cecilia has run into a failed producer named Mr. Schwartze (though sometimes he's "Schwartz") who explains to her that a writer is someone who "knows everything and at the same time he knows nothing." Cecelia/Cecilia thinks to herself that she likes writers because no matter what you ask them, you'll always get an answer. Then she explains, "Writers aren't people exactly. Or, if they're any good, they're a whole lot of people trying so hard to be one person."

This line has made its way onto the index cards I've stuck up over my various writing desks, and into the fronts of many of my little notebooks. It reminds me that to be any good, I'll need to be a whole lot of people too: friends, family, first readers, editors, agents, librarians, students, colleagues.

No one does it alone.

You are in good company, with the geniuses in this book. Hold them in your mind as you go. All the incredible things they've done and all the ridiculous mistakes that they've made. They strived for the same things as you, raced against the same clocks as you, beheld the same beauties and horrors, found the same bright lines to follow in the dark.

With all of that on your side, you are every bit the genius as anyone.

Bibliography

1. GENIUSES WRITE BAD DRAFTS

Brown, David S. *Paradise Lost: A Life of F. Scott Fitzgerald*. Harvard University Press. Cambridge, MA. 2017.

Bruccoli, Matthew J., ed. *F. Scott Fitzgerald: A Life in Letters*. Charles Scribner's Sons. New York, NY. 1994.

Fitzgerald, F. Scott. "Afternoon of an Author." *Esquire*. August 1, 1936. https://classic.esquire.com/article/1936/8/1/afternoon-of-an-author.

———. *The Love of the Last Tycoon: The Authorized Text*. Edited by Matthew Bruccoli. Scribner. New York, NY. 1994.

Irwin, John T. *F. Scott Fitzgerald's Fiction: An Almost Theatrical Innocence*. Johns Hopkins University Press. Baltimore, MD. 2014.

Meyers, Jeffrey. *Scott Fitzgerald: A Biography*. HarperCollins. New York, NY. 1994.

"Stories Scavenged for Tycoon." F. Scott Fitzgerald Papers. Manuscripts Division, Department of Special Collections, Princeton University Library. Princeton, NJ.

2. GENIUSES LACK CONFIDENCE

Balint, Benjamin. *Kafka's Last Trial: The Case of a Literary Legacy*. Norton. New York, NY. 2018.

Benjamin, Ross. "A Century On, the Search for the Real Franz Kafka Continues." *New York Times*. February 2, 2023. https://www.nytimes.com/2023/02/02/opinion/translating-franz-kafka-diaries.html.

Friedländer, Saul. *Franz Kafka: The Poet of Shame and Guilt*. Yale University Press. New Haven, CT. 2013.

Kafka, Franz. *The Trial*. Translated by Breon Mitchell. Schocken Books. New York, NY. 1995

———. *Amerika*. Translated by Edwin and Willa Muir. Doubleday. New York, NY. 1996.

———. *The Castle*. Translated by Edwin and Willa Muir. Schocken Books. New York, NY. 1995.

Stach, Reiner. *Kafka: The Years of Insight*. Translated by Shelley Frisch. Princeton University Press. Princeton, NJ. 2013.

Updike, John. "Foreword." *The Complete Stories*. Schocken Books. New York, NY. 1995.

3. GENIUSES GET OFF TO A BAD START

Alcott, Louisa May. "Aunt Nellie's Diary." *Strand*. Farmington Hills, MI. Summer 2020.

Cheever, Susan. *Louisa May Alcott: A Personal Biography*. Simon and Schuster. New York, NY. 2011.

Fortin, Jacey. "The End of This Louisa May Alcott Story May Disappoint You." *New York Times*. June 25, 2020. https://www.nytimes.com/2020/06/25/books/louisa-may-alcott-new-story-strand.html.

Publishers Weekly. Review of *The Inheritance*, by Louisa May Alcott. March 31, 1997. https://www.publishersweekly.com/9780525457565.

Reisen, Harriet. *Louisa May Alcott: The Woman Behind* Little Women. Henry Holt. New York, NY. 2009.

Shealy, Daniel. "Introduction to Aunt Nellie's Diary." *Strand*. Farmington Hills, MI. Summer 2020.

Sullivan, Walter. "Einstein Revealed as Brilliant in Youth." *New York Times*. February 14, 1984. https://www.nytimes.com/1984/02/14/science/einstein-revealed-as-brilliant-in-youth.html.

Stern, Madeleine B. *Louisa May Alcott: A Biography*. Northeastern University Press. Boston, MA. 1999.

Tanner, Nick. "Young, Gifted and Hack." *Guardian*. January 9, 2007. https://www.theguardian.com/books/booksblog/2007/jan/09/juvenilia.

4. GENIUSES DON'T MEASURE UP

Amis, Martin. "The Problem with Nabokov." *Guardian*. November 14, 2009.

Banville, John. "Save It." *Times Literary Supplement*. London, England. February 14, 2008. https://www.thetimes.co.uk/article/save-it-k2t3rzlmgck.

Coates, Steve. "Saving Laura, Part 2; Or, Nabokov's Walled Garden." *New York Times*. April 24, 2008. https://archive.nytimes.com/artsbeat

.blogs.nytimes.com/2008/04/24/saving-laura-part-2-or-nabokovs
-walled-garden.

McCrum, Robert. "The Final Twist in Nabokov's Untold Story." *Guardian*. October 24, 2009. https://www.theguardian.com/books/2009
/oct/25/nabokov-original-of-laura-mccrum.

Nabokov, Dmitri. "Nabokov's Final Literary Striptease." *Newsnight*.
BBC Two. London, England. November 18, 2008.

Nabokov, Vladimir. *The Original of Laura*. Edited and with an introduction by Dmitri Nabokov. Knopf. New York, NY. November 17, 2009.

Stoppard, Tom. "Burn It." *Times Literary Supplement*. London, England.
February 14, 2008. https://www.thetimes.co.uk/article/burn-it
-sqtglk2xmcj.

Theroux, Alexander. "In the Cards, a Last Hand." *Wall Street Journal*.
November 20, 2009. https://www.wsj.com/articles/SB10001424052748
7045762045745300528544454092.

Thurman, Judith. "Silent Partner." *New Yorker*. November 8, 2015.
https://www.newyorker.com/magazine/2015/11/16/silent-partner
-books-judith-thurman.

5. GENIUSES GET BLOCKED

Butler, Octavia. "A World Without Racism." Speech at UN World
Conference Against Racism. September 1, 2001. https://legacy.npr.org
/programs/specials/racism/010830.octaviabutleressay.html.

———. "'Devil Girl From Mars': Why I Write Science Fiction." Lecture
at Massachusetts Institute of Technology. February 19, 1998. https://
www.blackhistory.mit.edu/archive/transcript-devil-girl-mars
-why-i-write-science-fiction-octavia-butler-1998.

———. "Notes on Writing." Octavia Butler Archives at the Huntington
Library, Art Collections, and Botanical Gardens. https://huntington.
org/exhibition/octavia-e-butler-telling-my-stories.

———. *Parable of the Sower*. Grand Central Publishing. New York, NY.
2000.

———. *Parable of the Talents*. Grand Central Publishing. New York,
NY. 2019.

Canavan, Gerry. "'There's Nothing New / Under The Sun, / But There
Are New Suns': Recovering Octavia E. Butler's Lost Parables." *Los*

Angeles Review of Books. June 9, 2014. https://lareviewofbooks.org
/article/theres-nothing-new-sun-new-suns-recovering-octavia-e-butlers
-lost-parables.

Konnikova, Maria. "How to Beat Writer's Block." *New Yorker*. March
11, 2016. https://www.newyorker.com/science/maria-konnikova
/how-to-beat-writers-block.

Rilke, Ranier Maria. *Letters to a Young Poet*. Translated by M. D.
Herter Norton. W.W. Norton. New York, NY. 1993.

Steinem, Gloria. "A Celebration of Octavia Butler's Groundbreaking
Science-Fiction Novel." Early Bird Books. February 26, 2016. https://
earlybirdbooks.com/gloria-steinem-on-octavia-butler.

Warrick, Pamela. "An Alternative Universe." *Los Angeles Times*. October
18, 1998. https://www.latimes.com/archives/la-xpm-1998-oct-18-tm
-33581-story.html.

6. GENIUSES DON'T GET IT RIGHT THE FIRST TIME

Burns, Marian. "The Chronology of Flannery O'Connor's 'Why Do the
Heathen Rage?'" *Flannery O'Connor Bulletin* 11 (Autumn 1982):
58–75. Accessed through JSTOR.

Burns, Stuart L. "How Wide Did 'The Heathen' Range?" *Flannery
O'Connor Bulletin* 4 (Autumn 1975): 25–41. Accessed through
JSTOR.

Davies, Peter Ho. *The Art of Revision: The Last Word*. Graywolf. New
York, NY. 2021.

O'Connor, Flannery. *The Complete Stories*. Introduction by Robert
Giroux. Farrar, Straus & Giroux. New York, NY. 1971.

Wilson, Jessica Hooten. "*Why Do the Heathen Rage?* Flannery O'Connor's Unfinished Novel: Presented by Dr. Jessica Hooten Wilson."
Dallas Institute of Humanities and Culture. YouTube. September 14,
2020. https://www.youtube.com/watch?v=B0RThHhgBSs.

7. GENIUSES OFTEN QUIT

Austen, Jane. *Lady Susan, The Watsons, Sanditon*. Edited by Margaret
Drabble. Penguin Classics. New York, NY. 1974.

Morris, Edmund. *Edison*. Random House. New York, NY. 2019.

Stillman, Whit. *Love and Friendship: In Which Jane Austen's Lady Susan Vernon Is Entirely Vindicated*. Little, Brown & Company. New York, NY. 2016.

Tomalin, Claire. *Jane Austen: A Life*. Vintage. New York, NY. 1999.

8. GENIUSES STILL HAVE TO DO THE DISHES

Alexander, Paul. *Rough Magic: A Biography of Sylvia Plath*. Penguin Books. New York, NY. 1992.

Hughes, Ted. "The Art of Poetry, no. 71." Interview with Drue Heinz. *Paris Review*, Spring 1995. https://www.theparisreview.org/interviews/1669/the-art-of-poetry-no-71-ted-hughes.

Hughes, Ted, Frances McCullough, and Sylvia Plath. *The Journals of Sylvia Plath*. Anchor. New York, NY. 1998.

Kean, Danuta. "Unseen Sylvia Plath Letters Claim Domestic Abuse by Ted Hughes." *Guardian*. April 11, 2017. https://www.theguardian.com/books/2017/apr/11/unseen-sylvia-plath-letters-claim-domestic-abuse-by-ted-hughes.

Plath, Sylvia. *The Letters of Sylvia Plath: Volume 1, 1940–1956*. Edited by Karen V. Kukil and Peter Steinberg. Harper. New York, NY. 2017.

———. *The Letters of Sylvia Plath: Volume 2, 1956–1963*. Edited by Karen V. Kukil and Peter Steinberg. Faber & Faber. London, England. 2019.

———. *The Unabridged Journals of Sylvia Plath*. Edited by Karen V. Kukil and Peter Steinberg. Anchor. New York, NY. 2000.

Sylvia Plath Collection. Smith College Special Collections. Neilson Library. Northampton, MA.

Waldman, Katy. "A Lost Story by Sylvia Plath Contains the Seeds of the Writer She Would Become." *New Yorker*. January 7, 2019. https://www.newyorker.com/books/page-turner/a-lost-story-by-sylvia-plath-contains-the-seeds-of-the-writer-she-would-become.

9. GENIUSES HOLD GRUDGES

Franklin, Ruth. *Shirley Jackson: A Rather Haunted Life*. Liveright. New York, NY. September 27, 2016.

Jackson, Shirley. *Come Along with Me.* Preface by Stanley Edgar Hyman. Viking Press. 1968.

———. *The Letters of Shirley Jackson.* Edited by Laurence Jackson Hyman. Random House. New York, NY. July 13, 2021.

10. GENIUSES STRUGGLE (BUT NOT BECAUSE THEY'RE GENIUSES)

Lipsky, David. *Although Of Course You End Up Becoming Yourself: A Road Trip with David Foster Wallace.* Broadway Books. New York, NY. 2010.

Max, D. T. *Every Love Story Is a Ghost Story: A Life of David Foster Wallace.* Viking. New York, NY. 2012.

Roberts, Sam. "On Acknowledgments, the Inquisition Was Easier." *New York Times.* November 27, 2003. https://www.nytimes.com/2003/11/27/books/on-acknowledgments-the-inquisition-was-easier.html.

Wallace, David Foster. *David Foster Wallace: The Last Interview and Other Conversations.* Melville House. New York, NY. 2012.

———. *Everything and More: A Compact History of Infinity.* Norton. New York, NY. 2003.

———. "Good People." *New Yorker.* January 28, 2007. https://www.newyorker.com/magazine/2007/02/05/good-people.

———. *Infinite Jest.* Tenth anniversary paperback ed. Back Bay Books. New York, NY. 2006.

———. *The Pale King.* Editor's note by Michael Pietsch. Little, Brown. New York, NY. 2011.

———. "Wiggle Room." *New Yorker.* February 28, 2009. https://www.newyorker.com/magazine/2009/03/09/wiggle-room.

11. GENIUSES GET LOST IN THE WEEDS

Barnes, Julian. "Flaubert, C'est Moi." *New York Review of Books.* May 25, 2006. https://www.nybooks.com/articles/2006/05/25/flaubert-cest-moi.

Borges, Jorge Luis. "A Defense of *Bouvard and Pécuchet.*" Essay translated by Esther Allen. In *Borges: Selected Non-Fictions.* Penguin. New York, NY. 2000.

Calvino, Italo. *Six Memos for the New Millennium*. Translated by Patrick Creagh. Mariner. Boston, MA. 2016.

Flaubert, Gustave. *Bouvard and Pécuchet*. Translated by Mark Polizzotti. Dalkey Archive Press. Funks Grove, IL. 2005

Frye, Northrop. *Anatomy of Criticism*. Princeton University Press. Princeton, NJ. 1971.

Hitchens, Christopher. "I'm with Stupide." *New York Times*. January 22, 2006. https://www.nytimes.com/2006/01/22/books/review /im-with-stupide.html.

Wood, James. *How Fiction Works*. Tenth anniversary ed. Picador. New York, NY. 2018.

12. GENIUSES BITE OFF MORE THAN THEY CAN CHEW

Callahan, John F. "Introduction." *Juneteenth*. Modern Library. New York, NY. 2021.

Ellison, Ralph. *Juneteenth*. Vintage. New York, NY. 2021.

———. *Three Days Before the Shooting . . .* Edited by John F. Callahan. Random House. New York, NY. 2010.

Remnick, David. "Visible Man." *New Yorker*. March 6, 1994. https://www.newyorker.com/magazine/1994/03/14/ralph-ellison-visible-man.

13. GENIUSES KEEP SECRETS

Highsmith, Patricia. "First Person Novel." Swiss Literary Archives. Bern, Switzerland.

Meaker, Marijane. *Highsmith: A Romance of the 1950s*. Cleis Press. San Francisco, CA. 2003.

Schenkar, Joan. *The Talented Miss Highsmith: The Secret Life and Serious Art of Patricia Highsmith*. St. Martin's Press. New York, NY. 2009.

14. GENIUSES BURN BRIDGES

Capote, Truman. *Answered Prayers*. Vintage. New York, NY. 1994.

Clarke, Gerald. *Capote: A Biography*. Simon and Schuster. New York, NY. 1988.

Clarke, Gerald, ed. *Too Brief a Treat: The Letters of Truman Capote.* Vintage. New York, NY. 2005.

Leamer, Laurence. *Capote's Women: A True Story of Love, Betrayal, and a Swan Song for an Era.* Putnam. New York, NY. 2021.

Schultz, William Todd. *Tiny Terror: Why Truman Capote (Almost) Wrote* Answered Prayers. Oxford University Press. New York, NY. 2011.

15. GENIUSES GET REJECTED

Rowley, Hazel. *Richard Wright: The Life and Times.* University of Chicago Press. Chicago, IL. 2008.

Wright, Richard. *The Man Who Lived Underground.* Library of America. New York, NY. 2021.

16. GENIUSES CAVE UNDER PRESSURE

Baldwin, James, and Raoul Peck. *I Am Not Your Negro: A Companion Edition to the Documentary Film Directed by Raoul Peck.* Vintage. New York, NY. 2017.

Cohen, Roger. "McGraw-Hill Drops Baldwin Suit." *New York Times.* May 19, 1990. https://www.nytimes.com/1990/05/19/books/mcgraw -hill-drops-baldwin-suit.html.

Hass, Nancy. "The People James Baldwin Knew." *T* magazine. December 11, 2020. https://www.nytimes.com/2020/12/11/t-magazine/the-people -james-baldwin-knew.html.

National Museum of African American History and Culture. "Chez Baldwin." https://nmaahc.si.edu/explore/exhibitions/chez-baldwin.

17. GENIUSES ASK FOR HELP

Lispector, Clarice. *A Breath of Life (Pulsations).* Translated by Johnny Lorenz. New Directions. New York, NY. 2012.

———. *The Hour of the Star.* Translated by Benjamin Moser. New Directions. New York, NY. 2011.

Moser, Benjamin. *Why This World: A Biography of Clarice Lispector.* Oxford University Press. Oxford, England. 2009.

18. GENIUSES TRY ANOTHER WAY

Hurston, Zora Neale. *Barracoon: The Story of the Last "Black Cargo."* Amistad. New York, NY. 2018.

Kaplan, Carla, ed. *Zora Neale Hurston: A Life in Letters.* Knopf. New York, NY. 2007.

Raines, Ben. *The Last Slave Ship: The True Story of How* Clotilda *Was Found, Her Descendants, and an Extraordinary Reckoning.* Simon and Schuster. New York, NY. 2022.

19. GENIUSES BOUNCE BACK

Cep, Casey. "Harper Lee's Abandoned True Crime Novel." *New Yorker.* March 17, 2015. https://www.newyorker.com/books/page-turner /harper-lees-forgotten-true-crime-project.

Corrigan, Maureen. "Harper Lee's 'Watchman' Is a Mess That Makes Us Reconsider a Masterpiece." *Fresh Air*, NPR. July 13, 2015. https:// www.npr.org/2015/07/13/422545987/harper-lees-watchman-is-a-mess -that-makes-us-reconsider-a-masterpiece.

Gopnik, Adam. "Sweet Home Alabama." *New Yorker.* July 15, 2015. https://www.newyorker.com/magazine/2015/07/27/sweet-home -alabama.

Kachka, Boris. "The Decline of Harper Lee." *Vulture.* July 22, 2014. https://www.vulture.com/2014/07/decline-of-harper-lee.html.

Kemp, Kathy. "In Search of Harper Lee." *Birmingham News.* November 10, 2010. https://www.al.com/birmingham-news-stories/2010/11/in _search_of_harper_lee.html.

Lee, Harper. *Go Set a Watchman.* HarperCollins. New York, NY. 2015.

Lewis, Paul. "Lawsuit Divides Town Which Inspired Classic Novel *To Kill a Mockingbird*." *Guardian.* November 1, 2013. https://www .theguardian.com/world/2013/nov/01/harper-lee-monroeville-museum -lawsuit-mockingbird.

Lind, Dara. "*Go Set a Watchman*: Why Harper Lee's New Book Is So Controversial." *Vox.* July 16, 2015. https://www.vox.com/2015/7/16 /8974447/harper-lee-go-set-a-watchman-racism-controversy.

Richter, Greg. "Friend Finds Why Harper Lee Didn't Write Again." AL.com. August 7, 2011. https://www.al.com/birmingham-news -stories/2011/08/friend_finds_why_harper_lee_di.html.

Shields, Charles. J. *Mockingbird: A Portrait of Harper Lee.* Henry Holt. New York, NY. 2006.

Toohey, Paul. "Miss Nelle in Monroeville." *Sunday Telegraph.* July 31, 2011. https://www.dailytelegraph.com.au/the-town-where-a -mockingbird-lives/story-fn6b3v4f-1226104905164.

20. GENIUSES ARE MERE MORTALS

Bell, Quentin. *Virginia Woolf: A Biography.* Mariner Books. New York, NY. 1972.

Briggs, Julia. *Virginia Woolf: An Inner Life.* Mariner Books. New York, NY. 2006.

Jamison, Kay Redfield. *Touched with Fire: Manic-Depressive Illness and the Artistic Temperament.* Free Press. New York, NY. 1993.

Lee, Hermione. *Virginia Woolf.* Knopf. New York, NY. 1997.

Woolf, Virginia. *Between the Acts.* Mariner Books. New York, NY. 1970.

21. GENIUSES ARE NEVER FINISHED

Cross, Charles. *Heavier Than Heaven: A Biography of Kurt Cobain.* Hyperion. New York, NY. 2001.

Dickens, Charles. *The Mystery of Edwin Drood.* Edited by David Paroissien. Penguin Classics. New York, NY. 2002.

Gilbert, Creighton E. "What Is Expressed in Michelangelo's 'Non-Finito.'" *Artibus et Historiae* 24, no. 48 (2003): 57–64. Accessed through JSTOR. https://www.jstor.org/stable/1483730.

Sulcas, Roslyn. "'Sanditon,' Unfinished No More." *New York Times.* March 20, 2022. https://www.nytimes.com/2022/03/20/arts/television /sanditon-pbs.html.

OTHER SOURCES

Baum, Kelly, Andrea Bayer, and Sheena Wagstaff. *Unfinished: Thoughts Left Visible.* Metropolitan Museum of Art. New York, NY. 2016.

Currey, Mason. *Daily Rituals: How Artists Work.* Knopf. New York, NY. 2013.

———. *Daily Rituals: Women at Work.* Knopf. New York, NY. 2019.

Index

X

Y

Z

Acknowledgments

In some ways I've been writing this book for more than twenty years, ever since that interest in Fitzgerald first sparked, and so the list of people I need to thank is endlessly long. I feel a bit like some actor who never imagined they'd reach the podium at an awards show, suddenly trying to recall the names of everyone they ever knew, sure that I'll forget the bulk of them. But I will try.

Once I read an interview where an author was asked what similarities their new book had to their previous one and the honesty of their answer sticks forever in my brain. They said the only similarity between the two books was the massive amount of time each took away from their loving family and to please forgive them.

So thank you first and foremost to my wife, Leah, and our children, for your understanding and support and patience. Thank you as well to the rest of my family, there for me in every way.

This book would not exist without the guidance and vision of my agent, Doug Stewart, and everyone at Quirk Books, especially Shaquona, Jhanteigh, Kassie, and of course my brilliant editor, Jess Zimmerman, who I've known and loved working with since some of these chapters were columns. To that end, I also need to thank quite a number of people at *Electric Literature*, which has been a home for my "Unfinished Business" pieces and so much more for well over a decade. Thank you to Halimah Marcus, Denne Michele Norris, Lincoln Michel, Benjamin Samuel, and Michael Seidlinger, who, over a bowl of Lower East Side ramen, first suggested that my strange fascination with lost novels might be something worth writing about.

Thank you to everyone at the writing programs at Johns Hopkins University, especially the late Professor John Irwin, for allowing me to sit in on "Faulkner, Fitzgerald, and Hemingway."

Thank you as well to Alan Ziegler and many others at Columbia University, who showed me what it means to be a teacher of creative writing. Thank you Jean-Pierre Montal for clueing me in to Flaubert's true intentions.

Thank you to the librarians at the Princeton Special Collections Department of the Firestone Library, and at the Harry Ransom Center at UT Austin, and to Dr. Ulrich Weber at the Swiss Literary Archives. Thank you to all of my dedicated colleagues at New Paltz, and particularly to the office of the Dean of Liberal Arts & Sciences for the assistance of a CRAAL grant to help complete this research. Thank you as well to everyone who has helped me dig through the archives and the stacks at the Chappaqua Library and the Columbia University Library.

Thank you to Garth Greenwell, Yiyun Li, James Hannaham, Matt Bell, Noah Gordon, Ed Park, Stephen Dixon, Alice McDermott, and Isaac Butler for various kinds of incredible assistance and inspiration along the way with this project.

Finally, to all my students—past, present, and future—this book is for you, and written mainly because our classes are only so long and I never have enough time to say everything I wanted to say when I have to let you go. It seems wild to me that my job really is teaching you about all the things I love, and that in doing so, you help me immeasurably to better understand those same things. For all you wonderful geniuses, thank you from the bottom of my heart.

QUIRK BOOKS